VISIONS
&REVISIONS

VISIONS & REVISIONS

THE POET'S PROCESS

BARRY WALLENSTEIN & ROBERT BURR

broadview press

Canadian Cataloguing in Publication Data
Visions and revisions : the poet's process

Includes bibliographical references.
ISBN 1-55111-325-2

1. English poetry.   2. American Poetry.   3. Poetics.   I. Walenstein, Barry.
II. Burr, Robert, 1944- .

PR1175.V58 2001   821.008   C2001-930425-0

An earlier version of this work was published by Thomas Crowell in 1971.

Broadview Press Ltd. is an independent, international publishing house, incorporated in 1985.

North America:
P.O. Box 1243, Peterborough, Ontario, Canada K9J 7H5
3576 California Road, Orchard Park, NY 14127
TEL: (705) 743-8990; FAX: (705) 743-8353;
E-MAIL: customerservice@broadviewpress.com

United Kingdom:
Thomas Lyster Ltd.
Unit 9, Ormskirk Industrial Park
Old Boundary Way, Burscough Road
Ormskirk, Lancashire L39 2YW
TEL: (01695) 575112; FAX: (01695) 570120; E-mail: books@tlyster.co.uk

Australia:
St. Clair Press, P.O. Box 287, Rozelle, NSW 2039
TEL: (02) 818-1942; FAX: (02) 418-1923

www.broadviewpress.com

Broadview Press gratefully acknowledges the financial support of the Book Publishing Industry Development Program, Ministry of Canadian Heritage, Government of Canada.

Book design and composition by George Kirkpatrick

PRINTED IN CANADA

CONTENTS

PREFACE

Visions and Revisions: An Approach to Poetry was originally published in 1971; this current edition, while not changing the basic ambitions of what essentially is a compilation of poetic revisions, is expanded to include a diverse population of well established contemporary voices along with the original list of time-revered poets. There are also minor changes in the presentation of the various versions of the poems, changes intended to make the book consistent and more user-friendly.

The new edition of *Visions and Revisions* remains a direct approach to poetry. Each poem included in the book is accompanied by at least one earlier draft or version of that poem. This format allows exploration of the poet's vision from various aesthetic, social, and political perspectives. The reader will always be delving into the nature of poetic language and the dynamic changes often found so necessary by those obsessed with language. This book, used in an academic setting or elsewhere, should serve everyone who is interested in poetry.

The poets represented were chosen primarily for their excellence and for the availability of materials needed for this study, namely, the drafts and revisions the poets have gone through to achieve their final versions. The poem selections for each chapter are not necessarily representative of the individual poet's life work. Their inclusion, rather, depends largely on the insights offered by their various versions. Generally, and throughout the book, the definitive or accepted version will be given the designation—"Final Version." Because many of the poems underwent an even more extensive process of reworking, variant words or lines are also included in these drafts. Further variants or deletions are indicated by brackets.

The book proceeds chronologically so that the sensitive reader may notice an historical development in the use of language, idiom, cadence, and tone. There are, however, exceptions: the Keats chapter, which examines a single lengthy work; the chapter entitled "Three Poets"; and the "Miscellany" chapter. Both the "Three Poets" and the "Miscellany" chapters are arranged chronologically within themselves. In addition, there is an appendix of translated poems that illustrates how one vision, the original poem, when filtered through the medium of another language and seen through another person's eyes, can give rise to a very different work because of the translator's unique perception and use of language.

This study of poetry and poetic composition is intended to encourage consistent inquiry about each poem; the reader may question why one version is preferred over another. Is this simply a matter of personal taste or are there objective, aesthetic criteria that come into play? Serious analysis of the different visions should eventually lead away from the reader's prejudices and toward the poem itself. Also not to be forgotten in the process of poetic and artistic decision-making are larger social and political considerations, as nothing is produced in isolation from real life pressures.

Each chapter includes brief commentaries along with questions following each set of poems. The first, the Emily Dickinson chapter, illustrates extensive editorial changes involving syntax and punctuation. The questions asked regarding the Dickinson material should serve as a further guide throughout the book. The reader's approach might profitably be a cumulative one, the observations gathered from one chapter enlarging the perspective for the ones to follow. Some questions may overlap, but others will drop off, and of course readers will initiate further inquiries. The commentary also includes biographical and historical information intended to guide and stimulate the reader.

Many people helped to make this book. First, I extend my gratitude to Professor Leo Hamalian of the City College of New York, who encouraged me to develop what was at first an idea and a classroom exercise into a book-length study. Also, I thank Professors Paul Oppenheimer and Robert Ghiradella of CCNY and Professor John Tytell of Queens College for their very careful and close reading of much of the material. I am indebted to Stephen and Elaine Aronoff for their special kindness and valuable suggestions. I am grateful to Eileen Penn, who provided editorial assistance. Also, I thank my original editor, Lloyd Scott, who encouraged this project, and Linda Lumley of the Crowell College Department, who was extremely helpful with the first-edition manuscript in its final stages. My wife, Lorna Harbus, has throughout been a constant and brilliant source of encouragement. I am also most fortunate that Bob Burr has joined me as co-editor on this new and expanded edition of *Visions and Revisions.*

B.W.

INTRODUCTION

Man can make statements about verifiable facts: that is science. He can develop extremely complex attitudes of self-adjustment towards those facts: that is poetry.

Stephen Spender

Maybe there's another possible meaning of 'deep' surfacing here— and the revisions suggest that writing is both highly artificial and highly intuitive, and that the first version maybe didn't get deep enough?

William Matthews

It's like trying to remove a baby from its mother with a faulty pair of forceps, getting it out without bashing its head or knocking off one of its ears.

Carolyn Kizer

Visions and Revisions presents various sets of poems, each set containing two or more versions, or stages, of the same poem. Frequently, one version will vary from another sufficiently to communicate a slightly different, or possibly vastly different, experience. The quality of this altered experience may not be easy to perceive, but the reader, whether or not able to articulate these perceptions, will nonetheless feel the change.

The process of revision involves working the initial conception or vision through a first pattern (the first version), then a second pattern, and so forth. The versions eventually achieved represent a kind of jockeying for position as the poets' attitudes toward their initial experiences or ideas shift. A minor change in rhythm, image, or tone often indicates a shift in attitude or a reorganizing of response.

Thus, a poet's perception or vision becomes reset as the language and music of the poetry change. The poem may contain a single idea or the retelling of an old story, which for each version remains fundamentally unchanged. However, the experience changes each time the words change. Reading the different versions makes it clear that it is not necessarily the idea on which the poem rests, nor the story it tells, that determines the poem's essence, but rather the language. A poem is created by how the poet presents individual experience, imagined or real, through vital language. Of course, other factors condition a poem's life as it gains from and is informed by the reader's life.

We are looking at revisions to get close to poetry as experience, poetry as a particular kind of knowledge of the real world. Since our attention will be directed to technical details, the illusion may be created that through these details alone we can understand why or how a poem moves or affects us. Just as the poet has no set rules, often succeeding in the most outrageous and unexpected ways, the reader must not expect to learn a right way to respond to a poem or analyze how it is effective.

Some poets create finished works without going through an extremely laborious process of revision. Some do work through copious drafts; others work from prose sheets. Sometimes the final draft, while far superior to the first version, differs only in a few details. Sometimes poets produce a final version that barely resembles the first draft.

When presented as pieces in a museum, poems may become cold, perfect, and distant objects. There is little sense of the aesthetic process, or indeed the aesthetic reality of a poem, because the first contact with the poem is with a finished and apparently inspired work. The popular conception of the poet as madman or divinely inspired artist needs to be dispelled, and studying the poetic process can do this, as well as enhance the appreciation of the poem.

Through the examination of poetic composition, the separation of the reader from the poem is diminished. Getting closer to the poem—opening it up—is similar to getting closer to the artistic experience. This could include a study of those techniques that control and create the poem, using illustrations from the various versions of the poem. Specifically, it is possible to observe how sound changes through the revision of merely a word or syllable, or through the shifting of a stress. Also, we may notice the effectiveness of different figures of speech, as, for example, when the extension of a metaphor throughout a stanza intensifies the language while leaving the prose meaning alone. Thus, the reader is able to see the poet as a builder, mechanic, and craftsman, as well as a thinker, feeler, and creator.

Often another barrier to discovering poetry is the obligation to provide a prose paraphrase in order to understand a poem. Interestingly, looking at different versions of a poem will absorb many questions concerned with matters of literal or intellectual meaning, lessening the need to say in prose what the poem is about. Earlier versions sometimes more explicitly express a point of view, tone, or story, and a combination of versions can make the direction of the poet's intentions more apparent.

Poetry demands a concentration that can accept a language of ideas and emotion which is untranslatable. A paraphrase or summation is reductive—it keeps us from both poetry and experience. A love affair examined only in terms of needs, desires, and facts does not describe what the participants feel. Poetry is difficult when we allow conventionality to bully us, to assign formulas, rules, or slogans to experience. Rather, poetry is so specific that it must be left as written, so that the poem's meaning or meanings remain suggestive as well as true.

Asking questions about a poet such as "What kind of statement is he making?", "What does she believe in?", "Where does he stand philosophically?", "Is she an optimist or a pessimist?"—however interesting they may be—will rarely lead the student to the actuality of the poem itself. A comparison of early drafts to their final versions will, on the other hand, show that philosophy, ideas, and opinions do not define the poet or the art.

The poem's philosophical position or motivating idea can be a guide for the presentation of a reality that holds up a strange mirror to the original conception, fracturing it into several possible developments. The final poem, especially one that is the culmination of many manuscript drafts, may capture a more complex or more exact truth than the original version. An exact poetic utterance, a demonstrable truth when we apply those standards found in the world of the poem itself, is realized when the weight of systematic reasoning has been eliminated. The beauty that results from clear, logical thought is still present, but the evidence of the ponderous labor necessary for its achievement has been removed.

This book is an inquiry into poetic pleasure. At the center of the pleasure is the poem's elusiveness and, at the same time, its simplicity. This simplicity is often overlooked because we have generally felt that great poetry ought to contain noble, broad, and powerful statements about the condition of human affairs. Those questions—"What is the poet saying?", "What is the message of the poem?"—are often masks for "Which popular or unpopular platitude can I ascribe to this or that poem?" The kind of truth a poet reveals is most difficult to para-phrase, not because of its profundity or obscurity, but because it is particular to the poet and to a very short space of experience in the poet's life. It is this uniqueness that may anticipate the large questions of human nature.

When I. A. Richards wrote that since "good poetry owes its value in a large measure to the closeness of its contact with reality, it may thereby become a powerful weapon for breaking up unreal ideas and responses," he was speaking of a relationship with reality that is encouraged by the poet's accommodating several feelings, responses, ideas, and levels of experience at the same time. As the poet's vision may include opposing positions and sympathies, he must also be able to express the often paradoxical nature of his relationship to experience. The poet's ability to include such variety and reality pro-duces poetry's elusiveness, its freedom from artificiality, that is, its simplicity, beauty, and power.

Intimacy with the poem itself is the primary reason for this book; all of the discussions are directed toward achieving this end. Our imagination, as it is exposed in many ways to the poet's art, may con-struct a creative process. When an image in an earlier draft is replaced by another in a later draft, we can imagine why the poet chose to do such a thing. While never fully identifying the mental or internal activity of the poet, these conjectures help us to discover the develop-ment of poetic objectivity.

In the revision of earlier and more autobiographical drafts, the development of an anti-self or objective expression of the poet's own self is revealed. It is helpful to observe what the poet works away from. By deleting certain passages or striking out single words, the poet not only demonstrates a mastery over the craft, but at times shows an impatience or dissatisfaction with an earlier perspective, even if the vision under the knife of correction is only five minutes old.

To go slightly further, each poem a poet writes is in some way a version of an earlier one, and in the same sense, all the poems repre-sent an attempt to write the poem that will best record the individual self, his or her experience and vision. In the various versions the poet charts a life and eventually the conditions of the age and locale.

II

Just as poems are records of the experience of individuals in their times, the changes a poet makes over a period of time will in many cases expose more than just an increasing technical efficiency as a craftsman and self-critic. The changes will record how and in what ways language is alive and in flux, reflecting many facets of our shifting mores, customs, and attitudes. The use of language is a gauge of how we live in the world. It, perhaps more than any other human invention, exposes the evolution of a society, not so much in the definitions of words, but in their implied communications.

Yeats used the expression "full round moon" in 1893, though by the time he collected his poems in 1933, the phrase was eliminated. Possibly Yeats decided it was a cliché or no longer romantically effective. Perhaps the change could even indicate a shift in the way we look at celestial bodies—an entire system of faith may be at the root of the poet's decision! One generation may feel a certain way toward an event, story, or condition, and the next can either topple or intensify this attitude.

W. H. Auden's poetry offers another illustration. During the 1930s, the poet was involved in left-wing politics, an involvement reflecting a generation's hopes, aspirations, and frustrations. By the early 1950s Auden deleted lines, stanzas, and even whole poems from his *Collected Poetry,* indicating his, and his generation's, political disillusionment. The values and the tensions of a particular era reveal themselves to the analytical eye of a literary historian or critic of poetry. A close reading of contemporary poetry intensifies one's understanding of patterns of order, or chaos, in the contemporary world. The order poets perceive and construct out of the chaos and fertility of their own imaginations is the very order applied by "scientist, statesman, professional classes and eventually tradesmen," to use Stephen Spender's listing. The poets see this order first, and similarly are among the first to detect, or at least expose, national disorder. They present the words and rhythms that imitate such disorder. The imitation of life in art need not be construed as disorderly poetry imitating disorder in the world or complex poetry following the recognition of complexity. Rather, it is a reciprocal relationship, revealing the ground of reality in the poet's achievement.

For these reasons, contemporary poetry is often unpopular. After all, if the sounds and patterns of new ideas and evolving order or disorder are not yet generally manifest, the reader is likely to resist these patterns in poetry. The reader must be a participant in a world that seems unfamiliar, strange, or even grotesque, a world that is not mirroring traditional reality. This new world, an artificial construct, is the poem. However, the individual may perceive that the poem is an image of the actual world, not perceived until now. The intensified perception comprises aesthetic pleasure, a reaction that remains the most important reason for looking at art, or anything else for that matter.

If the poet's vision is a true one, in the sense of seeing into the essential as well as the substantial level of experience, the vision will evoke in the reader a response something like a "moment of recognition." This powerful recognition is not of what the reader has already known, but of what is being experienced at the moment of reading the poem. The reader of a Shakespearean sonnet is denied a higher pleasure if he or she believes the enjoyment comes from having had a similar experience. Shakespeare's experience, however mundane or however noble, was unique, and the reader, however worldly, has never felt it. Once the life inherent in the poem is felt by the reader, the reader can have that poem's unique sensation forever. The finest poetry is new life experience.

A reader may ask, "If the poet's vision is such a powerful one, then why all these stumblings to express what he is trying to say?" One answer is that while the matter or theme may not be overly complicated—about a man stopping by woods, or a woman cutting her finger—the poet has the double task of envisioning and communicating the felt experience and transforming language into art. In order to do this, the poet must labor to reproduce experience in such a fashion that it remains personal while not being private, and public without being obvious and predictable. At their best, poets provide surprises that enrich our entire sensibility.

The most familiar poem will, if it is a good one, continue to surprise us and continue to be new. This is a mysterious and beautiful phenomenon in art, not entirely fathomed by our psychological sophistication. For this reason, the so-called "right reading" of a poem is not only difficult to prove but is perhaps beside the point. Some poems have about as many readings as there are critics. The poem may not be particularly obscure, but as with every new thing, we must reassess our own values when contacting it. While many critics will agree on the poem's basic meaning, tone, and structure, there may be facets to it that remain wonderfully elusive. In literary criticism, as in the study of the creative process, the clues that emerge in the earlier drafts are illuminating. However, this should not be overemphasized. Early versions are richer than when used solely as tables to comprehend the complex experience of the final draft.

We often take it for granted that the final version is the best poem. We assume that though the poet may sacrifice many lovely touches, or lines, the poem will be improved by the process. If the reader follows this assumption too religiously, the point will be missed that the two versions often will present not merely a poem getting better, but two separate experiences, each valuable and interesting in its own right. It is also possible that the poet, with eyes and sensibilities controlled by many concerns, will make the final poem best in relation to the developing vision, but inferior to the earlier version. Again, we are asking for fresh attention not only to each final poem, but to each revision.

III

A Poem ... is in every sense a teaching machine for the training of perception and judgment.

Marshall McLuhan

Criticism, as I understand it, is the endeavor to discriminate between experiences and evaluate them.

I.A. Richards

There is a final question: Why bother with these poems at all? Or, more explicitly: What is the ultimate value of poetry and criticism? Or, as I.A. Richards asks the question, "Why are [poems] worth the devotion of the keenest hours of the best minds, what is their place in this system of human endeavors?" The answer requires strong convictions about poetry's values. For instance, the poet writes:

Ah, love, let us be true
To one another! for the world, which seems
To lie before us like a land of dreams,
So various, so beautiful, so new,

Hath really neither joy, nor love, nor light,
Nor certitude, nor peace, nor help for pain;
And we are here as on a darkling plain
Swept with confused alarms of struggle and flight,
Where ignorant armies clash by night.

Clearly, he is doing something very different from making a statement such as "Certain difficult periods in history produce a desperate need for love." This statement, while implying the meaning of the poem, is, like most prose statements, a generalization that could include a great variety of possible human experiences. It contains no heightened or deepened emotion, little form or rhythm, and less impact.

The state of mind poetry generates, how the activity of the poem affects us, is a different consideration from how the poem develops into art, which involves poetry's technical qualities. Since it is through these techniques that the poem is formed, we must pay close attention to the details, analytical attention version to version, as our states of mind are affected.

Through the method of making critical discriminations regarding various objects, in this case, poems, and by noting our responses to the poems' components, we approach an awareness of why and how different things affect us. In our responses to the special features of a poem lie the clues to how we feel first about the poem, next about our own lives in relation to the poem, and ultimately about the world.

Even the barest poetry works through images. Words that can devise something new out of their own being are like wonderful tools used to create a new entity. While "making it new" in this way, the poet, at the same time, is consciously or unconsciously storing, preserving, and possibly transcending the values of the age. Reading poetry not only extends our world through images, but also delivers and connects us to various systems of values. In learning to make intimate contact with value systems, we may be better able to make free choices. If we are able to evaluate another's vision, perception, or system of beliefs, it is less likely that we will be the unwitting, unwilling recipients of a system of values imposed on us.

WILLIAM BLAKE

1757-1827

WILLIAM BLAKE, PERHAPS THE FIRST TRUE ROMANTIC
poet, was largely neglected during his lifetime by both
the public and critics, and it was not until forty years
after his death that scholars began to take an interest in
his life, his poetry, and his art. He epitomized what was later to
become the Romantic ideal in his varied and individual genius.
He was a lyric poet, as demonstrated by the *Songs of Innocence and of
Experience*; a prophetic visionary, as exemplified by his epics and satires;
a revolutionary, as expressed in *America, a Prophecy* and *The French Revolu-
tion*; and an artist and craftsman who illustrated and engraved the cop-
per plates from which his poems were printed according to his own
method of "illuminated printing."

Among those who did recognize his genius, the frequenters of
Joseph Johnson's bookshop, including the radical thinkers Thomas
Paine, William Godwin, and Mary Wollstonecraft, there were few, if
any, who could understand his ideas and the intense, abiding joy
embedded in his mysticism. Blake's mysticism, influenced by the writ-
ings of Emmanuel Swedenborg, a religious mystic, teacher, scientist,
and Neo-Platonist, eventually led him to repudiate the doctrines of
rationalism, systematic philosophy, and the orthodoxy of the
Church. That is, he rejected all processes or methodologies that he
felt interfered with man's direct apprehension of God and Truth. He
was truly a free spirit, determined to liberate the body and soul:

> Abstinence sows sand all over
> The ruddy limbs & flaming hair,
> But Desire Gratified
> Plants fruits & beauty there.

Though Blake admired radical political and literary figures for
their revolutionary temperament, libertarianism, and opposition to
conformity, he believed their faith in rationalism and the benefits of
science, law, analysis, and discipline separated them from the virtues

of freedom. These virtues are symbolized by love, innocence, imagina-tiveness, and the primal unity with Spiritual Truth. In the childlike state of "unfallen mortality" these virtues are realized, but of course such an ideal state is impossible to maintain. The contrary state, the real as opposed to the ideal, is a part of life, and the light, laughter, and glee of the innocent state are tempered by the awareness of forth-coming experience, darkness, and evil. There are two sides to Blake's thought, and, indeed, for an understanding of his primary concern, Dualism is necessary. His primary concern is with the finiteness of man compared to the whole universe and, ultimately, the correspon-dence of the material creation with man's spiritual insight to form a unity, or reality. The soul moves through a cycle of contrary states, good and evil. Yet the Dualism, even the darkness, arises from God, the Divine Reality. As Blake stated, "Without Contraries is no progres-sion," and "To be in Error, and to be Cast out, is a part of God's design."

This chapter is made up of selections from the *Songs of Innocence* (1789), and the *Songs of Experience* (1794). Reflecting the contraries of the human condition without presenting a systematic philosophy, these poems, instead, illustrate the ways in which the contrary states mani-fest themselves. Though it may not be apparent, if one considers these poems solely from the point of view of Blake's Dualistic ideas, these poems are masterpieces of simplicity and lyricism. Many of them have been put to music and have been sung. There is a certain tension in them, especially noticeable if one reads about the contrary states of a single subject, for example, God's creativity in "The Tyger" and "The Lamb." But this tension is the underlying human struggle for the recognition of ambiguities and, because of the very universality of this struggle, the poems, in expressing the tension, in no way lose their beauty, clarity, or simplicity.

The following paragraph is by David Wagenknecht,[1] noted Blake scholar and editor of *Studies in Romanticism*:

It has already been suggested that in Blake's case we are interest-ed in a somewhat wider range of revision than is the case with our other poets; it's worth remembering that Blake is unique among the poets represented in this book, since he was an artist in two mediums, or perhaps a "composite artist." None of his poems except the early collection *Poetical Sketches* (1783) were ever printed in the black-letter common to books of poems of the period (e.g., *Lyrical Ballads*) and their reproduction here; all the *Songs of Innocence & of Experience* and all his other published poems were printed from copper, etched plates which, rather like the potato-prints some of us practiced in childhood, bore the raised letters of the words *and* the outlines of Blake's illustrations (or "illuminations") of the words. Texts and illustrations were printed together (Blake owned his own small press, and did multiple runs of his books, working with his wife at home), sometimes in colored ink, and then washed or colored in by hand individually before the poems were gathered in home-made books and sold. These facts are not only interesting in themselves; they have a bearing on the whole issue of "revision." Since Blake's texts were etched into relatively expensive copper, once this was done their "plate state" was a great disincentive to revision. Blake sometimes revised his long narrative prophetic poems by changing the order of the plates, or weaving in new ones between plates that already existed, rather than change the words on the plates already extant; he sometimes seemed interested in changing the tone of a long finished poem by adding "arguments" or "preludiums" to their beginnings, or attaching relatively independent pieces to their conclusions. In the case of the *Songs*, in addition to adding poems of "Experience" to his songs of "Innocence," Blake seemed to be constantly experimenting with the orders of the poems in his collections, something that changes not only the reader's sense of relationship between contiguous poems but that also tends to change her sense of correspondences between certain "Songs of Innocence" and their experienced counterparts. Moreover—and just as importantly— though some changes in the poems' decoration may represent accidental effects of Blake's modest efforts at mass-production on his press, others are clearly deliberate, and poems which are obviously associated with each other in some copies by means of similar coloration of characters common to more than one illustration (say a solicitous or over-solicitous nurse) will be disassociated in other copies by using very different colors for these same illustrations. Again Blake seems not to be attempting anything systematic by these means, which can be as subtle as his verbal revisions, and what was remarked earlier about his taste for contradiction and ambiguity applies to these visual elements of his work as well. And, in fact, one might want to think of "revision by illustration" in a given instance by means of some conception other than variation: sometimes the words of a poem might appear in the sky, or be indissociable from the leaves on a tree (as in the second illustration to "Night"), and it might occur to a reader that their representation had a bearing on their meaning. Illustrations may exert subtle or blatant influence on how one interprets a text; they can as well take the place of stanzas of certain poems that are readable in their drafts or notebook versions but that are not allowed to appear in publication. "Revision" therefore might extend to the capacity of an illustration to suppress certain elements of a text as well as possibly underlining them or influencing their interpretation. That these very sophisticated poems purport to be intended for children (partly by way of their pictures) may serve ironic or privative intentions as well as earnestness and openness. Blake is passionately intense in his (apparent) convictions, but his methods of expression *and* revision cause one to become thoughtful about the relationship between very-great-finality in the finish and subtlety of his forms and a curious lack of finality in the meanings these forms convey.

In this chapter, each of the poems included from *Songs of Innocence* is presented along with a complement from *Songs of Experience,* with the exception of "London," which is from *Songs of Experience.* In a number of instances, there are first drafts or first versions as well. This is in exception to the general format of the book, which concentrates on different versions alone. Here the reason for giving two different poems instead of only versions of a single poem is to emphasize that there may be multiple approaches to a particular conception, idea, or experience and, again, to permit the reader to accept this idea even when confronted with B and C versions of a single poem. This is an attempt to blur the concept of versions of poems with that of separate poems, for each different creation, even variants, requires separate attention.

The text used is *The Complete Poetry and Prose of William Blake,* edited by David V. Erdman.[2] Two more recent studies of Blake's *Songs* are *Songs of Innocence and of Experience,* edited by Andrew Lincoln, and Zachary Leader's *Reading Blake's Songs.*[3]

A   *Introduction*

Piping down the valleys wild,
Piping song of pleasant glee,
On a cloud I saw a child,
And he laughing said to me:

"Pipe a song about a Lamb!"   5
So I piped with merry cheer.
"Piper, pipe that song again;"
So I Piped: he wept to hear.

"Drop thy pipe, thy happy pipe;
Sing thy songs of happy cheer:"   10
So I sung the same again,
While he wept with joy to hear.

"Piper, sit thee down and write
In a book, that all may read."
So he vanish'd from my sight,   15
And I pluck'd a hollow reed,

And I made a rural pen,
And I stain'd the water clear,
And I wrote my happy songs
Every child may joy to hear.

            Songs of Innocence

A   *Introduction*

Hear the voice of the Bard!
Who Present, Past, & Future, sees;
Whose ears have heard
The Holy Word
That walk'd among the ancient trees,   5

Calling the lapsed Soul,
And weeping in the evening dew;
That mighty controll

The starry pole,
And fallen, fallen light renew!   10

"O Earth, O Earth, return!
Arise from out the dewy grass;
Night is worn,
And the morn
Rises from the slumberous mass.   15
"Turn away no more;
Why wilt thou turn away?
The starry floor,
The wat'ry shore,
Is giv'n thee till the break of day."

Songs of Experience

1. Both poems contain a note of optimism. How is this attitude directed in each instance?

2. The poet acts as hero or main figure in both poems. Yet clearly his poetic function is different in the two contexts. In the *Songs of Experience* Introduction the context is a religious one with the bard as a God-inspired man and the voice of prophecy. He is calling to Adam, if we follow that symbolic association, as he is affirming the cyclical order in the natural world. Discuss the poet's role in the *Songs of Innocence* Introduction.

3. In the earlier poem the language is direct, almost childlike. The repetition and simplicity of design suggest the innocence of childhood. The control evident in the poem, however, is not youthful and should indicate the association of the piper with the wise and watchful innocence of Christ. The figure of Christ dominates the *Songs of Innocence* and acts as a bridge or unifier between the helpless child and the wise poet-adult. Discuss.

4. A dramatic form is used in both of these songs. The drama is more clearly felt between the child and the piper, however, than in the song of experience. Discuss dialogue and dramatic expectancy in both poems.

A   *The Lamb*

Little Lamb, who made thee?
Dost thou know who made thee?
Gave thee life, & bid thee feed
By the stream & o'er the mead;
Gave thee clothing of delight,   5
Softest clothing, wooly, bright;
Gave thee such a tender voice,
Making all the vales rejoice?
Little Lamb, who made thee?
Dost thou know who made thee?   10

Little Lamb, I'll tell thee,
Little Lamb, I'll tell thee:
He is called by thy name,
For he calls himself a Lamb.
He is meek, & he is mild;   15
He became a little child.
I a child, & thou a lamb,
We are called by his name.
Little Lamb, God bless thee!
Little Lamb, God bless thee!   20

Songs Of Innocence

B   *The Tyger*

Tyger, Tyger, burning bright
In the forests of the night,
What immortal hand or eye
[Could] [Dare] frame thy fearful symmetry?
[In what] [Burnt in] distant deeps or skies   5
[Burnt the] [The cruel] fire of thine eyes?
On what wings dare he aspire?
What the hand dare seize the fire?

And what shoulder & what art
Could twist the sinews of thy heart?   10
And when thy heart began to beat
What dread hand & what dread feet

[Could fetch it from the furnace deep
And in thy horrid ribs dare steep
In the well of sanguine woe?   15
In what clay & in what mould
Were thy eyes of fury roll'd?]

[What] Where the hammer? [What] Where the chain?
In what furnace was thy brain?
What the anvil? What [the arm] [arm] [grasp] [clasp] dread grasp?   20
[Could] Dare its deadly terrors [grasp] clasp?

Tyger, Tyger, burning bright
In the forests of the night,
What immortal hand & eye
Dare [form] frame thy fearful symmetry?   25
(3) And [did he laugh] dare he [smile] [laugh] his work
to see?
[What the (shoulder) ankle? What the knee?]
(4) [Did] Dare he who made the lamb make thee?
(1) When the stars threw down their spears
(2) And water'd heaven with their tears

Note-book, 1793

A   *The Tyger*

Tyger! Tyger! burning bright
In the forests of the night,
What immortal hand or eye
Could frame thy fearful symmetry?

In what distant deeps or skies   5
Burnt the fire of thine eyes?
On what wings dare he aspire?
What the hand dare seize the fire?

And what shoulder, & what art.
Could twist the sinews of thy heart?   10
And when thy heart began to beat,
What dread hand? & what dread feet?

What the hammer? what the chain?
In what furnace was thy brain?
What the anvil? what dread grasp   15
Dare its deadly terrors clasp?

When the stars threw down their spears,
And water'd heaven with their tears,
Did he smile his work to see?
Did he who made the Lamb make thee?   20

Tyger! Tyger! burning bright
In the forests of the night,
What immortal hand or eye,
Dare frame thy fearful symmetry?

Songs of Experience

1. "The Lamb" is one of a number of songs that incorporate a question-answer method. Here the questioner and the one questioned are identical. How is this identity made manifest?

2. Note that couplets open and close each stanza. Each line contains four stresses, stress being the emphasis given to a syllable or word. Can you detect the difference in rhythm in the central couplets? The contrast in rhythm parallels other contrasting elements in the poem. Comment.

3. "The Tyger" demonstrates Blake's art of the lyric. The language is lively and simple yet there is immense complexity and ambiguity of meaning. Compare "forests of the night" with "clothing of delight." Both are highly suggestive; they are not different kinds of phrases, yet one is more complex in thought and tone.

4. Unlike "The Lamb" in the *Songs of Innocence,* "The Tyger" answers none of its own questions. Here the questions are rhetorical; that is, the grand and ultimate answers are implicit in the questions themselves. Demonstrate and discuss.

5. "The Tyger," in its acceptance of the terror of life, is, in part, a satire of "The Lamb," which excludes what is fearful from our experience. In the song of experience terror may be positive. The illusion that the

poem satirizes is that in a state of innocence fear and terror are emotions that can and should be transcended. The Tyger is as natural, as fundamental as the Lamb. The satire is not the biting kind, for Blake wants not to mock the Lamb but to combine the positive forces of experience with it. Discuss.

6. Note in the B version of "The Tyger" such canceled phrases as "cruel fire," "horrid ribs," and "sanguine woe." How do such phrases interfere with the powerful affirmative motif in the poem?

7. The notebook version demonstrates a shifting around of stanzas and lines within the stanzas as well. It is most interesting to perceive Blake's hesitancy with individual key words. In the draft he occasionally preferred words that were later changed back to the original version, namely, lines 18, 21, and 28. Discuss.

A   *Chimney Sweeper*

> When my mother died I was very young,
> And my father sold me while yet my tongue
> Could scarcely cry "'weep! 'weep! 'weep! 'weep!"
> So your chimneys I sweep, & in soot I sleep.
>
> There's little Tom Dacre, who cried when his head   5
> That curl'd like a lamb's back, was shav'd: so I said
> "Hush, Tom! never mind it, for when your head's bare
> You know that the soot cannot spoil your white hair."
>
> And so he was quiet, & that very night,
> As Tom was a-sleeping, he had such a sight!   10
> That thousands of sweepers, Dick, Joe, Ned, & Jack,
> Were all of them lock'd up in coffins of black.
>
> And by came an Angel who had a bright key,
> And he open's the coffins & set them all free;
> Then down a green plain leaping, laughing, they run   15
> And wash in a river, and shine in the Sun.
>
> Then naked & white, all their bags left behind,
> They rise upon clouds and sport in the wind;

And the Angel told Tom, if he'd be a good boy,
He'd have God for his father, & never want joy.   20

And so Tom awoke; and we rose in the dark,
And got with our bags & our brushes to work.
Tho' the morning was cold, Tom was happy & warm;
So if they all do their duty they need not fear harm.

Songs of Innocence

A   *The Chimney Sweeper*

A little black thing among the snow,
Crying "'weep! 'weep!" in notes of woe!
"Where are thy father & mother? say?"
"They are both gone up to the church to pray.

                                                                   5

"Because I was happy upon the heath,
And smil'd among the winter's snow,
They clothed me in the clothes of death,
And taught me to sing the notes of woe.

"And because I am happy & dance & sing   10
They think they have done me no injury,
And are gone to praise God & his Priest & King,
Who make up a heaven of our misery."

Songs of Experience

1. In the song of innocence the sweep is an orphan. In the later poem
no such detail is given. There Blake presents his victim of social injus-
tice exclusively as an object of exploitation. Discuss the poet's role as
reformer in the one poem and his avoidance of such questions in the
other. How does Blake employ satire to attack the complacency of
the first poem?

2. Discuss Tom Dacre's function in the first song and his absence in the
second.

3. Despite his woe, Tom Dacre is made happy as a vision descends
upon him. The sweep in the shorter poem is happy too, for he recog-
nizes (maybe not consciously) the strength of life and the union with

nature (lines 5 and 6) that lies within him. Despite the song of experience's satire, how is Tom's vision affirmed in both poems?

4. Taking a clue from the word "thing" in line 1 of the song of experience, discuss the different approaches to life's misery and sorrow in the two poems.

5. In the first draft version of this song of experience from the 1793 Note-book there is an interesting variant for the last line: "Who wrap themselves up in our misery." Comment on this and the revised line 12.

A   *The Little Boy Lost*

    "Father! father! where are you going?
    O do not walk so fast.
    Speak, father, speak to your little boy,
    Or else I shall be lost."

    The night was dark, no father was there;   5
    The child was wet with dew;
    The mire was deep, & the child did weep,
    And away the vapour flew.
                               Songs of Innocence

B   ["Then] And father [I cannot] how can I love you   5
    [Nor] Or any of my brothers more?
    I love [myself, so does the bird]
    you like the little bird
    That picks up crumbs around the door."

    The Priest sat by and heard the child.
    In trembling zeal he siez'd his hair: 10
    [The mother follow'd, weeping aloud:
    "O, that I such a fiend should bear."]
    [Then] He led him by his little coat
    [To show his zealous, priestly care.]
    And all admir'd his priestly care.   15

. . . . .

The weeping child could not be heard;   20
The weeping parents wept in vain.
[They bound his little ivory limbs
In a cruel Iron chain.]
[And] They strip'd him to his little shirt
& bound him in an iron chain.   25
[They] And burn'd him in a holy [fire] place,

*Stanzas selected from first
draft of "A Little Boy Lost," in* Songs of Experience, Note-book *(1793).*

A   *Little Boy Lost*

"Nought loves another as itself,
Nor venerates another so,
Nor is it possible to Thought
A greater than itself to know:

"And Father, how can I love you   5
Or any of my brothers more?
I love you like the little bird
That picks up crumbs around the door."

The Priest sat by and heard the child,
In trembling zeal he siez'd his hair: 10
He led him by his little coat,
And all admir'd the Priestly care.

And standing on the altar high,
"Lo! what a fiend is here!" said he,
"One who sets reason up for judge   15
Of our most holy Mystery."

The weeping child could not be heard,
The weeping parents wept in vain;
They strip'd him to his little shirt,
And bound him in an iron chain;   20

And burn'd him in a holy place,
Where many had been burn'd before:
The weeping parents wept in vain.
Are such things done on Albion's shore?

Songs of Experience

1. Is Blake implying, in the last words of the song of innocence, that a child's weeping is magical and affirmative? "Vapour" could be construed as mere nothingness, illusion. How does this understanding of the word illuminate the poem's ambiguous close?

2. Line 5 of the song of innocence suggests the orphan motif we have already seen in "The Chimney Sweeper." With no father, the little boy adopts God the Father as his own in a very human sense. Note how this developing idea prepares us for the song's *Song of Experience* counterpart.

3. In the song of experience, the little boy is not lost in the dark, but is lost to the world after the sacrificial fire. Here, unlike most of the contrary poems, there is no satire or parody offered to the song of innocence. This poem may not have been originally intended for *Songs of Experience*. The title came last and it was not etched for the original issue of the *Songs of Experience*. Discuss.

4. The ironic spirit of experience (namely, line 12) is opposed to innocence. Discuss.

5. The little boy in both poems is innocent and, therefore, must speak the truth. What kind of truth is spoken in the song of experience and how does such truth infuriate the Priest? The child is clearly a religious martyr. In what way is his religion subversive?

6. Note how in the early draft the developing idea of self love was carried into line 7. Is the idea clearer and more emphatic in the earlier draft?

7. Note the interesting change in line 11. Discuss.

8. There is a loss in graphic detail by the deletion of line 22. Does this

change, in any way, improve the poem? How does it alter our vision of the particular experience in this stanza?

A
Holy Thursday

'Twas on a Holy Thursday, their innocent faces clean,
The children walking two & two, in red & blue & green,
Grey-headed beadles walk'd before, with wands as white as snow,
Till into the high dome of Paul's they like Thames' waters flow.

O what a multitude they seem'd, these flowers of London town!   5
Seated in companies they sit with radiance all their own.
The hum of multitudes was there, but multitudes of lambs,
Thousands of little boys & girls raising their innocent hands.

Now like a mighty wind they raise to heaven the voice of song,
Or like harmonious thunderings the seats of Heaven among.   10
Beneath them sit the aged men, wise guardians of the poor;
Then cherish pity, lest you drive an angel from your door.

Songs of Innocence

Holy Thursday

Is this a holy thing to see
In a rich and fruitful land,
Babes reduc'd to misery,
Fed with cold and usurous hand?

Is that trembling cry a song?   5
Can it be a song of joy?
And so many children poor?
It is a land of poverty!

And their sun does never shine,
And their fields are bleak & bare,   10
And their ways are fill'd with thorns:
It is eternal winter there.

For where-e'er the sun does shine,
And where-e'er the rain does fall,

Babe can never hunger there,   15
Nor poverty the mind appall.

Songs of Experience

1. The song of innocence is set in London, as was "The Chimney Sweeper." Authenticity is sought through the inclusion of various physical details. Discuss setting and naturalistic detail in both the song of innocence and the song of experience.

2. By placing the "aged men" (usually guardians—shepherds) "beneath" the children (lambs—to be guarded) Blake has turned the religious order upside down. Such a perversion of natural order is prepared for throughout the poem. Discuss.

3. The experience poem is clearly a parody or satire of the earlier poem. Discuss the development of images in both songs. Has the imagined perception of the experience poem suffered from the social indignation or partisanship of its attack? Where are the sympathies concrete; where are they abstract?

4. Discuss complexity and simplicity in both of the songs.

5. Line 7 of the 1793 draft of the song of experience read "And so great a number poor?" Discuss this deletion.

A   *Infant Joy*

              "I have no name:
              I am but two days old."
              What shall I call thee?
              "I happy am,
              Joy is my name."   5
              Sweet joy befall thee!

              Pretty joy!
              Sweet joy but two days old,
              Sweet joy I call thee:
              Thou dost Smile,   10

                    I sing the while,
                    Sweet joy befall thee!

                                            Songs of Innocence

B   ...
                When I saw that rage was vain,
[*Infant*   And to sulk would nothing gain,   10
Sorrow]   [I began to so] [Seeking many an artful wile]
                Turning many a trick & wile,
                I began to soothe & smile.

                And I [grew] [smil'd] sooth'd day after day
                Till upon the ground I stray: 15
                And I [grew] smil'd night after night,
                Seeking only for delight.

                [But upon the nettly ground
                No delight was to be found]
                And I saw before me shine   20
                Clusters of the wand'ring vine
                [And beyond a mirtle tree]
                And many a lovely flower & tree
                Stretch'd [its] their blossoms out to me.

                [But a] [But many a Priest]   25
                My father then with holy look,
                In [their] his hands a holy book,
                Pronounc'd curses on [his] my head
                [Who the fruit or blossoms shed]
                And bound me in a mirtle shade.   30

                [I beheld the Priests by night;
                They embrac'd [my mirtle] the blossoms bright:
                I beheld the Priests by day;
                [Where beneath my]
                Underneath the vines [he] they lay]

                [(3) Like [a] to serpents in the night,   35
                (4) They [*altered to* He] embrac'd my [mirtle] blossoms bright]
                (1) Like [a] to [serpents in the] holy men by day,

(2)   Underneath [my] the vines [he] they lay.
So I smote them & [his] their gore   40
Stain'd the roots my mirtle bore;
But the time of youth is fled,
And grey hairs are on my head.

From the first draft of "Infant Sorrow," Note-book *(1793)*.

A   *Infant Sorrow*

My mother groaned, my father wept;
Into the dangerous world I leapt,
Helpless, naked, piping loud,
Like a fiend hid in a cloud.

Struggling in my father's hands   5
Striving against my swaddling bands,
Bound & weary, I thought best
To sulk upon my mother's breast.

Songs of Experience

1. The first stanza of "Infant Joy" is a dialogue, and the second, a song sung by the adult. How are these different forms integrated? Note how the parts of the dialogue are not separated by "she said" or "the child replied." How are empathy and parental (maternal) love expressed through the combined form?

2. Is there an acknowledgment of sorrow or fearfulness in the word "befall"? Explain.

3. Originally "Infant Sorrow" was a much longer poem. It is printed here as B without the first two stanzas which later became the song of experience. The shortened version is more clearly polemical or contrary to the song of innocence. Regarding B, show how the first two stanzas act as an introduction to a history of the speaker from birth to old age.

4. These two short songs belong together, as do "The Lamb" and "The Tyger." While the song of experience does offer ironic or satiric commentary to the earlier song, it also complements it by demonstrating

the human need for a balanced view. The willfulness, vigor, and sorrow of the song of experience is as much a part of Blake's world view as the passive loveliness of "Infant Joy." What the song of experience does satirize is a one-sided view of man and the human condition. Illustrate.

5. In view of "The Tyger," how is "dangerous" (line 2 of "Infant Sorrow") a positive word? Discuss the affirmative nature of the full version of "Infant Sorrow."

B   *London*

    I wander thro' each dirty street,
    Near where the dirty Thames does flow,
    And [see] mark in every face I meet
    Marks of weakness, marks of woe.

    In every cry of every man   5
    In [every voice of every child]
    every infant's cry of fear
    In every voice, in every ban
    The [german] mind forg'd [links I hear] manacles I hear.

    [But most] How the chimney sweeper's cry
    [Blackens o'er the churches' walls]   10
    Every black'ning church appalls,
    And the hapless soldier's sigh
    Runs in blood down palace walls.

    [But most the midnight harlot's curse
    From every dismal street I hear,   15
    Weaves around the marriage hearse
    And blasts the new born infant's tear.]

    But most [from every] thro' wintry streets I hear
    How the midnight harlot's curse
    Blasts the new born infant's tear,   20
    And [hangs] smites with plagues the marriage hearse.

But most the shrieks of youth I hear
But most thro' midnight & ....
How the youthful ...

Note-book (1793)

A   *London*

Final   I wander thro' each charter'd street,
version   Near where the charter'd Thames does flow,
                 And mark in every face I meet
                 Marks of weakness, marks of woe.

                 In every cry of every Man,   5
                 In every Infant's cry of fear,
                 In every voice, in every ban,
                 The mind-forg'd manacles I hear.

                 How the Chimney-sweeper's cry
                 Every blackening Church appalls;   10
                 And the hapless Soldier's sigh
                 Runs in blood down Palace walls.

                 But most thro' midnight streets I hear
                 How the youthful Harlot's curse
                 Blasts the new born Infant's tear,   15
                 And blights with plagues the Marriage hearse.

1. This great poem is about human squalor and misery peculiar to large cities, yet it is not indicting London itself. Blake's scathing ironies are reserved for man in a graceless state. He is against the chartering of human lives, which is to say, he is against slavery and tyranny in all their institutional manifestations. To charter is to "hire out." How is this a more appropriate word than the earlier "dirty"? How can the Thames, a free-flowing river, be "chartered"?

2. Discuss linguistic daring in this poem. Use the B version to illuminate Blake's care with phrasing and individual words.

3. The poem offers revolutionary faith that the human spirit may be transformed. What is needed is the removal of institutional tyrannies.

As if these institutions are not explicit enough in this poem, Blake offers a fragment from the Rossetti Manuscript, no. 33:

> Remove away that black'ning church:
> Remove away that marriage hearse:
> Remove away that man of blood
> You'll quite remove the ancient curse.

Notes

1. David Wagenknecht, *Blake's Night: William Blake and the Idea of Pastoral* (Cambridge, MA: Harvard University Press, 1973).
2. *The Complete Poetry and Prose of William Blake*, ed. David V. Erdman, commentary by Harold Bloom, rev. ed. (Berkeley and Los Angeles: University of California Press, 1982).
3. *Songs of Innocence and of Experience*, ed. Andrew Lincoln; Volume 2, *The Illuminated Books of William Blake* (Princeton, NJ: Princeton University Press, 1998); and Zachary Leader, *Reading Blake's Songs* (Boston: Routledge & Kegan Paul, 1981).

EMILY DICKINSON

1830–1886

Tell all the Truth but tell it slant—
Success in Circuit lies
Too bright for our infirm Delight
The Truths superb surprise.

As Lightning to the Children eased
With explanation kind
The Truth must dazzle gradually
Or every man be blind—

W E HAVE THOMAS H. JOHNSON TO THANK FOR HIS excellent variorum edition of *The Poems of Emily Dickinson*,[1] which finally enabled readers of Emily Dickinson to study her poems as she had written them down, though not in the sequence she intended. For an insightful study of her notebooks (facsimiles)—these were handwritten in small handbound notebooks, 4–5 sheets each—see *The Modern Poetic Sequence* by M.L. Rosenthal and Sally M. Gall.[2] In the various editions that followed her death in 1886, editors altered and "regularized" the poems to suit the demands of popular taste. Only twelve poems were published in her lifetime.

Emily Dickinson lived her entire life in Amherst, Massachusetts, a village of stern Puritan origins, making only brief visits to South Hadley and Washington, D.C. Her father, a lawyer and congressman, was a friend of Ralph Waldo Emerson, and it is quite possible that as a young girl Emily may have met and listened to this leading American thinker and poet. It is necessary to remind ourselves that Emily Dickinson was involved in the literary and cultural world of her day. Because her life eventually became reclusive, the tendency is to imagine it, inaccurately, as "a buried life." Emily Dickinson reached out to many people, largely through correspondence, and many of them were aware of her poems. It is evident through her letters that she knew her poetic strength, which is attested to by her central question to her literary friend T.W. Higginson. She wanted to know if her verse was "alive," if it "breathed."

In his introduction, Johnson provides us with the reliable text of Dickinson's poems, and details the various editorial problems encountered in working with the manuscripts and various editions:

The manuscripts of nearly all the poems survive. The text is always in one of three stages of composition: a fair copy, a semi-final draft, or a workshop draft. It sometimes had been set down in two or more various fair copies, sent to different friends. On occasion it is found in all three stages, thus affording the chance to watch the creative spirit in action.

Johnson makes the point that one version is as valid, or as final, as another. The so-called authoritative version is often arbitrarily chosen. Occasionally there is evidence that the original inspiration produced a poem complete in its first draft, and that the poet was completely satisfied with it, for example, the famous "Humming Bird." But generally, there is no such indication as to which version the poet preferred, or if she was ever completely satisfied with the last version.

The external and, perhaps more important, internal events of Emily Dickinson's life are charted in her poems. Her many losses, her daily involvement with her natural surroundings, her growing and acute sensitivity to relationships—all are there. Yet an overemphasis on the autobiographical nature of her poetry tends to make one less aware of the revelation of a psychological dilemma that is truly universal in nature, a dilemma exemplified by her love of paradox—a bitter perception of contraries within single experiences. Both the short, epigrammatic line and the strange punctuation—her use of the dash—communicate a world in which certainty and faith are being constantly disturbed.

Her poems can be divided into general themes. Many of her love poems are about renunciation while others are much more sensual. In the nature poems, one feels her sensibility reaching out for truth through the creation of relationships with all things beyond the self, that is, with the eternal. This extension to include the infinite contained in spirit, nature, and man is part of her concept of "circumference":

Circumference, Thou Bride of Awe
Possessing thou shalt be,

Possessed by every hallowed knight
That dares to covet thee.

Her intent was to elicit awe, not dread (though fear is a dominant emotion in her poetry), and to send this awe out through circumference. We can find analogies to her sense of awe in the most religious poetry, yet her own sense is particularly secular and metaphysical. Still, she is also moved by a sense of the Creator. Awe in this sense also finds constant expression in her poetry. There are also poems having to do with psychological pain and death. These divisions are only convenient ways to categorize many overlapping themes; many of her poems are invested with them all.

Emily Dickinson is a nineteenth-century poet with many of the characteristics typical of the late Romantic and Victorian ages. Stylistically, there is an obvious debt to Emerson and to the seventeenth-century poet Sir Thomas Browne, but more so to the Bible in her use of biblical cadence and rhythm. It has been said of her that "the Bible was her lexicon." She relied on "common meter," usually iambic, from Protestant hymnals. Still, modern critics and readers have embraced her poetry as if it were modern. Cries of priggishness or lady-like poetry can hardly apply, and her poems can undergo the careful examination that one would afford John Donne or T.S. Eliot. Her imagery is both suggestive and vivid and invites the reader to participate in the experience of the poem in a way that only the most well-wrought poetry does.

The chronological arrangement here, as in Johnson's variorum edition, is merely an approximation. I have followed his direction along with the scholarly wisdom of Ralph William Franklin's *The Editing of Emily Dickinson, a Reconsideration*,[3] a book which raises interesting questions about the editing of the poems. Dickinson's poems are generally without titles. Johnson assigned numbers to them, and for the ease of finding the poems in the collected edition, or in the selected poems, we have retained Johnson's numbering. The A version, in general, is the definitive poem as Johnson chooses to present it, though it is not necessarily the final version the poet wrote. In like fashion, and in this chapter only, B and C are not indicators of chronological order, but merely of the poet's variant versions. Poems marked X contain alterations made by one or another of Emily Dickinson's editors. When relevant, notes, sources, and dates of publication will be given following the poem.

A

[*Definitive
version*]

Heart! We will forget him!
You and I—tonight!
You may forget the warmth he gave—
I will forget the light!

When you have done, pray tell me   5
That I may straight begin!
Haste! lest while you're lagging
I remember him!

X

Heart! We will forget him!
You and I tonight!
You may forget the warmth he gave
I will forget the light!

When you have done, pray tell me   5
That I my thoughts may dim
Haste! lest while you're lagging
I may remember him!

1. Emily Dickinson's use of dashes and other punctuation is often idiosyncratic, though it's been appreciated as a kind of musical notation or clue as to how the voice might sound. When the editors regularized the punctuation here, did they make an easier flowing poem? In the poetry that follows, one might consider when her poetry invites editorial interference by its unconventionality. What else, other than tempo, is disturbed by the elimination of dashes? Why retain all exclamation points?

2. Why did the editors tamper with line 6? Is its tone at variance with the rest of the poem? Does it change the meaning?

3. Elements of emotional conflict are as essential to dramatic poetry as are the multiple voices and characters in a play. Multiple voices and characters, however, may be implied if not actually present. Discuss this poem as a drama. Such a discussion must consider the tone of

voice of one or another dramatic parts. In order for dramatic tension to be upheld, the dramatic voice must be consistent.

B   *Called Back*

Just lost, when I was saved!
Just heard the world go by!
Just girt me for the onset with Eternity,
When breath drew back,
And on the other side   5
I heard recede the disappointed tide!

Therefore, as One returned, I feel,
Odd secrets of "the Line" to tell!
Some Sailor, skirting novel shores
Some pale "reporter" from the awful doors   10
Before the Seal!

Next time, to stay!
Next time, the things to see
By Ear unheard.
Unscrutinized by Eye   15
Next time, to tarry,
While the Ages steal
Tramp the slow centuries,
And the Cycles wheel!

A   [*160*]

efinitive
version

Just lost, when I was saved!
Just felt the world go by!
Just girt me for the onset with Eternity.
When breath blew back,
And on the other side   5
I hear recede the disappointed tide!

Therefore, as One returned, I feel,
Odd secrets of the line to tell!
Some Sailor, skirting foreign shores—

Some pale Reporter, from the awful doors   10
Before the Seal!

Next time, to stay!
Next time, the things to see
By Ear unheard,
Unscrutinized by Eye—   15
Next time, to tarry,
While the Ages steal—
Slow tramp the Centuries,
And the Cycles wheel!

1. "Novel shores" in B9, while carrying the same literal meaning as "foreign shores" in A9, is a very different construction. The phrase used in A is less strange. After all, we understand "novel" only in terms of the shores' being foreign (new to sailors) in the first place. Because the one is more metaphysical, less direct, than the other does not mean it produces better poetry. Certain metaphors offer false attractiveness. Discuss.

2. Line 18 is different in each version. How different is the meaning of each? Consider whether or not this is a significant change. Discuss the question of consistency of diction or language usage in the poem regarding this change in line 18.

3. What is implied about the author's attitude toward the words in quotation marks?

B

[214]

I taste a liquor never brewed—
From Tankards scooped in Pearl—
Not all the Frankfort Berries
Yield such an Alcohol!

Inebriate of Air—am I—   5
And Debauchee of Dew—
Reeling—thro endless summer days—
From inns of Molten Blue—

When "Landlords" turn the drunken Bee
Out of the Foxglove's door—   10

When Butterflies—renounce their "drams"—
I shall but drink the more!

Till Seraphs swing their snowy Hats—
And Saints—to windows run—
To see the little Tippler   15

From Manzanilla come!

A   [*214*]

efinitive   I taste a liquor never brewed—
version   From Tankards scooped in Pearl—
Not all the Vats upon the Rhine
Yield such an Alcohol!

Inebriate of Air—am I—   5
And Debauchee of Dew—
Reeling—thro endless summer days—
From inns of Molten Blue—

When "Landlords" turn the drunken Bee
Out of the Foxglove's door—   10
When Butterflies—renounce their "drams"—
I shall but drink the more!

Till Seraphs swing their snowy Hats—
And Saints—to windows run—
To see the little Tippler   15
Leaning against the—Sun—

In an edition published after her death, editors altered the first stanza to read:

I taste a liquor never brewed,
From tankards scooped in pearl;
Not Frankfort berries yield the sense
Such a delirious whirl.

1. The editors in 1861 felt the need to alter line B4. Is the original line

objectionable? What conjectures can be made about editorial taste during this period?

2. "Manzanilla" in B16 is a better sounding word in the context of line 15. The line is more melodious than A16. However, while A16 may seem more prosaic, the language being direct, it does achieve a necessary image. It is a difficult image to imagine, but in the context of the whole last stanza, it does make sense. After all, the Saints are doing the seeing here. Is there something about the second stanza or the general mood of the entire poem that accounts for the last line in A?

3. Is the rhythm improved or disturbed by the alteration of line 3? Which line holds richer imagery? Specificity is lost when "Frankfort Berries" is abandoned. What is gained?

C

[216]

Safe in their Alabaster Chambers—
Untouched by Morning
And untouched by Noon—
Sleep the meek members of the Resurrection—
Rafter of satin,   5
And Roof of stone.

Light laughs the breeze
In her Castle above them—
Babbles the Bee in a stolid Ear,
Pipe the Sweet Birds in ignorant cadence—   10
Ah, what sagacity perished here!

B

Safe in their Alabaster Chambers
Untouched by Morning—
And untouched by Noon—
Sleep the meek members of the Resurrection,
Rafter of Satin—and Roof of Stone—   5

Grand go the Years,
In the Crescent above them—
Worlds scoop their Arcs—
And Firmaments—row—
Diadems—drop—   10

And Doges—surrender—
Soundless as Dots,
On a Disc of Snow.

A

*efinitive
version*

Safe in their Alabaster Chambers,
Untouched by Morning—
And Untouched by Noon—
Lie the meek members of the Resurrection—
Rafter of Satin—and Roof of Stone—   5

Grand go the Years—in the Crescent—above them—
Worlds scoop their Arcs—
And Firmaments—row—
Diadems—drop—and Doges—surrender
Soundless as dots—on a Disc of Snow—   10

*This poem was enclosed in a letter to Sue Dickinson in 1861. The following substitutes for
the second stanza were also sent to her:*

Springs—shake the sills—
But—the Echoes—stiffen—
Hoar—is the window—
And numb the door—
Tribes of Eclipse—in Tents—of Marble—   5
Staples—of Ages—have buckled—there—

Springs—shake the Seals—
But the silence—stiffens—
Frosts unhook—in the Northern Zones—
Icicles—crawl from the Polar Caverns—
Midnight in Marble—Refutes—the Suns—   5

X

Safe in their Alabaster Chambers—
Untouched by Morning
And untouched by Noon—
Sleep the meek members of the Resurrection—
Rafter of satin, And Roof of Stone.   5

Light laughs the breeze
In her Castle of sunshine
Babbles the Bee in a stolid Ear.
Pipe the Sweet Birds in ignorant cadence—
Ah, what sagacity perished here!   10

Grand go the Years—in the Crescent—above them—
Worlds scoop their Arcs—
And Firmaments—row—
Diadems—drop—and Doges surrender
Soundless as dots—on a Disc of Snow—   15

1. The lyric is a short poem, often on a theme of personal love or sorrow. It is marked by its personal tone as well as its apparent spontaneity. It is like a short burst of song, sudden and "lyrical. " In the above versions we see many changes, changes that actually embody different kinds of poetry. Where is Emily Dickinson practising lyrical poetry with the particular intensity of that mode? When is she less lyrical, more intellectual? What kind of poem is finally achieved?

2. Which attempt at the second stanza is more musical? Consider all versions of the stanza. How is this an important consideration in this particular poem?

3. In her attempts to embody a vision that must have been shifting, she writes with entirely different images, movement, and ideas. The reconstructed version X is most interesting for it brings together two versions of the second stanza as its second and third stanzas. Do you think this is successful or is it an awkward construction?

4. "Castle of sunshine" in X7 sounds like a cliché and not very much like an Emily Dickinson metaphor. Can you characterize her metaphors?

B

[273]

He put the Belt around my life
I heard the Buckle snap—
And left his process satisfied
My Lifetime folding up—
Deliberate, as a Duke would do   5
A Kingdom's Title Deed—

Henceforth, a Dedicated sort—
A Member of the Cloud.

Yet near enough to come at call—
And do the little Toils 10
That make the Circuit of the Rest—
And deal occasional smiles
To lives as stoop to notice mine—
And kindly ask it in—
Whose invitation, For this world   15
For Whom I must decline?

Incorporating suggested variants.

A   [273]

efinitive
version
He put the Belt around my life
I heard the Buckle snap—
And turned away, imperial,
My Lifetime folding up—
Deliberate as a Duke would do   5
A Kingdom's Title Deed—
Henceforth, a Dedicated sort—
A Member of the Cloud.

Yet not too far to come at call—
And do the little Toils 10   10
That make the Circuit of the Rest—
And deal the occasional smiles
To lives that stoop to notice mine—
And kindly ask it in—
Whose invitation, know you not   15
For Whom I must decline?

In Poems *(1891), one word is altered: l. 15: know/knew.*

1. The two versions are from one manuscript poem. The B version includes the poet's cancelled or marginal lines and words. What results from this editorial process are two versions of the same poem, when in fact there were not two versions intended but rather one

poem with certain undecided parts.

2. In B3 "process" is an interesting word when referring to an act of love or human contact—both of which are implied in the first two lines. Yet the word "process" is extremely cold. There may be a built-in slur in her usage. The line, however, is difficult to read aloud and in respect to euphony A3 sounds much better. Belt/life/Buckle/imperial form a lovely pattern of sounds. Is more lost than gained in line 3? Does "imperial" do more than merely sound good?

3. Note how the action and attention in A3 remain with the "He" of the first line. In the B version "He" is dismissed earlier.

4. What does the apparently minor change in line 9 indicate about the speaker's attitude toward her situation? Discuss the other changes.

B

[*280*]

    I felt a Funeral, in my Brain,
    And Mourners to and fro
    Kept treading—treading—till it seemed
    That Sense was breaking through—

    And when they all were seated,   5
    A Service, like a Drum—
    Kept beating—beating—till I thought
    My mind was going numb—

    And then I heard them lift a Box
    And creak across my Soul   10
    With those same Boots of Lead, again,
    Then Space—began to toll,

    As all the Heavens were a Bell,
    And Being, but an Ear,
    And I, and Silence, some strange Race   15
    Wrecked, and solitary, here—

    And then a Plank in Reason, broke,
    And I dropped down, and down—

And hit a World, at every Crash
And Got through—knowing then—   20

Incorporating suggested variants.

A   [*280*]

Definitive   I felt a Funeral, in my Brain,
version   And Mourners to and fro
                   Kept treading—treading—till it seemed
                   That Sense was breaking through—

                   And when they all were seated,   5
                   A Service, like a Drum—
                   Kept beating—beating—till I thought
                   My mind was going numb—

                   And then I heard them lift a Box
                   And creak across my Soul   10
                   With those same Boots of Lead, again,
                   Then Space—began to toll,

                   As all the Heavens were a Bell,
                   And Being, but an Ear,
                   And I, and Silence, some strange Race 1   15
                   Wrecked, and solitary, here—

                   And then a Plank in Reason, broke,
                   And I dropped down, and down—
                   And hit a World, at every plunge,
                   And Finished knowing—then—   20

In Poems *(1896), this poem was printed with stanza 5 omitted.*

1. This often-reprinted poem conveys psychological pain. The pain felt
in the first stanza is perceived in a context of disorder and is later
organized through images of the funeral service and intensified in the
terrifying stanza 3. From this point, the poem moves toward the
reception of stanza 5. In 1896 the editors omitted this fifth stanza. Does
stanza 4 seem to offer a solution as to why they did this "chopping"?

2. A different idea develops because of the few variants in the last lines. The shift in tone suggests a psychological difference as well. Discuss.

B   There came a Day—at Summer's full—
       Entirely for me—
[322] I thought that such—were for the Saints—
       Where Resurrections [Revelations]—be—
       The Sun—as Common—went abroad   5
       The Flowers accustomed blew
       While our two Souls that [As if no Souls the] Solstice passed—
       Which [that] maketh all things new.

       The time was scarce profaned—by speech—
       The falling [figure/symbol] of a word   10
       Was needless—as at Sacrament—
       The wardrobe—of our Lord—

       Each was to each—the sealed church—
       Permitted to commune—this time—
       Lest we too awkward—show—   15
       At "Supper of the Lamb."

       The hours slid fast—as hours will—
       Clutched tight—by greedy hands—
       So—faces on two Decks—look back—
       Bound to opposing lands—   20

       And so—when all the time had leaked [failed]—
       Without external sound—
       Each—bound the other's Crucifix—
       We gave no other bond—

       Sufficient troth—that we shall rise—   25
       Deposed—at length—the Grave—
       To that New Marriage—
       Justified—through Calvaries of Love!

There came a Day at Summer's full,
Entirely for me—
I thought that such were for the saints,
Where Resurrections—be—
The Sun, as common, went abroad,   5
The flowers, accustomed, blew,
As if no soul the solstice passed
That maketh all things new—

The time was scarce profaned, by speech—
The symbol of a word   10
Was needless, as at Sacrament,
The Wardrobe—of our Lord—

Each was to each The Sealed Church,
Permitted to commune this—time—
Lest we too awkward show
At Supper of the Lamb.   15

The Hours slid fast—as Hours will,
Clutched tight, by greedy hands—
So faces on two Decks, look back,
Bound to opposing lands—   20

And so when all the time had leaked,
Without external sound
Each bound the Other's Crucifix—
We gave no other Bond—

Sufficient troth, that we shall rise—   25
Deposed—at length, the Grave—
To that new Marriage,
Justified—through Calvaries of Love—

This poem was published in Scribner's Magazine, *VIII (August, 1890), titled
"Renunciation." Stanza 4 was omitted. The following words were altered: 1.3: were/was,
1.7: soul/sail, 1.17: fast/past, 1.25: shall/should.*

1. The editor's alteration (see note below A) generally makes the language more predictable, as if he suspects the poet of being mad. For example, l.17: Slid "fast" is a rather startling substitution for the more standard "slid past. " Yet it *does* much more, whatever problems the reader may encounter.

2. Emily Dickinson's use of initial capital letters has caused much wondering. How is the poet using capitalization as a device?

3. Discuss the intellectual struggle apparent in B10. Comment on the other variants bracketed in B.

4. Line 7 is different in meaning in the two versions. Here the difference betrays the speaker's emotion rather than her religious point of view.

5. Action and movement are finally sacrificed in A10. Is "symbol" a better word?

B   *Dying*

[465]
        I heard a Fly buzz—when I died—
        The Stillness round my form
        Was like the Stillness in the Air—
        Between the Heaves of Storm—

        The Eyes beside—had wrung them dry—   5
        And Breaths were gathering sure
        For that last Onset—when the King
        Be witnessed—in his power—

        I willed my Keepsakes—Signed Away
        What portion of me—I   10
        Could make assignable—and then
        There interposed a Fly—

        With Blue uncertain stumbling Buzz—
        Between the light—and me—
        And then the Windows failed—and then   15
        I could not see to see—

A

Definitive
version

[465]

I heard a Fly buzz—when I died—
The Stillness in the Room
Was like the Stillness in the Air—
Between the Heaves of Storm—

The Eyes around—had wrung them dry—   5
And Breaths were gathering firm
For that last Onset—when the King
Be witnessed—in the Room—

I willed my Keepsakes—Signed away
What portion of me be   10
Assignable—And then it was
There interposed a Fly—

With Blue-uncertain stumbling Buzz—
Between the light—and me—
And then the Windows failed—and then   15
I could not see to see—

1. In X₂ "round" *is* more dramatic. Is the word preferred for this reason? How are other words, as in the second stanza, affected by the change?

2. What are the editors aiming at in the rewriting of line 8?

3. Note the editors' attempt to make lines 10 and 11 "easier." Both are difficult to read. Is this a weak point in the poem?

4. Dickinson veered from conventional rhymes to use vowel, slant, or "suspended" rhymes. Comment on whatever specific changes affect the rhyming in this poem.

B

[365]

Dare you see a soul at the "White Heat?"
Then crouch within the door—
Red—is the Fire's common tint—
But when the quickened Ore

Has sated Flame's conditions— 5
She quivers from the Forge
Without a color, but the Light
Of unannointed Blaze—

Least Village, boasts its Blacksmith—
Whose Anvil's even ring 10
Stands symbol for the finer Forge
That soundless tugs—within—

Refining these impatient Ores
With Hammer, and with Blaze
Until the designated Light 15
Repudiate the Forge—

This version was published in the Atlantic Monthly (*October, 1891*) *with Emily Dickinson's suggested variants: 1.4: quickened/vivid; l.6: Its quivering substance plays; 1.10: ring/din.*

In Poems (*1991*), *the version of the poem is the same as that in the* Atlantic Monthly, *but it is titled "The White Heat."*

A   [*365*]

Definitive   Dare you see a Soul *at the White Heat?*
version   Then crouch within the door—
                  Red —is the Fire's common tint—
                  But when the vivid Ore
                  Has vanquished Flame's conditions, 5
                  It quivers from the Forge
                  Without a color, but the light
                  Of unannointed Blaze.
                  Least Village has its Blacksmith
                  Whose Anvil's even ring 1 10
                  Stands symbol for the finer Forge
                  That soundless tugs—within—
                  Refining these impatient Ores
                  With Hammer, and with Blaze
                  Until the Designated Light 15
                  Repudiate the Forge—

1. Does this poem naturally fall into stanzas or is the single sixteen-line unit more consistent with the poem's design? If both are acceptable but create different responses in the reader, what is it about typography that does this?

2. Comment on the length and sound as well as the meanings of the two words changed in lines 4 and 5.

3. Why the change in pronoun in line 6? This may be a matter of style, but the poet's choice could trigger a change of attitude in the reader.

4. "Boasts" is a better word in line 9. But like a dominant line in a painting, a word may pull too much attention toward an action the poet does not want emphasized. Is this the case here?

5. What is the dominant action or concern of the poem? Is it the same—on all levels—in both versions?

A

efinitive
version

[712]

Because I could not stop for Death—
He kindly stopped for me—
The Carriage held but just Ourselves
And Immortality.

We slowly drove—He knew no haste   5
And I had put away
My labor and my leisure too,
For His Civility—

We passed the School, where Children strove
At Recess—in the Ring—   10
We passed the Fields of Grazing Grain—
We passed the Setting Sun—

Or rather—He passed Us—
The Dews drew quivering and chill—
For only Gossamer, my Gown—   15
My Tippet—only Tulle—

We paused before a House that seemed
A Swelling of the Ground—
The Roof was scarcely visible—
The Cornice—in the Ground—   20

Since then—'tis Centuries—and yet
Feels shorter than the Day
I first surmised the Horses Heads
Were toward Eternity—

X   *The Chariot*

Because I could not stop for Death—
He kindly stopped for me—
The Carriage held but just Ourselves
And Immortality.

We slowly drove—He knew no haste   5
And I had put away
My labor and my leisure too,
For His Civility—

We passed the School, where Children played
Their lessons scarcely done.   10
We Passed the Fields of Grazing Grain—
We passed the setting Sun—

We paused before a House that seemed
A Swelling of the Ground—
The Roof was scarcely visible—   15
The Cornice—but a Mound—

Since then—'tis Centuries—but each
Feels shorter than the Day
I first surmised the Horses Heads
Were toward Eternity—   20

1. For years critics of Emily Dickinson's poetry were distressed by the
fact that editors had mangled her poetry. Mr. Johnson's text reveals
qualities in many of the poems which had been obscured by earlier

editors. Note the changes in lines 9 and 10. What has the poet—not the editors—done to vary the rhythm of the line? How do the editors create an image with one word in line 9 that the poet could not possibly have intended?

2. There is an interesting play of mind missed by the editorial omission of stanza 4. Discuss.

3. There are a few other changes in certain short words. Do these count in terms of our responses?

B
I felt a Cleaving in my Mind
As if my Brain had split
I tried to match it Seam by Seam
But could not make them fit.

The thought behind, I tried to join   5
Unto the thought before
But Sequence ravelled out of reach
Like Balls—upon a Floor.

Variant of second stanza:

The Dust behind I strove to join
Unto the Disk before—
But Sequence ravelled out of Sound
Like Balls upon a Floor—

A   [937]

efinitive
version
I felt a Cleaving in my Mind—
As if my Brain had split—
I tried to match it Seam by Seam—
But could not make them fit.

The thought behind, I strove to join   5
Unto the thought before—
But sequence ravelled out of Sound
Like Balls—upon a Floor.

A version of this poem, titled "The Last Thought," was published in Poems *(1896).*
The change in line 7 was adopted. Word altered: 1.1: Cleaving/cleavage.

1. The B version of the second stanza introduces an interesting conceit, or elaborated idea. Does this merely intensify or build upon the already metaphysical imagery of the poem, or is the pattern of imagery somehow changed?

2. What purpose is served by giving a poem a title? Is "The Last Thought" an appropriate title?

3. Discuss the change of the first line in the version published in *Poems* (1896). Does the poem's "activity" demand a participle? Would the noun be the more conservative choice?

4. Which version of line 7 is most consistent with the development of imagery in the poem?

B

Worksheet
draft

To Pity those who [that] know her not
Is helped [soothed] by the regret
That those who know her know her less
The nearer her they get—
How adequate the Human Heart   5
To its emergency
Intrenchments stimulate [Intrenchment stimulates] a friend
And stem [stems] [balk] an enemy

[*1400*]

A

Definitive
version

What mystery pervades a well!
The water lives so far—
A neighbor from another world
Residing in a jar

Whose limit none have ever seen,   5
But just his lid of glass—
Like looking every time you please
In an abyss's face!

The grass does not appear afraid,
I often wonder he   10
Can stand so close and look so bold
At what is awe to me.

Related somehow they may be,
The sedge stands next the sea—
Where he is floorless   15
And does not timidity betray

But nature is a stranger yet;
The ones that cite her most
Have never passed her haunted house
Nor simplified her ghost.   20

To pity those that know her not
Is helped by the regret
That those who know her, know her less
The nearer her they get.

X   *A Well*

What mystery pervades a well!
The water lives so far—
Like neighbor from another world
Residing in a jar

The grass does not appear afraid,   5
I often wonder he
Can stand so close and look so bold
At what is dread to me.

Related somehow they may be,
The sedge stands next the sea—   10
Where he is floorless, yet of fear
No evidence gives he.

But nature is a stranger yet;
The ones that cite her most
Have never passed her haunted house   15
Nor simplified her ghost.

To pity those that know her not
Is helped by the regret
That those who know her, know her less
The nearer her they get. 20

1. What is lost by the omission of the second stanza? Is it a smoother poem without this difficult quatrain? What difficulties arise within the quatrain? Discuss fear in this stanza.

2. Again the editors have corrected the poet. "Like" in line X3 is better syntactically. The editorial change in syntax turns the metaphor into a simile. "Like" makes the analogy explicit, whereas the metaphor implies the analogy, thus bringing the reader into active participation in the poem's development. The simile here makes less of a demand on our imaginations.

3. The editors replaced Dickinson's "awe" (AI_2) with "dread" (X8). "Awe" had a special meaning to the poet. "Dread" may or may not be more concrete. A concrete noun evokes an *image* of something with an objective existence; a concrete illustration brings what is abstract into the range of personal, usually sensory, experience. Discuss concrete language in Dickinson's poetry.

4. Discuss rhythm, meter, and rhyme in A's fourth stanza (X's stanza 3), taking into consideration the poet's use of imperfect rhymes. Does the worksheet draft betray a different vision from the one that the final poem contains?

B

[1540]

As imperceptibly as Grief
The Summer lapsed away—
Too imperceptibly at last
To feel like Perfidy—

A Quietness distilled— 5
As Twilight long begun—
Or Nature—Spending with Herself
Sequestered Afternoon—

Sobriety inhered
Through gaudy influence 10

The Maple lent unto the Road
And graphic Consequence

Invested sombre place—
As suddenly be worn
By sober Individual   15
A Homogeneous Gown.

Departed was the Bird—
And scarcely had the Hill—
A flower to help His straightened face
In stress of Burial   20

The Winds came closer up—
The Cricket spoke so clear
Presumption was—His Ancestors
Inherited the Floor—

The Dusk drew earlier in—   25
The Morning foreign shone—
The courteous, but harrowing Grace
Of Guest who would be gone—

And thus, without a Wing
Or service of a Keel—   30
Our Summer made her light Escape
Unto the beautiful—

A

                              [*1540*]

efinitive
version

As imperceptibly as Grief
The Summer lapsed away
Too imperceptible at last
To seem like Perfidy—
A Quietness distilled   5
As Twilight long begun,
Or Nature spending with herself
Sequestered Afternoon—
The Dusk drew earlier in—
The Morning foreign shone—   10

A courteous, yet harrowing Grace,
As Guest, that would be gone—
And thus, without a Wing
Or service of a Keel
Our Summer made her light escape   15
Into the Beautiful!

1. Here the two versions are two separate poems. The omission of portions in A provides a tightness and concision not in B. Compared to the A version, the B version seems to have an added poem in its middle. Viewed independently, however, do the materials of the B version cohere? Do all its parts function toward an achieved end?

Notes

1. Thomas H. Johnson, *The Poems of Emily Dickinson* (Cambridge, MA: Harvard University Press, 1955).
2. M.L. Rosenthal and Sally M. Gall, *The Modern Poetic Sequence* (Oxford: Oxford University Press, 1983).
3. Ralph William Franklin, *The Editing of Emily Dickinson, a Reconsideration* (Madison, WI: University of Wisconsin Press, 1967).

WILLIAM BUTLER YEATS

1865-1939

> The friends that have it I do wrong
> Whenever I remake a song,
> Should know what issue is at stake:
> it is myself that I remake.

BORN IN IRELAND, WILLIAM BUTLER YEATS WAS THE son of the Pre-Raphaelite painter John Butler Yeats. He had no formal university education, although he did read widely. By the late 1890s, Yeats was considered a leading poet in both England and Ireland. In addition, he was one of the leaders of the Irish Renaissance, a nationalistic movement that insisted on self-realization and freedom from English domination. He was also one of the founders of the Abbey Theatre and Senator in the Irish Free State (1922-28). In 1923, Yeats received the Nobel Prize for literature. His writings on occultism and Irish folklore provide essential commentary on his poetry.

Any study of Yeats' poetry will reveal astonishing growth in terms of style and total performance. While the middle and late poems recall many of the concerns and habits of mind, facts of locale, and general sympathies of the very earliest poems, the changes are so great that one might doubt the same poet was at work. Growing up in the "romantic Ireland" of the late nineteenth century, Yeats had to strive to get away from personal commentaries and from an overly elaborate style, heightened to the point of extreme artificiality, which would be characterized by the terms (inadequate though they may be) "romantic agony" or romantic vagueness. Yeats' poetry grew more direct, the line "harder" and more like ordinary speech. He confronted the problems that younger, twentieth-century poets, especially those who came of age immediately following World War I, were facing; that is, how can humanity survive or face its future in a world that is shattered and rapidly losing all meaning? Many of his best poems have at their center a striving for some absolute or positive value that could lend a continuity and/or unity to an age in which "the center cannot hold." Throughout his poetry, the reader feels Yeats' need for a comprehensive mythology or system that would order or organize history, as well as a vision that would enable him to see his age and moment clearly. His solution, expressed in the book *A Vision,* is both personal and complex. In the poetry, the symbols, now developed and clear, remain personal, though they simultaneously expand to afford meanings that are publicly available and have a constant bearing on social conditions.

Yeats provides a cogent example for the modern reader's search for relevance in literature. His poetry, arising from personal experiences, nevertheless suggests, through a series of "symbolic actions," those eternal, ever current, and pressing problems that the truly alive individual faces in his social and political existence, as well as the private life of his own heart.

The "definitive" edition of poetry is *The Poems: The Collected Works of W. B. Yeats,* edited by Richard J. Finneran.[1] This volume contains the final versions of all the poetry that the poet wished to preserve. There is a problem in that Yeats was constantly revising his poetry, especially the early poetry, and the final version often presents a mature Yeats in the guise of an early Yeats poem. Though the final collection of poetry is beautifully organic, it does not demonstrate the total development of the poet. For a fuller awareness of the growth of his poems the reader may consult *The Variorum Edition of the Poems of W.B. Yeats.*[2] This great work carefully records all the revisions of the published poetry of Yeats.

Curtis B. Bradford, in *Yeats at Work,*[3] carries the study of Yeats' revisions one key step further. This study considers the various changes in manuscript form prior to publication. Yeats labored endlessly before he considered his poems ready for publication, and Bradford's book presents the evidence of that labor.

M.L. Rosenthal prepared *Selected Poems and Four Plays of William Butler Yeats,*[4] which has a fine introduction and helpful selective bibliography.

Many general statements have been made about Yeats' revisions. It is acknowledged, for example, that he worked toward greater concision in his rewriting, and that he worked from prose notes. The work stands on its own and it is for each individual student to decide on the virtue or otherwise of these changes. Yeats said in 1927 that "one is always cutting out the dead wood." We see this cutting process in the study of his poetic revisions. Also, the changes in syntax, choice of words, rhythm, and structure indicate more than the wish to be more concise or clearer in meaning. Often the very persona behind the voice in a poem changes as the poet responds differently, at a later date, to his own experience and to the contemporary world.

For our selection of Yeats' poems, we have followed Bradford's method in the handling of draft revisions. Revisions within a line are bracketed. Dates do not appear beneath the A versions, as they are reprinted from the 1956 Macmillan edition of *The Collected Poems.* The B version dates are those of original publication.

B   *A Cradle Song*

The angels are bending
Above your white bed,
They weary of tending
The souls of the dead.

God smiles in high heaven   5
To see you so good;
And the old planets seven
Grow sweet with His mood.

I kiss you and kiss you,
My arms round my own;   10
Ah! how I shall miss you,
My dear, when you're grown!

1890

A   *A Cradle Song*

Final   The angels are stooping
version   Above your bed;
                 They weary of trooping
                 With the whimpering dead.

                 God's laughing in Heaven   5
                 To see you so good;

The Sailing Seven
Are gay with His mood.

I sigh that kiss you,
For I must own   10
That I shall miss you
When you have grown.

1. The early version is clearly the more romantic. While the subject of
the final poem is still romantic, the handling, its use of language and
cadence, has grown tougher, the emotion less vague. Line 11 offers
illumination of this process.

2. Words such as "bending" (B1) and "stooping" (A1) indicate a change
in attitude rather than merely a shift in style. There is an edge to the
word in the final version that determines, or foretells, other changes
in the poem. While the words are close in literal meaning, they do
create different images. Discuss.

3. Also, "tending" (B3) and "trooping" (A3) lead to similar observa-
tions. The "trooping" angel presents a curious image. Can this
abstract conception be seen concretely or realistically?

4. There is clearly no satire or irony in the early poem. Can such tones
be detected in the final poem?

5. Where does Yeats change the meter or the rhythm in his revision?
Note any added or subtracted syllables to the measure and your own
reading speed in each line.

6. Does the astrological allusion introduced in line 7 add to or detract
from the final version?

B   *The Sorrow of Love*

The quarrel of the sparrows in the eaves,
The full round moon and the star-laden sky,
And the loud song of the ever-singing leaves,
Had hid away earth's old and weary cry.

And then you came with those red mournful lips   5
And with you came the whole of the world's tears
And all the trouble of her labouring ships,
And all the trouble of her myriad years.

And now the sparrows warring in the eaves
The curd-pale moon, the white stars in the sky,   10
And the loud chanting of the unquiet leaves,
Are shaken with earth's old and weary cry.

1893

A   *The Sorrow of Love*

Final   The brawling of a sparrow in the eaves,
Version   The brilliant moon and all the milky sky,
               And all that famous harmony of leaves,
               Had blotted out man's image and his cry.

               A girl arose that had red mournful lips   5
               And seemed the greatness of the world in tears,
               Doomed like Odysseus and the labouring ships
               And proud as Priam murdered with his peers;

               Arose, and on the instant clamorous eaves,
               A climbing moon upon an empty sky,   10
               And all that lamentation of the leaves,
               Could but compose man's image and his cry.

1. The final version is a total rewriting of the earlier poem. How does the expression in the final poem alter the entire experience of "The Sorrow of Love"?

2. Which version is more "poetic"? This calls for a close consideration of the poet's diction. Most of Yeats' alterations lie in this area. However, is the total design or structure affected by questions of language and diction? When speaking of design and structure the first consideration is how the lines fall on the page—for example, length of stanza, length of line within each stanza. After that is settled and *felt*, other considerations arise, such as how the action or plot progresses

through the verses, how the tempo and varieties of emotional content are expressed.

3. Is not "quarrel" a more melodious word than "brawling," and the idea of many sparrows quarreling a more interesting image than the image of one sparrow "brawling"? Is "brawling" more acceptable because of the new development in line 2? Or does the change to a single sparrow suggest the evolving emotion of loss better than the possibly more exciting earlier first line? Is the poet simply gaining precision through a tightening up of his diction (viz. line 10) or is the precision an indication of a perception becoming sharper?

4. Line 3 is a substitution of a difficult and vague idea for a rather simple, yet possibly stale, nineteenth-century image. In line 4 the entire vision is shifted. The language is less predictable. Discuss this effect.

5. The image in A6 is a difficult one, but it announces the theme of the rest of the poem. When the image is altered in A, is the theme affected? Discuss the total effect.

6. Note the repetition of "arose" in A. Does the repetition influence the total action in the poem? Note how the romantic conception in the image of B9 fulfills the action in the first line of B. Yeats replaces the image with a different figure of speech—one more difficult to translate.

7. The repetition in the last stanza follows a similar pattern in both versions. What are the differences?

8. Discuss tense in the last line of each version.

B   *A Dream of Death*

> I dreamed that one had died in a strange place
> Near no accustomed hand,
> And they had nailed the boards above her face
> The peasants of that land,
>
> And wondering planted by her solitude   5
> A cypress and a yew.

I came and wrote upon a cross of wood—
Man had no more to do—

'She was more beautiful than thy first love,
This lady by the trees';   10
And gazed upon the mournful stars above,
And heard the mournful breeze.

1891

A

A Dream of Death

Final
Version   I dreamed that one had died in a strange place
              Near no accustomed hand;
              And they had nailed the boards above her face,
              The peasants of that land,
              Wondering to lay her in that solitude,   5
              And raised above her mound
              A cross they had made out of two bits of wood,
              And planted cypress round;
              And left her to the indifferent stars above
              Until I carved these words:
              She was more beautiful than thy first love,
              But now lies under boards.

1. The earlier version is in the ballad tradition. The ballad is conventionally a form of verse adopted for singing or recitation and primarily characterized by its presentation in simple narrative form of a dramatic or exciting episode. When the quatrains are destroyed in A, the ballad movement is altered, the tempo is faster, and the drama movement advances less by acts or stages. Does this effect better suit the content of the poem?

2. One rhyme is done away with in A; a slant rhyme replaces it. What effect has this on the ear? The italics, used instead of quotation marks, effect a very different kind of change. Discuss.

3. How does the voice change in the final version? (The change begins with the omission of the conjunction in A5.)

4. How does the poet indicate a change of feeling about nature being sympathetic to the dead lady?

D

"The great of the old times are among the Tribes of Danu, and are kings and queens among them. Caolte was a companion of Frann; and years after his death he appeared to a king in a forest, and was a flaming man, that he might lead him in the darkness. When the king asked him who he was, he said, 'I am your candlestick.' I do not remember where I have read this story ... Niam was a beautiful woman of the tribes of Danu that led Oisin to the country of the Young, as their country is called; ... and he came back, at last, to bitterness and weariness."

"Knocknarea is in Sligo, and the country people say that Maeve, still a great queen of the Western Sidhe, is buried in the cairn of stones upon it. Cloothna-Bare ... went all over the world, seeking a lake deep enough to drown her faery life, of which she had grown weary, leaping from hill to hill, and setting up a cairn of stones where her feet lighted, until, at last, she found the deepest water in the world in little Lough Ia, on the top of the bird mountain, in Sligo."

C They call from the cairn on Knocknarea
They are calling calling from Knocknarea
They call from the grave of Clooth-na-Bare
And the pool [water] that is over Clooth-na-Bare
Caolte tosses his burning hair.   5
But Niam murmurs 'away come away'

2

Linger no more [Why dost thou brood] where the fire burns bright
Filling thy heart with a mortal dream
[White Our Her] For hands wave to them [are waving] and eyes [are]
    a gleam
'Away, come away [To draw it away] to the dim twilight'   10

3

White arms glimmer and red lips are apart
If any man gaze on the Danaan band
They come between him and the deed of his hand
They come between him and the hope of his heart

[But come afar on their way]   15
Ah somewhere afar on their ringing way
—No hope or deed was a whit so fair
And no hope or deed is

Manuscript Version

B   *The Faery Host*

The host is riding from Knocknarea
And over the grave of Clooth-na-bare,
Coulte tossing his burning hair
And Niam calling, 'away come away.'

'And brood no more where the fire is bright   5
Filling thy heart with a mortal dream,
For breasts are heaving and eyes a-gleam; Away, come away, to
     the dim twilight.

'Arms are a-waving and lips apart
And if any gaze on our rushing band   10

We come between him and the deed of his hand,
We come between him and the hope of his heart.'

The host is rushing 'twixt night and day,
And where is there hope or deed as fair?
Coulte tossing his burning hair   15
And Niam calling 'away, come away.'

1893

A   *The Hosting of the Sidhe*

Final   The host is riding from Knocknarea
Version   And over the grave of Clooth-na-Bare;
                 Coulte tossing his burning hair,
                 And Niam calling *Away, come away:*
                 Empty your heart of its mortal dream.   5
                 The winds, awaken, the leaves whirl round,

Our cheeks are pale, our hair is unbound,
Our breasts are heaving, our eyes are agleam,
Our arms are waving, our lips are apart;
And if any gaze on our rushing band,   10
We come between him and the deed of his hand,
We come between him and the hope of his heart.
The host is rushing 'twixt night and day,
And where is there hope or deed as fair?
Coulte tossing his burning hair,   15
And Niam calling *Away, come away.*

1. Note the change of title, and that the ballad feeling, which is primarily narrative rather than dramatic, is replaced with a more dramatic structure. Also, italics replace quotation marks: an immediacy is gained. There is a different usage of the pronoun in each version. Here may be a good opportunity for "adjective" study. "Mortal" in "mortal dream" is retained in all three versions, while the adjectives "white" and "red" ("White arms glimmer and red lips are apart") are dropped after C. Why?

2. Perhaps "mortal" is essential to the poem's vision, while "white" and "red" are mainly descriptive. Again, why does Yeats use so many predicate adjectives in A?—"Our cheeks are pale," "Our breasts are heaving … our eyes are agleam," and so on.

5. Does the change of the line "Filling thy heart" to "Empty your heart" indicate a change in the poet's relation to the call of the Fairy Band? Again, how is the poem's immediacy affected? Can we consider immediacy in itself a virtue in poetry?

B   *The Two Trees*

Beloved, gaze in thine own heart,
The holy tree is growing there;
From joy the holy branches start,
And all the trembling flowers they bear.
The changing colours of its fruit   5
Have dowered the stars with merry light;
The surety of its hidden root,

Has planted quiet in the night;
The shaking of its leafy head,
Has given the waves their melody,   10
And made my lips and music wed,
Murmuring a wizard song for thee.
There, through bewildered branches, go
Winged Loves borne on in gentle strife,
Tossing and tossing to and fro   15
The flaming circle of our life.
When looking on their shaken hair,
And dreaming how they dance and dart,
Thin eyes grow full of tender care:
Beloved gaze in thin own heart.   20

Gaze no more in the bitter glass
The demons with their subtle guile,
Lift up before us as they pass,
Or only gaze a little while;
For there a fatal image grows,   25
With broken boughs and blackened leaves
And roots half hidden under snows,
Driven by a storm that ever grieves.
All things turn to barrenness
In the dim glass the demons hold—   30
The glass of outer weariness,
Made when God slept in times of old.
There, through the broken branches, go
The ravens of unresting thought;
Peering and flying to and fro,   35
To see men's souls bartered and bought.
When they are heard upon the wind,
And when they shake their wings-alas!
Thy tender eyes grow all unkind:-
Gaze no more in the bitter glass.   40

1892

The Two Trees

Beloved, gaze in thin own heart,
The holy tree is growing there;
From joy the holy branches start,
And all the trembling flowers they bear.
The changing colours of its fruit   5
Have dowered the stars with merry light;
The surety of its hidden root
Has planted quiet in the night;
The shaking of its leafy head
Has given the waves their melody,   10
And made my lips and music wed,
Murmuring a wizard song for thee.
There the Loves a circle go,
The flaming circle of our days,
Gyring, spiring to and fro   15
In those great ignorant leafy ways;
Remembering all that shaken hair
And how the wingéd sandals dart,
Thine eyes grow full of tender care:
Beloved, gaze in thine own heart.   20

Gaze no more in the bitter glass
The demons, with their subtle guile,
Lift up before us when they pass,
Or only gaze a little while;
For there a fatal image grows   25
That the stormy night receives,
Roots half hidden under snows,
Broken boughs and blackened leaves.
For all things turn to barrenness
In the dim glass the demons hold,   30
The glass of outer weariness,
Made when God slept in times of old.
There, through the broken branches, go
The ravens of unresting thought;
Flying, crying, to and fro,   35
Cruel claw and hungry throat,
Or else they stand and sniff the wind;

And shake their ragged wings; alas!
Thy tender eyes grow all unkind:
Gaze no more in the bitter glass.   40

1. In version A, line 13 introduces the image of the circle. In the earlier
version, this image is not developed until line 16. Note the difference
in vision between the circles of version A and version B. How is our
response guided by the introduction of the circle image? Is the
response different in each case? How is the language in the poem
determined by the image and the vision behind the image, which
surely seeps through? Note the change in words—"gyring" for "toss-
ing." How is this consistent with the change of the circle?

2. In version A, note the word "ignorant" in line 16. Is this a clue to
future changes in the poem? Are there any such clues in version B?

3. There is an extension in A36 of the movement in line 35 In the earlier
version a different action is suggested. Comment on how this change,
which includes two lines, affects the close of the poem.

4. Note the differences in punctuation. Are they significant?

B   *Cap and Bell*

The Cap
nd Bells]
                  A Queen was loved by a jester,
                  And once, when the owls grew still,
                  He made his soul go upward
                  And stand on her window sill.
                  In a long and straight blue garment   5
                  It talked, ere the morn grew white.
                  It had grown most wise with thinking
                  On a foot-fall hushed and light,
                  But the young Queen would not listen;
                  She rose in her pale night-gown,   10
                  She drew in the brightening casement,
                  She snicked the brass bolts down.
                  He bade his heart go see her.
                  When the bats cried out no more:
                  In a garment red and quivering,   15
                  It sang to her through the door,

The tongue of it sweet with dreaming
On a flutter of flower-like hair;
But she took her fan from the table
And waved it out on the air.   20
'I've cap and bells,' (he pondered),
'I will send them to her and die.'
And as soon as the morn had whitened,
He left them where she went by.
She took them into her bosom,   25
In her heart she found a tune,
Her red lips sang them a love-song,
The night smelled rich with June.
She opened her door and her window,
The heart and the soul came through: 30
To her right hand came the red one,
To her left hand came the blue.
They set a noise like crickets,
A chattering wise and sweet;
And her hair was a folded flower,   35
And the quiet of love in her feet.

                                              1894

A   *The Cap and Bells*

Final   The jester walked in the garden:
Version   The garden had fallen still;
                 He bade his soul rise upward
                 And stand on her window-sill.

                 It rose in a straight blue garment,   5
                 When owls began to call;
                 It had grown wise-tongued by thinking
                 Of a quiet and light footfall;

                 But the young queen would not listen;
                 She rose in her pale night-gown;   10
                 She drew in the heavy casement
                 And pushed the latches down.

He bade his heart go to her,
When the owls called out no more;
In a red and quivering garment
It sang to her through the door.

It had grown sweet-tongued by dreaming
Of a flutter of flower-like hair;
But she took up her fan from the table
And waved it off on the air.

'I have cap and bells,' he pondered,
'I will send them to her and die';
And when the morning whitened
He left them where she went by.

She laid them upon her bosom,
Under a cloud of her hair,
And her red lips sang them a love-song
Till stars grew out of the air.

She opened her door and her window
And the heart and the soul came through,
To her right hand came the red one,
To her left hand came the blue.

And they set up a noise like crickets,
A chattering wise and sweet,
And her hair was a folded flower
And the quiet of love in her feet.

1. Discuss whether the action of this poem is more effectively expressed in the version without stanzas or in the final version.

2. In version A Yeats omits the introductory statement "A Queen was loved by a jester." What is gained by allowing the poem to imply this statement?

3. Discuss the shifts in rhythm. In your discussion consider line length and questions of stress; that is, note where the accents fall in each line and which syllable in a word is stressed. What do these considerations

have to do with theme? A particular rhythm will determine the way we attend to the content.

4. Note the shifts in language. What kind of words are "brightening" in B11 and "snicked" in B12? Why did Yeats change the figure of speech in line 13? Is it merely that A13 is more direct? Why "owls" for "bats"?

5. Why is the inverted word order of B15 sacrificed for direct word order?

6. Compare stanza 7 in the final poem with line 25 and what follows in B. How has the quality of expression changed?

7. The last eight lines are mostly unchanged. Is the central vision of the poem implicit in these lines?

Notes

1. Richard J. Finneran, ed., *The Poems: The Collected Works of W.B. Yeats* (New York: Simon & Schuster, 1997).
2. Peter Allt and Russell K. Alspach, eds., *The Variorum Edition of the Poems of W.B. Yeats* (New York: Macmillan, 1957)
3. Curtis B. Bradford, *Yeats at Work* (Carbondale, IL: Southern Illinois University Press, 1965).
4. M.L. Rosenthal, ed., *Selected Poems and Four Plays of William Butler Yeats,* 4th ed. (New York: Simon & Schuster, 1996).

WILFRED OWEN

1893–1918

This book is not about heroes. English poetry is not yet fit to speak of them.

Nor is it about deeds, or lands, nor anything about glory, honour, might, majesty, dominion, or power, except War.

Above all I am not concerned with Poetry. My subject is War, and the pity of War. The Poetry is in the pity.

Yet these elegies are to this generation in no sense consolatory. They may be to the next. All a poet can do today is warn. That is why the true Poets must be truthful.

Preface to Wilfred Owen's *War Poems*

I was a boy when I first realized that the fullest life livable was a poet's, and my later experience ratifies it.

Wilfred Owen to his mother

WILFRED OWEN WAS BORN IN SHROPSHIRE, ENGLAND, in the house of his maternal grandfather, Edward Shaw. But the date and circumstances of his death are far more central to the study of his poetry. He was killed in action in World War I at the age of 25 while trying to get his men across a canal. The bulk of his poetry was written in the trenches between August 1917 and September 1918, and the brevity of his own life provides a quiet commentary on the bitter ironies and themes of death and war which make up the substance of his poetry.

The tone of modern poetry was permanently affected by the war experience. This can best be seen in the poetry of those generally neglected poets, the Trench poets of 1914–1918, among them Rupert Brooke, Siegfried Sassoon, Charles Sorley, Robert Graves, Isaac Rosenberg, and Wilfred Owen. Owen was not the only one who died young on the battlefield; an entire generation of talented young men was lost. The infinite despair generally felt by these World War I poets produced a kind of poetry that was new for the English. The poet could no longer view war as a glorious contest with national pride as emotional ballast. The human condition received a reappraisal as a result of the vast blood-letting.

It is difficult to speak of Owen as a major poet in the same sense as we would speak of Yeats or Dickinson. The volume of his verses is slim, and there has long been speculation about Owen's potential had he lived longer. Nevertheless, though only four of his poems were published in his lifetime, his war poems are believed by many to be the finest of their kind in our language.

What is most characteristic of Owen's poems of war is that he emerges as an outstanding poet of peace; love of life emerges beyond the imagery of despair.

His development as a poet directly parallels his war experience. In 1914, like so many young men, he was an idealistic soldier, full of notions about the grandeur of war. Keats was his model and a "weak luxuriousness" marked his early verses. In a very short time he moved away from the comfortable niceties of nineteenth-century verse to a harsher realism, yet he retained the sensuousness that early and late link him to Keats.

Though the realism is marked, Owen is never merely journalistic. The power of his imagination informs the pointed observations, as in "Strange Meeting":

> It seemed that out of the battle I escaped
> Down some profound dull tunnel, long since scooped
> Through granite which titanic wars had grained,
> Yet also there encumbered sleepers groaned,
> Too fast in thoughts or death to be bestirred.

The achievement of the imagination is that it carries us beyond ourselves, and the art clearly transcends the immediate personal situation, while holding on to the immediate world.

Pity is a dominant emotion in his poems, as his preface to a projected book remarks. The pity is clear in the famous poem "Greater Love":

> Red lips are not so red
> As the stained stones kissed by the English Dead.

Kindness of Wooed and Wooer
Seems shame to their love pure.
O love, your eyes lose lure
When I behold eyes blinded in my stead!

Heart, you were never hot
Nor large, nor full like hearts made great with shot;
And though your hand be pale,
Paler are all which trail
Your cross through flame and hail:
Weep, you may weep, for you may touch them not.

Owen's pity is not for himself or his miserable lot, but for the general condition of misery. Thus there is no loss of urgency as the poetry moves away from private experience and remains as relevant to our present condition as it was in 1917.

Like Keats, Owen loved the sound of language. In the genesis of an individual poem we shall see simple rhyme patterns replaced by internal rhyming and stretches of assonances. This is rich poetry, finely embellished, while at the same time it is clear and hard. Discordant sounds are not a failure of the poet's ear, but echoes of war's strident music.

The changes he made in his poetry between 1914 and shortly before his death in 1918 record the poet's seriousness toward his craft, just as the staccato-like sentences in his preface record the seriousness with which he regarded war. The ironies become more concise. In many instances, the language tightens and grows more certain of its power. The poetry becomes wider in its application, less tied to the event, while remaining rooted in actions in the most fundamental way.

Most of Wilfred Owen's autographed poems are in the British Museum, and editions or manuscript drafts exist in at least five other locations. Before the Collected Poems of Wilfred Owen, edited by C. Day Lewis,[1] which contains a biographical memoir by Edmund Blunden, the available editions were Siegfried Sassoon's Poems (1920) and E. Blunden's Poems (1931). Lewis brings together all of the known textual materials in what amounts to a variorum edition, and it is to this text that we refer. No dates appear beneath the poems because most exact dates are unknown. The war poems were composed between January 1917 and November 1918 when Owen was killed. The ordering of all drafts here follows that of Lewis.

What passing-bells for these who die so fast?
    —Only the monstrous anger of our guns.
Let the majestic insults of their iron mouths
    Be as the requiem of their burials.
Of choristers and holy music, none;   5
    Nor any voice of mourning, save the wail
The long-drawn wail of high far-sailing shells.

What candles may we hold to light these lost?
    —Not in the hands of boys, but in their eyes
Shall shine the many flames: holy candles.   10
    Women's wide-spread arms shall be their wreaths,
And pallor of girls' cheeks shall be their palls.
    Their flowers, the tenderness of rough men's minds.
And each slow Dusk, a drawing-down of blinds.

B   *Anthem for Dead Youth*

What passing-bells for you who die in herds?
    —Only the monstrous anger of the guns!
    —Only the stuttering rifles' rattled words
Can patter out your hasty orisons.
No chants for you, nor balms, nor wreaths, nor bells,   5
    Nor any voice of mourning, save the choirs,
And long-drawn sighs of wailing shells;
    And bugles calling for you from sad shires.

What candles may we hold to speed you all?
    Not in the hands of boys, but in their eyes   10
Shall shine [the] holy lights of our goodbyes.
    The pallor of girls' brows must be your pall.
Your flowers, the tenderness of comrades' minds,
And each slow dusk, a drawing-down of blinds.

Other drafts give alternates for the word "comrades" in line 13: patient/silent. In another draft an alternate to line 5 is: "No mockeries for them from prayers or bells."

A

A

Final
Version

Anthem for Doomed Youth

What passing-bells for these who die as cattle?
    Only the monstrous anger of the guns.
    Only the stuttering rifles' rapid rattle
Can patter out their hasty orisons.
No mockeries now for them; no prayers nor bells,   5
    Nor any voice of mourning save the choirs,—
The shrill, demented choirs of wailing shells;
    And bugles calling for them from sad shires.

What candles may be held to speed them all?
    Not in the hands of boys, but in their eyes   10
Shall shine the holy glimmers of good-byes.
    The pallor of girls' brows shall be their pall;
Their flowers the tenderness of patient minds,
And each slow dusk a drawing-down of blinds.

1. The final version achieves greater objectivity and control than the two earlier drafts. The poet has stepped back from the action while still close enough to see and intensely feel it. In what way do we feel the poet has stepped away from the action? Note the change in line 9 and the elimination of the second person "you" throughout stanza 1.

2. The B version is more interesting than C as it shows the poet feeling his way into the final vision by discarding much that was objectionable to him in C and, also, by making use of the material in C. To what degree does C differ from A in terms of how these poems affect the reader? How are they alike?

3. The expression "die so fast" in C1 is abandoned in the B and A versions. Owen may be picking up on the deleted phrase in the opening line of the second stanza. What idea suggested in this phrase is transmitted to the final version of the second stanza?

4. Is there a shifting attitude toward religious conventions observed in the changing imagery from C to A?

5. Which poem is more realistic? Could realism be considered a value here? Note how an artful handling of language, highly contrived as in

A3, can produce the necessary illusion of reality, at least in terms of sound effects.

E   1

[The   "Down the deep, darkening lanes they sang their way
Send-Off]   To the waiting train,
                 And filled its doors with faces grimly gay,
                 And heads and shoulders white with wreath and spray,
                 As men's are, slain."   5

                                    4

                 Will they return, to beatings of great bells,
                 In wild train-loads?
                 A few, a few, too few for drums and yells,
                 May walk back, silent, to their village wells,
                 Up half-known roads.   10

D   Down the wet darkening lanes they sang their way to the cattle-shed
      And lined the train with faces grimly gay.
      Their breasts were stuck all white with wreath and spray
      As men's are, dead.

The final stanzas of The Send-Off *were well established in Owen's mind. The opening stanza, however, went through extensive rewriting as can be seen in this draft and the two that follow.*

C   Low-voiced through darkening lanes they sang their way to the
                                                  cattle-shed.
          And filled the train with faces grimly gay.
       Their breasts were stuck all white with wreath and spray,
          as men's are, dead.

B   Softly down darkening lanes they sang their way
             And no word said.
             They filled the train with faces vaguely gay
             And shoulders covered all white with wreath and spray
             As men's are, dead.   5

The Send-Off

Down the close, darkening lanes they sang their way
To the siding-shed,
And lined the train with faces grimly gay.

Their breasts were stuck all white with wreath and spray
As men's are, dead.   5

Dull porters watched them, and a casual tramp
Stood staring hard,
Sorry to miss them from the upland camp.
Then, unmoved, signals nodded, and a lamp
Winked to the guard.   10

So secretly, like wrongs hushed-up, they went.
They were not ours:
We never heard to which front these were sent.

Nor there if they yet mock what women meant
Who gave them flowers.   15

Shall they return to beatings of great bells
In wild train-loads?
A few, a few, too few for drums and yells,
May creep back, silent, to still village wells
Up half-known roads.   20

1. These many attempts to embody one central experience suggest a
great deal about the relationship of the poet to that particular experi-
ence. Poetic revision here is an index not only to craftsmanship but to
human experience as well. Discuss this statement.

2. The first line of these five versions or drafts demonstrates the poet's
attitude toward an action and a place (*going* "down … *lanes*"). It is
through the choice of adjectives that Owen particularizes this action,
this place. I doubt that it is possible to account for the groping evident
here, but some quality of the poetic process certainly is revealed. Dis-
cuss.

3. In draft E, the first stanza ends with the word "slain." This is a more dramatic word than "dead" (in most cases) and it lines up nicely with "spray" in the line above. Finally, however, Owen chose the word "dead." The question must not be "why?" but "to what end?" Also, how are these two words different?

4. Discuss the evolution of the final stanza.

B

Last Words

> "O Jesus Christ!" one fellow sighed.
> And kneeled, and bowed, tho' not in prayer, and died.
> And the Bullets sang "In Vain,"
>   Machine Guns chuckled "Vain,"
>   Big Guns guffawed "In Vain."   5
>
> "Father and mother!" one boy said.
> Then smiled—at nothing, like a small child; being dead.
> And the Shrapnel Cloud
>   Slowly gestured "Vain,"
>   The falling splinters muttered "Vain."   10
>
> "My love!" another cried, "My love, my bud!"
> Then, gently lowered, his whole face kissed the mud.
> And the Flares gesticulated, "Vain,"
>   The Shells hooted, "In Vain,"
>   And the Gas hissed, "In Vain."   15

A

The Last Laugh

Final Version

> 'O Jesus Christ! I'm hit,' he said; and died.
> Whether he vainly cursed, or prayed indeed,
> The Bullets chirped—In vain! vain! vain!
> Machine-guns chuckled,—Tut-tut! Tut-tut!
> And the Big Gun guffawed.   5
>
> Another sighed,—'O Mother, mother! Dad!'
> Then Smiled, at nothing, childlike, being dead.
>   And the lofty Shrapnel-cloud

Leisurely gestured,——Fool!
And the falling splinters tittered.   10

'My Love!' one moaned. Love-languid seemed his mood,
Till, slowly lowered, his whole face kissed the mud.
      And the Bayonets' long teeth grinned;
      Rabbles of Shells hooted and groaned;
      And the Gas hissed.   15

1. This poem is an elegy but differs from that traditional form in its use of discords and development of tone that is more satirical than elegiac. The elegy is a sustained and formal poem setting forth the poet's meditations upon death or upon a grave theme. The meditation often is occasioned by the death of a particular person, but it may be a generalized observation or the expression of a solemn mood. A few famous and conventional elegies are Gray's "Elegy Written in a Country Churchyard," Tennyson's "In Memoriam," and Whitman's "When Lilacs Last in the Dooryard Bloom'd." Discuss this comparison.

2. The "In vain" motif or refrain in B is handled like rapid-fire. The repetition of the phrase may create a "literary" tone in the poem. It is abandoned in the final version for a different kind of development. Is the *idea* of "In vain" abandoned or simply changed in the final draft?

3. Owen's use of consonantal end-rhyme is related to his use of assonance. Consonantal end-rhyme is often called half-rhyme or slant rhyme. Note the use at the end of words in which the final consonants in the stressed syllables agree but the vowels that precede them differ. Likewise, assonance is the resemblance or similarity between vowels followed by different consonants in two or more stressed syllables. Find illustrations in this poem.

4. How does the placing of lower-pitched vowels after higher-pitched vowels affect our response to the poem in general?

5. Discuss the shortening of the last line in the final poem.

B   *The Dead-Beat (TRUE, in the incidental)*

He dropped, more sullenly than wearily,
    Became a lump of stench, a clot of meat,
    And none of us could kick him to his feet.
He blinked at my revolver, blearily.

He didn't seem to know a war was on,   5
    Or see or smell the bloody trench at all ...
    Perhaps he saw the crowd at Caxton Hall,
And that is why the fellow's pluck's all gone—

Not that the Kaiser frowns imperially.
    He sees his wife, how cosily she chats;   10
    Not his blue pal there, feeding fifty rats.
Hotels he sees, improved materially;

Where ministers smile ministerially.
    Sees Punch still grinning at the Belcher bloke;
    Bairnsfather, enlarging on his little joke,   15
While Belloc prophesies of last year, serially.

We sent him down at last, he seemed so bad,
    Although a strongish chap and quite unhurt.
    Next day I heard the Doc's fat laugh: "That dirt
You sent me down last night's just died. So glad!"   20

Against lines 13 and 16, Owen has written, "These lines are years old!!" Against lines 19-20, "Those are the very words!"

A   *The Dead-Beat*

*Final
Version*

He dropped,—more sullenly than wearily,
Lay stupid like a cod, heavy like meat,
And none of us could kick him to his feet;
Just blinked at my revolver, blearily;
—Didn't appear to know a war was on,   5
Or see the blasted trench at which he stared.
"I'll do 'em in," he whined. "If this hand's spared,
I'll murder them, I will."

<pre>
                        A low voice said,
        "It's Blighty, p'raps, he sees; his pluck's all gone,   10
        Dreaming of all the valiant, that aren't dead:
        Bold uncles, smiling ministerially;
        Maybe his brave young wife, getting her fun
        In some new home, improved materially.
        It's not these stiffs have crazed him; nor the Hun."   15

        We sent him down at last, out of the way.
        Unwounded;—stout lad, too, before that strafe.
        Malingering? Stretcher-bearers winked, "Not half!"

        Next day I heard the Doc.'s well-whiskied laugh:
        "That scum you sent last night soon died. Hooray."   20
</pre>

1. There are fewer direct references to persons and places in A than in B, fewer proper nouns. Does this make B the more realistic poem? Note that the assurance that this event is "true" is missing, and that the Doc's "very words" are changed in the final version.

2. Discuss the rhyme pattern in both versions. Note the use of consonantal rhyme in A6-7 and slant rhyme in A16-18.

3. Abandoning the use of quatrains in the final version, Owen may have been accommodating the use of dialogue and creating a faster movement. Dialogue rather than indirect discourse produces the illusion of reality. Discuss indirect discourse in B.

4. Is our attitude toward the "dead-beat" any different in the two versions?

B   *He Died Smiling*

S.I.W.]   Patting goodbye, his father said, "My lad,
                       You'll always show the Hun a brave man's face.
                       I'd rather you were dead than in disgrace.
                   We're proud to see you going, Jim, we're glad."

                   His mother whimpered, "Jim, my boy, I frets   5
                       Until ye git a nice safe wound, I do."

His sisters said: why couldn't they go too.
His brothers said they'd send him cigarettes.

For three years, once a week, they wrote the same,
  Adding, "We hope you use the Y.M. Hut."   10
  And once a day came twenty Navy Cut.
And once an hour a bullet missed its aim.

And misses teased the hunger of his brain.
  His eyes grew scorched with wincing, and his hand
  Reckless with ague. Courage leaked, like sand   15
From sandbags that have stood three years of rain.

A   *S.I.W.* [2]

Final   I will to the King,
Version   And offer him consolation in his trouble,
                 For that man there has set his teeth to die,
                 And being one that hates obedience,
                 Discipline, and orderliness of life,
                 I cannot mourn him.

                                        W.B. Yeats

I. The Prologue

Patting good-bye, doubtless they had told the lad
He'd always show the Hun a brave man's face;
Father would sooner him dead than disgrace,—
Was proud to see him going, aye, and glad.
Perhaps his mother whimpered how she'd fret   5
Until he got a nice safe wound to nurse.
Sisters would wish girls too could shoot, charge, curse;
Brothers—would send his favourite cigarette.
Each week, month after month, they wrote the same,
Thinking him sheltered in some Y.M. Hut,   10
Because he said so, writing on his butt
Where once an hour a bullet missed its aim
And misses teased the hunger of his brain.
His eyes grew old with wincing, and his hand
Reckless with ague. Courage leaked, as sand   15

From the best sand-bags after years of rain.
But never leave, wound, fever, trench-foot, shock,
Untrapped the wretch. And death seemed still withheld
For torture of lying machinally shelled,
At the pleasure of this world's Powers who'd run amok.   20
He'd seen men shoot their hands, on night patrol.
Their people never knew. Yet they were vile.
"Death sooner than dishonour, that's the style!"
So Father said.

II. The Action

One dawn, our wire patrol   25
Carried him. This time, Death had not missed.
We could do nothing but wipe his bleeding cough.
Could it be accident?—Rifles go off . . .
Not sniped? No. (Later they found the English ball.)

III. The Poem

It was the reasoned crisis of his soul   30
Against more days of inescapable thrall,
Against infrangibly wired and blind trench wall
Curtained with fire, roofed in with creeping fire,
Slow grazing fire, that would not burn him whole
But kept him for death's promises and scoff,   35
And life's half-promising, and both their riling.

IV. The Epilogue

With him they buried the muzzle his teeth had kissed,
And truthfully wrote the Mother, "Tim died smiling."

Alternate version of Part III:

It was the reasoned crisis of his soul.
Against the fires that would not burn him whole
But kept him for death's perjury and scoff
And life's half-promising, and both their riling.

1. The immediate drama of B is consciously exchanged for a different kind of movement. Which opening do you prefer? In which version are we more involved in the speaker's vision, in his imagination?

2. The sentiment of B7 is intensified in A7. What else happens here? Line 13 remains the same. Comment on this line of poetry.

3. The final poem extends version B to about twice the length. Discuss the poetry in A. How has the reading experience changed?

4. Comment on how the elimination of the ballad form in the final version affects the reader's response to the poem.

B

[*Smile, Smile, Smile*]

Head to limp head, sunk-eyed wounded scanned
Yesterday's news: the casualties (typed small)
And (large) Vast Booty from our Latest Haul.
Also they read of Cheap Homes, not yet planned,
"For," said the paper, "when the war is done   5
The men's first instinct will be for their homes.
Meanwhile our need is ships, tanks, aerodromes,
It being certain war is but begun.
Peace would do wrong to our undying dead,
Our glorious sons might even regret they died   10
If we got nothing lasting in their stead
But lived on, tired and indemnified.
All will be worthy victory, which all bought.
Yet we who labour on this ancient spot
Would wrong our very selves if we forgot   15
The greatest glory will be theirs, who fought—
Who kept the nation in integrity."
NATION? The half-legged, half-lunged did not chafe
But smiled at one another curiously
Like secret men who know their secret safe.   20
(This is the thing they know and never speak—
This Nation, one by one, has fled to France
And none lay elsewhere now, save under France.)
Pictures of their broad smiles appear in sketches,
And people say, "They're happy now, poor wretches."   25

Smile, Smile, Smile

Head to limp head, the sunk-eyed wounded scanned
Yesterday's Mail; the casualties (typed small)
And (large) Vast Booty from our Latest Haul.
Also, they read of Cheap Homes, not yet planned
"For," said the paper, "when this war is done   5
The men's first instinct will be making homes.
Meanwhile their foremost need is aerodromes,
It being certain war has but begun.
Peace would do wrong to our undying dead,—
The sons we offered might regret they died   10
If we got nothing lasting in their stead.
We must be solidly indemnified.
Though all be worthy Victory which all bought,
We rulers sitting in this ancient spot
Would wrong our very selves if we forgot   15
The greatest glory will be theirs who fought,
Who kept this nation in integrity."
Nation?—The half-limbed readers did not chafe
But smiled at one another curiously
Like secret men who know their secret safe.   20
(This is the thing they know and never speak,
That England one by one had fled to France,
Not many elsewhere now, save under France.)
Pictures of these broad smiles appear each week,
And people in whose voice real feeling rings   25
Say: How they smile! They're happy now, poor things.

1. A number of changes occur in the use of pronouns from B to A (line 5 and following), creating a shift in the reader's attitude. The change in line 7 also falls in with this general shift. What new tone is developed as a result of these changes?

2. Discuss the adjectival change in line 10. Which produces a more consistent rhythm, consistent with either metrical pattern or development of action?

3. Discuss the shift in emphasis in line 14. How is this carried through to the end? Discuss the developing irony here.

4. In line 18, the A version is softer, smoother. B18, while richer in image, does not move as clearly into the following line. Discuss.

Dirt[3]

B

"Rear rank one pace step back. March!"
    I shouted; and inspected the Platoon.
Their necks were craned like collars stiff with starch;
    All badges glittered like the great bassoon.

Boots dubbined; rifles clean and oiled;   5
    Belts blancoed; straps—The sergeant's cane
Prodded a lad whose haversack was soiled
    With some disgraceful muddy stain.

A

Inspection

Final
Version

"You! What d'you mean by this?" I rapped.
"You dare come on parade like this?"
"Please, Sir, it's—" "'Old yer mouth," the sergeant snapped.
"I takes 'is name, sir?"—"Please, and then dismiss."

Some days "confined to camp" he got,   5
For being "dirty on parade."
He told me, afterwards, the damned spot
Was blood, his own. "Well, blood is dirt," I said.

"Blood's dirt," he laughed, looking away
Far off to where his wound had bled [he'd lain and bled/his body
                                had bled]   10
And almost merged for ever into clay.
"The world is washing out its stains," he said.
"It doesn't like our cheeks so red:
Young blood's its great objection.
But when we're duly white-washed [pipe-clayed], being dead,   15
The race will bear Field-Marshal God's inspection."

1. Were B attached to A, as was once intended, the entire conflict would be shifted. The dramatic movement would have a kind of grad-

ual introduction, and the poem would obviously also be longer. What other differences in total effect would result?

2. Discuss the change in language between the early draft and the final poem.

3. Comment on the few canceled passages in the A version.

B   *The Last Piece from Craiglockhart*

I dreamed that Christ had fouled the big-gun gears,
And made a permanent stoppage in all bolts
And buckled, with a smile, Mausers and Colts,
And rusted every bayonet with His tears.

And there were no more bombs, of ours or Theirs.   5
So we got out, and gathering up our plunder
Of pains, and nightmares for the night, in wonder!—
Leapt the communication trench like flares.

But at the port, a man from U.S.A.
Stopped us, and said: You go right back this minute.   10
I'll follow. Christ, your miracle ain't in it,
I'll get those rifles mended by today.

A   *Soldier's Dream*

Final   I dreamed kind Jesus fouled the big-gun gears;
Version   And caused a permanent stoppage in all bolts;
             And buckled with a smile Mausers and Colts;
             And rusted every bayonet with His tears.

And there were no more bombs, of ours or Theirs,   5
Not even an old flint-lock, nor even a pikel.
But God was vexed, and gave all power to Michael;
And when I woke he'd seen to our repairs.

1. The basic development between B and A is away from the particular, political, geographic situation (note the title) to a more general "Soldier's Dream." Discuss.

2. In A, the vision, as well as the language, is more concise, with fewer particularizing details. Note the omission of B9. Is it significant that the poet identified the dream as belonging to a soldier?

3. Both are antiwar poems, but from different perspectives. Is there a clue to perspective in the change of "made" in B2 to "caused" in A2?

4. The "kind Jesus" of A is handled differently from the "Christ" of B. The difference also establishes a dichotomy between Jesus and God. Is there such a clear dichotomy in B? How is it different?

5. There is definite irony in the word "vexed." After all, this is hardly an emotion we attribute to the Deity.

6. How would one argue for B as the superior poem?

B   *To My Friend*

    If ever I had dreamed of my dead name
    High in the heart of London; unsurpassed
    By Time forever; and the fugitive, Fame,
    There taking a long sanctuary at last,
    —I'll better that. Yea, now, I think with shame   5
    How once I wished it hidd'n from its defeats
    Under those holy cypresses, the same
    That mourn around the quiet place of Keats.

    Now rather let's be thankful there's no risk
    Of gravers scoring it with hideous screed.   10
    For let my gravestone be this body-disc
    Which was my yoke. Inscribe no date, nor deed.
    But let thy heart-beat kiss it night and day ...
    Until the name grow vague and wear away.

A later draft has the following alternate to line 11:

    But let my death be memoried on this disc

On a separate folio we find the following lines:

Well, here's a meeter tombstone; and no risk
Of mason's marring it with florid ill-scored screeds.
For let my inscription be this soldier's disc.

To My Friend

(With an Identity Disc)

If ever I had dreamed of my dead name
    High in the heart of London, unsurpassed
By Time for ever, and the Fugitive, Fame,
    There seeking a long sanctuary at last,—

Or if I onetime hoped to hide its shame,   5
  —Shame of success, and sorrow of defeats,—
Under those holy cypresses, the same
    That shade always the quiet place of Keats,

Now rather thank I God there is no risk
    Of gravers scoring it with florid screed.   10
Let my inscription be this soldier's disc....
    Wear it, sweet friend. Inscribe no date nor deed.
But may thy heart-beat kiss it, night and day,
    Until the name grow blurred and fade away.

1. The dramatic quality of the poem resides in the tension between speaker and the silent friend. In the A version the friend is addressed directly in line 12. We do know, from the title at least, that the poem is meant for a particular person, but the expression "sweet friend" in A draws us into the situation more directly. Discuss.

2. The middle quatrain in A presents a different tone and development of the idea than B. The contextual shift is accompanied by a typographical one. Comment on the use of typography. Draw from other poets as well.

3. Line 11 has three versions. None of the choices seems particularly successful. What is the difficulty with this line?

B   *1914*

War broke: and now the Winter of the world
With perishing great darkness closes in.
The cyclone of the pressure on Berlin
Is over all the width of Europe whirled,
Rending the sails of progress. Rent or furled   5
Are all Art's ensigns. Verse wails. Now begin
Famines of thought and feeling. Love's wine's thin.
The grain of earth's great autumn rots, down-hurled.

For after Spring had bloomed in early Greece,
And Summer blazed to perfect strength   10
There fell a slow grand age, a harvest home,
Quiet ripening, [rich with all increase.]
But now the exigent winter and the need
Of sowings for new Spring, and blood for seed.

A   *1914*

*Final
Version*   War broke: and now the Winter of the world
With perishing great darkness closes in.
The foul tornado, centered at Berlin,
Is over all the width of Europe whirled,
Rending the sails of progress. Rent or furled   5
Are all Art's ensigns. Verse wails. Now begin
Famines of thought and feeling. Love's wine's thin.
The grain of human Autumn rots, down-hurled.

For after Spring had bloomed in early Greece,
And Summer blazed her glory out with Rome,   10
An Autumn softly fell, a harvest home,
A slow grand age, and rich with all increase.
But now, for us, wild Winter, and the need
Of sowings for new Spring, and blood for seed.

1. The two versions of the third line contain different language, yet the
same idea is developed. The change in line 8, however, while clearly a
rhythmic change, also offers a shift in emphasis. Discuss.

2. The second stanza of B is particularly rough in comparison with the final version. Words are used differently in the earlier draft. Note the particular use of "blazed." Line 13 in B is a difficult line to read aloud. In the corrected version, the line is smoother and more consistent with the developing theme. Discuss.

Notes

1. C. Day Lewis, ed., *Selected Poems of Wilfred Owen* (New York: New Directions, 1963).
2. Self-inflicted wound.
3. This version is a manuscript draft that was intended as the opening of the A version. C. Day Lewis writes, "This version then continues, in four-line stanzas, with the sense of the (A) text."

W.H. AUDEN

1907-1973

BEFORE EMIGRATING TO THE UNITED STATES FROM England in 1939, Wystan Hugh Auden taught school and was a leading figure of the socially conscious left-oriented poetry movement of the 1930s with other poets such as Stephen Spender, C. Day Lewis, and Louis MacNeice. Once he became an American citizen, his poetry and the revisions of earlier poems revealed a more conservative position than his earlier, more widely known poetry. Joseph Warren Beach's *The Making of the Auden Canon*[1] is a valuable study of the poet and his revisions.

In the late 1930s, Auden moved from a left-wing political faith to orthodox Christianity, and critics have made much of the shift in his poetry around that time. The reader must watch the changes closely before generalizing about the overall pattern of development in Auden's poetry. Auden maintained that there was no easy or definitive line of development, and in at least one edition, *Collected Poems* (1945), the poems were printed in a nonchronological arrangement deliberately in order to prevent any such tracing of a course. But readers generally enjoy tracing courses, however meaningful or however irrelevant the activity. The poems here are chronologically arranged.

Auden wrote a great deal of light verse, and although not represented in this text, the tone of lightness is present in many of the serious and morally instructive poems. Growing out of the tradition of social protest poetry, much of the poetry not in this genre of light verse shares the rhetoric of a poetry of instruction—though it is rarely didactic or propagandistic. The poetry is engaged in confrontation with the poet's own self, an activity that allows the most socially conscious poetry its private or subjective appeal.

Auden constantly revised his poems, primarily for aesthetic reasons. The poet was always aiming at a better-made work of art, and questions of political, social, and religious ideology were secondary. Often, the changes we see, technical and stylistic, social and political, occur in the same poem and the reader need not bother to point to one and say, "this change is because the poet has changed politically," but rather, "in this revision the poet is trying to approximate his altered vision which, indeed, includes art as well as social considerations."

In the foreword to the 1967 edition of *Collected Shorter Poems 1927-1957*, which is chronologically arranged, Auden states his dislike for dishonest poetry, or dishonest language in his earlier poems. Through the process of revision he stripped his poetry of what he considered "rhetorically effective" yet untrue, untrue to his own experience or belief. The reader, aware of what occurs when one changes beliefs after many years, will often suspect earlier phrases of being dishonest as they do not represent current beliefs. Thus we read Auden's preface on his revisions with extreme care, perhaps even with skepticism. He writes, "... I have never, consciously at any rate, attempted to revise my former thoughts or feelings, only the language in which they were first expressed, when on further consideration, it seemed to me inaccurate, lifeless, prolix, or painful to the ear."

The presentation of the poems in this chapter differs from the rest of the book in general, in that at times we present only the final version in its entirety. The bracketed words are earlier variants that were replaced in the final version by the underlined words. Unless otherwise noted, all A versions are taken from the 1945 *Collected Poetry* and/or the 1967 *Collected Shorter Poems* (these two volumes contain many identical poems).

Taller To-day

A

*Final
Version
with
earlier
variants in
brackets*

Taller to-day, we remember similar evenings,
Walking together in a windless orchard
Where the brook runs over the gravel, far from the glacier.

Nights come bringing the snow, and the dead howl
Under [the] headlands in their windy dwelling   5
Because the Adversary put too easy questions
On the lonely roads.

But happy now, though no nearer each other,
We see [the] farms lighted all along the valley;
Down at the mill-shed hammering stops   10
And men go home.

Noises at dawn will bring
Freedom for some, but not this peace
No bird can contradict; <u>passing but here</u>,
                            [passing, but is] sufficient now
For something fulfilled this hour, loved or endured.   15

The bracketed words above and additional stanzas below are from a version published in
Poems *(1930).*

Between stanzas 1 and 2:

Again in the room with the sofa hiding the grate,
Look down to the river when the rain is over,
See him turn to the window, hearing our last
Of Captain Ferguson.

It is seen how excellent hands have turned to commonness.
One staring too long, went blind in a tower,
One sold all his manors to fight, broke through, and faltered.

1. There is specific detail in the several lines omitted from the A version. How are these lines different from the rest of the poem? A possible answer is that they are obscure in a way that nothing in the final version is obscure. This is an obscurity of allusion. Whatever difficulty the final version may offer, it is not one of literary or personal allusions.

2. The deletion of the article in lines 5 and 9 gives these lines and the entire stanza a quality they did not have earlier. Can you explain why? (Reading aloud helps.)

Consider

Consider this and in our time
As the hawk sees it or the helmeted airman:
The clouds rift suddenly—look there
At cigarette-end smouldering on a border
At the first garden party of the year.   5
Pass on, admire the view of the massif
Through plate-glass windows of the Sport Hotel;

Join there the insufficient units
Dangerous, easy, in furs, in uniform,
And constellated at reserved tables, 10
Supplied with feelings by an efficient band,
Relayed elsewhere to farmers and their dogs
Sitting in kitchens in the stormy fens.

Long ago, supreme Antagonist,
More powerful than the great northern whale, 15
Ancient and sorry at life's limiting defect,
In Cornwall, Mendip, or the Pennine moor
Your comments on the highborn mining-captains,
Found they no answer, made them wish to die
—Lie since in barrows out of harm. 20
You talk to your admirers every day
By stilted harbours, derelict works,
In strangled orchards, and a silent comb
Where dogs have worried or a bird was shot.
Order the ill that they attack at once: 25
Visit the ports and, interrupting
The leisurely conversation in the bar
Within a stone's throw of the sunlit water,
Beckon your chosen out. Summon
Those handsome and diseased youngsters, those women 30
Your solitary agents in the country parishes;
And mobilize the powerful forces latent
In soils that make the farmer brutal
In the infected sinus, and the eyes of stoats.
Then, ready, start your rumour, soft 35
But horrifying in its capacity to disgust
Which, spreading magnified, shall come to be
A polar peril, a prodigious alarm,
Scattering the people, as torn-up paper
Rags and utensils in a sudden gust, 40
Seized with immeasurable neurotic dread.

Seekers after happiness, all who follow
The convolutions of your simple wish,
It is later than you think; nearer that day
Far other than that distant afternoon 45

Amid rustle of frocks and stamping feet
They gave the prizes to the ruined boys.
You cannot be away, then, no
Not though you pack to leave within an hour,
Escaping humming down arterial roads: 50
The date was yours; the prey to fugues,
Irregular breathing and alternate ascendancies
After some haunted migratory years
To disintegrate on an instant in the explosion of mania
Or lapse for ever into a classic fatigue.   55

Between lines 41 and 42:

Financier, leaving your little room
Where money is made but not spent,
You'll need your typist and your boy no more;
The game is up for you and for the others,
Who, thinking, pace in slippers on the lawns
Of College Quad or Cathedral Close,
Who are born nurses, who live in shorts
Sleeping with people and playing fives.

1. Beginning with line 42, Auden is speaking to the financier, confronting him with all the weight of the warnings implied in the poem up to that point. The allusions have been topical as well as universal. The imagery is suggestive rather than direct and the didactic turn of the poem is everywhere muted by this suggestiveness of language. Discuss.

2. The omitted lines contain an even more direct confrontation, not with the reader but with a particular social type. Surely the poem builds in its rhetoric, its frequent violent images, toward the specific social comment. Without the lines the poet later deleted, the "you" in line 49 becomes a more general "you" and the reader is drawn in, in a way unlikely in the earlier version. Discuss.

3. What is it about the tone in the omitted material that Auden may have found unacceptable at the time of revision? Does one regret the omission of colloquial constructions such as "the game is up" that appear in the missing stanza?

At the Grave of Henry James

The snow, less intransigeant than their marble,
Has left the defence of whiteness to these tombs;
    For all the pools at my feet
Accommodate blue now, and echo such clouds as occur
To the sky, and whatever bird or mourner the passing   5
    Moment remarks they repeat

While the rocks, named after singular spaces
Within which images wandered once that caused
    All to tremble and offend,
Stand here in an innocent stillness, each marking the spot   10
Where one more series of errors lost its uniqueness
    And novelty came to an end.

To whose real advantage were such transactions
When words of reflection were exchanged for trees?
    What living occasion can   15
Be just to the absent? O noon but reflects on itself,
And the small taciturn stone that is the only witness
    To a great and talkative man

Has no more judgment than my ignorant shadow
Of odious comparisons or distant clocks   20
    Which challenge and interfere
With the heart's instantaneous reading of time, time that is
A warm enigma no longer in you for whom I
    Surrender my private cheer

Startling the awkward footsteps of my apprehension,   25
The flushed assault of your recognition is
    The donnée of this doubtful hour:
O stern proconsul of intractable provinces,
O poet of the difficult, dear addicted artist,
    Assent to my soil and flower.   30

As I stand awake on our solar fabric,
That primary machine, the earth, which gendarmes, banks,
    And aspirin pre-suppose.

On which the clumsy and sad may all sit down, and any who will
Say their a-ha to the beautiful, the common locus   35
          Of the master and the rose.

Our theatre, scaffold, and erotic city
Where all the infirm species are partners in the act
          Of encroachment bodies crave,
Though solicitude in death is de rigueur for their flesh   40
And the self-denying hermit flies as it approaches
          Like the carnivore to a cave.

That its plural numbers may unite in meaning,
Its vulgar tongues unravel the knotted mass
          Of the improperly conjunct,   45
Open my eyes now to all its hinted significant forms,
Sharpen my ears to detect amid its brilliant uproar
          The low thud of the defunct.

O dwell, ironic at my living centre,
Half ancestor, half child; because the actual self   50
          Round whom time revolves so fast
Is so afraid of what its motions might possibly do
That the actor is never there when his really important
          Acts happen. Only the past

Is present, no one about but the dead as,   55
Equipped with a few inherited odds and ends,
          One after another we are
Fired into life to seek that unseen target where all
Our equivocal judgments are judged and resolved in
          One whole <u>Alas or Hurrah</u>. [alas or hurrah]   60

And only the unborn <u>remark</u> [mark] the disaster
When, though it makes no difference to the pretty airs
          The bird of Appetite sings,
And Amour Propre is his usual amusing self,
Out from the jungle of an undistinguished moment   65
          The flexible <u>shadow</u> [Shadow] springs.

Now more than ever, when torches and snare-drum
Excite the squat women of the saurian brain
        Till a milling mob of fears
Breaks in insultingly on anywhere, when in our dreams   70
Pigs play on the organs and the blue sky runs shrieking
        As the Crack of Doom appears,

Are the good ghosts needed with the white magic
Of their subtle loves. War has no ambiguities
        Like a marriage; the result   75
Required of its affaire fatale is simple and sad,
The physical removal of all human objects
        That conceal the Difficult.

Then remember me that I may remember
The test we have to learn to shudder for is not   80
        An historical event,
That neither the low democracy of a nightmare nor
An army's primitive tidiness may deceive me
        About our predicament.

That catastrophic situation which neither   85
Victory nor defeat can annul; to be
        Deaf yet determined to sing,
To be lame and blind yet burning for the Great Good Place,
To be radically [essentially] corrupt yet mournfully attracted
        By the Real Distinguished Thing.   90

And shall I not specially bless you as, vexed with
My little inferior questions, today I stand
        Beside the bed where you rest
Who opened such passionate arms to your Bon when It [it] ran
Towards you with its overwhelming reasons pleading   95
        All beautifully in Its [its] breast?

O with what innocence your hand submitted
To these [those] formal rules that help a child to play,
        While your heart, fastidious as
A delicate nun, remained true to the rare noblesse   100

Of your lucid gift and, for its own sake, ignored the
        Resentful muttering Mass.

Whose ruminant hatred of all which cannot
Be simplified or stolen is still at large;
        No death can assuage its lust   105
To vilify the landscape of Distinction and see
The heart of the Personal brought to a systolic standstill,
        The Tall to diminished dust.

Preserve me, Master, from its vague incitement;
Yours be the disciplinary image that holds   110
        Me back from agreeable wrong
And the clutch of eddying muddle, lest Proportion shed
The alpine chill of her shrugging editorial shoulder
        On my loose impromptu song.

Suggest; so may I segregate my disorder   115
Into districts of prospective value: approve;
        Lightly, lightly, then, may I dance
Over the frontier of the obvious and fumble no more
In the old limp pocket of the minor exhibition,
        Nor riot with irrelevance.   120

And no longer shoe geese or water stakes, but
Bolt in my day my grain of truth to the barn
        Where tribulations may leap
With their long-lost brothers at last in the festival
Of which not one <u>had</u> [has] a dissenting image, and the   125
        Flushed immediacy sleep.

Into this city from the shining lowlands
Blows a wind that whispers of uncovered skulls
        And fresh ruins under the moon,
Of hopes that will not survive the secousse of this spring   130
Of blood and flames, of the terror that walks by night and
        The sickness that strikes at noon.

All will be judged. Master of nuance and scruple,
Pray for me and for all writers living or dead;

Because there are many whose works   135
Are in better taste than their lives; because there is no end
To the vanity of our calling: make intercession
        For the treason of all clerks.

Because the darkness is never so distant,
And there is never much time for the arrogant   140
        Spirit to flutter its wings,
Or the broken bone to rejoice, or the cruel to cry
For Him whose property is always to have mercy, the author
        And giver of all good things.

The bracketed words above and additional stanzas below are from a version published in
Horizon, III, 18 (1941).

Between stanzas 11 and 12:

Perhaps the honour of a great house, perhaps its
Cradles and tombs may persuade the bravado of
        The bachelor mind to doubt
The dishonest path, or save from disgraceful collapse
The creature's shrinking withness bellowed at and tickled
        By the huge Immodest Without.

Between stanzas 15 and 16:

Let this orchard point to its stable arrangement
Of accomplished bones as a proof that our lives
        Conceal a pattern which, shows
A tendency to execute formative movements, to have
Definite experiences in their execution,
        To rejoice in knowing it grows.

Between stanzas 21 and 22:

Knowing myself a mobile animal descended
From an ancient line of respectable fish,
        With a certain méchant charm,
Occupying the earth for a grass-grown interval between

Two oscillations of polar ice, engaged in weaving
　　His conscience upon its calm.

Despising Now yet afraid of Hereafter,
Unable in spite of his stop-watch and lens
　　To imagine the rising Rome
To which his tools and tales migrate, to guess from what shore
The signal will flash, to observe the anarchists gestation
　　In the smug constricted home.

A　　　　　　　　　　*At the Grave of Henry James*

Final　　The snow, less intransigeant than their marble,
Version　Has left the defence of whiteness to these tombs,
　　　　　　And all the pools at my feet
Accommodate blue now, echo clouds as occur
To the sky, and whatever bird or mourner the passing　　　　　5
　　　　　　Moment remarks they repeat.

While rocks, named after singular spaces
Within which images wandered once that caused
　　　　　　All to tremble and offend,
Stand here in an innocent stillness, each marking the spot　　　10
Where one more series of errors lost its uniqueness
　　　　　　And novelty came to an end.

To whose real advantage were such transactions,
When worlds of reflection were exchanged for trees?
　　　　　　What living occasion can　　　　　　　　　　15
Be just to the absent? Noon but reflects on itself,
And the small taciturn stone, that is the only witness
　　　　　　To a great and talkative man,

Has no more judgement than my ignorant shadow
Of odious comparisons or distant clocks　　　　　　　　　20
　　　　　　Which challenge and interfere
With the heart's instantaneous reading of time, time that is
A warm enigma no longer to you for whom I
　　　　　　Surrender my private cheer,

As I stand awake on our solar fabric   25
That primary machine, the earth, which gendarmes, banks
    And aspirin pre-suppose,
On which the clumsy and sad may all sit down, and any who will
Say their a-ha to the beautiful, the common locus
    Of the Master and the rose.   30

Shall I not especially bless you as, vexed with
My little inferior questions, I stand
    Above the bed where you rest,
Who opened such passionate arms to your Bon when It ran
Towards you with its overwhelming reasons pleading   35
    All beautifully in Its breast?

With what an innocence your hand submitted
To those formal rules that help a child to play,
    While your heart, fastidious as
A delicate nun, remained true to the rare noblesse   40
Of your lucid gift and, for its love, ignored the
    Resentful muttering Mass,

Whose ruminant hatred of all that cannot
Be simplified or stolen is yet at large:
    No death can assuage its lust   45
To vilify the landscape of Distinction and see
The heart of the Personal brought to a systolic standstill,
    The Tall to diminished dust.

Preserve me, Master, from its vague incitement;
Yours be the disciplinary image that holds   50
    Me back from agreeable wrong
And the clutch of eddying Muddle, lest Proportion shed
The alpine chill of her shrugging editorial shoulder
    On my loose impromptu song.

All will be judged. Master of nuance and scruple,   55
Pray for me and for all writers, living or dead:
    Because there are many whose works
Are in better taste than their lives, because there is no end

To the vanity of our calling, make intercession
　　For the treason of all clerks.　　　　　　　　　　　　　　　60

1. An entirely different pattern of action is presented in the A and B versions. By omitting stanzas that contain such direct appeals as "O stern proconsul ... " and so forth, and by waiting until stanza 9 of the final version for the affectionate "Preserve me, Master ... ," the poet creates a tension or drama not present in the earlier version. In what other ways has this poem been reconstructed?

2. In stanza 7 of A, what emotion does the addition of the "child" passage evoke?

3. Discuss the stanzas omitted from both the A and B versions. Do you think there is a connection between the two major revisions?

4. In version B, do stanzas 7 and 8 offer anything significant to the development of theme?

A　　　　　　　　　　　　*In Memory of W.B. Yeats*
　　　　　　　　　　　　　　(D. Jan 1939)

　　　　　　　　　　　　　　　　I

Final　He disappeared in the dead of winter:
version　The brooks were frozen, the airports almost deserted,
with　And snow disfigured the public statues;
earlier　The mercury sank in the mouth of the dying day.
variants　<u>What instruments we have agree</u> [O all the instruments agree]
in　The day of his death was a dark cold day.　　　　　　　5
brackets

Far from his illness
The wolves ran on through the evergreen forests,
The peasant river was untempted by the fashionable quays;
By mourning tongues
The death of the poet was kept from his poems.　　　　　10

But for him it was his last afternoon as himself,
An afternoon of nurses and rumours;

The provinces of his body revolted,
The squares of his mind were empty,   15
Silence invaded the suburbs,
The current of his feeling failed; he became his admirers.

Now he is scattered among a hundred cities
And wholly given over to unfamiliar affections,
To find his happiness in another kind of wood   20
And be punished under a foreign code of conscience.
The words of a dead man
Are modified in the guts of the living.

But in the importance and noise of to-morrow
When the brokers are roaring like beasts on the floor of the Bourse,   25
And the poor have the sufferings to which they are fairly accustomed,
And each in the cell of himself is almost convinced of his freedom,
A few thousand will think of this day
As one thinks of a day when one did something slightly unusual.
<u>What instruments we have agree</u> [O all the instruments agree]   30
The day of his death was a dark cold day.

II

You were silly like us; your gift survived it all;
The parish of rich women, physical decay,
Yourself. Mad Ireland hurt you into poetry.
Now Ireland has her madness and her weather still,   35
For poetry makes nothing happen: it survives
In the valley of its <u>making</u> [saying] where executives
Would never want to tamper, <u>flows on</u> [it flows] south
From ranches of isolation and the busy griefs,
Raw towns that we believe and die in; it survives,   40
A way of happening, a mouth.

III

Earth, receive an honoured guest:
William Yeats is laid to rest.
Let the Irish vessel lie
Emptied of its poetry.   45

In the nightmare of the dark
All the dogs of Europe bark,
And the living nations wait,
Each sequestered in its hate;

Intellectual disgrace   50
Stares from every human face,
And the seas of pity lie
Locked and frozen in each eye.

Follow, poet, follow right
To the bottom of the night,   55
With your unconstraining voice
Still persuade us to rejoice;

With the farming of a verse
Making a vineyard of the curse,
Sing of human unsuccess   60
In a rapture of distress;

In the deserts of the heart
Let the healing fountain start,
In the prison of his days
Teach the free man how to praise.   65

Collected Shorter Poems (1967).
*The bracketed words above and additional stanzas below are from
a version published in* Collected Poetry *(1945).*

Between stanzas 1 and 2 of section III:

Time that is intolerant
Of the brave and innocent,
And indifferent in a week
To a beautiful physique,

Worships language and forgives
Everyone by whom it lives;
Pardons cowardice, conceit,
Lays its honours at their feet.

Time that with this strange excuse
Pardoned Kipling and his views,
And will pardon Paul Claudel,
Pardons him for writing well.

1. Part One of this most famous of modern elegies is non-elegiac in tone. Nowhere does the poet communicate remorsefulness over the death of W.B. Yeats. That is, the implicit sympathy is immediately understated and general. The only change in the text of the first part is one appropriate to the mood of uncommitted pessimism. Only in the light of such a contrived mood could line 26 be understood. There is a fairly realistic basis here. Indeed, only "a few thousand" at most would be personally moved by the death of the great poet—nature is not moved. Discuss.

2. It is clear that the idea "poetry makes nothing happen" is the central motivation or impetus to Auden's handling of this occasional poem. How is this idea developed and finally modified or qualified by the end of the poem?

3. In section III a new rhythm, one most often encountered in light verse or jingles, enters the elegy. (Blake too employs a musical tone in "The Tyger.") How can we account for this movement at this stage in the action?

4. Following line 54, Auden develops the final affirmation, —it is an affirmation not only of Yeats' poetic activity or poetry itself, but also of the human condition generally. Discuss.

5. The omitted stanzas may be somewhat didactic in the announcement that "time ... worships language"; however, anthologies continue to print the poem with these three stanzas. Can you provide a defense on either or both sides?

Note

1. Joseph Warren Beach, *The Making of the Auden Canon* (Minneapolis: University of Minnesota Press, 1957).

DYLAN THOMAS

1914–1953

D YLAN THOMAS WAS BORN IN SWANSEA, WALES, AND
died 39 years later in a hospital in New York. The quiet
countryside of his early youth, rich in folk tradition and
simple faith, illuminates our enduring picture of Thomas
the lyricist, the poet of wonder and childhood. Urban America, how-
ever, with its "terminal hospitals," in both the literal and metaphori-
cal sense, fills out the picture of an irascible poet who was somehow
doomed.

Thomas is one of the most popular of modern English poets, espe-
cially among young readers. *Child's Christmas in Wales* and *Under Milkwood,*
two long dramatic poems, have a following far out of proportion to
the accessibility of his total work. Thomas is not an easy poet. He does
not speak directly as if to a large audience, and yet it is a large audience
indeed that responds to his poetry. There is little mystery in all this.
Much of Thomas's fame rests upon his reputedly wild and bawdy per-
sonality, and his early death and a clearly self-destructive life style add
to or satisfy the romantic imagination. This, and the more important
fact that his poetry, both early and late, communicates an exuberant
energy and soaring lyricism with which young readers can identify,
suggests reasons to embrace the poetry of Dylan Thomas.

Unlike much romantic poetry, Thomas's is never vague. He writes
often of his childhood and his style is intensely lyrical, but his images,
even when so elaborate as to seem obscure, are sharp and specific. Fre-
quently the poetry is quite intellectual in the special way it makes
demands on our ability to unravel or reorder complicated patterns of
experience. He is rarely intellectual or philosophical in the sense of
imposing an already oriented system of thought on a wide range of
human experience.

The study of Thomas's poetry in this chapter should separate the
popular image of Thomas—the wild, drunken Welshman, or the
poet of fine sentiment—from the poet whose work is carefully
wrought and finely conceived, though it is often resonant with moods
of defiance and celebration. His poetry is, at times, associated with the

early-nineteenth-century romantic style, but his is frequently more like the elaborate poetry of the seventeenth century, with exaggerated metaphor and paradox. We will read oddly connected imagery that lends a surrealistic element to his work. Yet there is an intensity and sureness of direction to his art that separates him from the surrealists. Also, his attitude toward his art is of a different order from those poets, or any modernistic school for that matter.

We will also note that Thomas is a master of sound. He himself said that "poetry is sound," and often our appreciation of the wonderful sound patterns makes the sometimes private meanings easier to accept, or less bothersome. Though the materials of Thomas's poetry are public—for example, the Bible, images and ideas out of Freud, actual recorded events—there is always a subjective awareness shaping these materials. This subjectivity creates, at times, privacy rather than indirect communication, but as at least one critic has observed, that special or private vision, impossible to translate out of the poetry, is, in itself, something communicated.

The poems reprinted here are from *Collected Poems* (1952), and the earlier drafts are from Ralph Maud's edition of Dylan Thomas's *Notebooks.*[1] This last volume is made up of four manuscript exercise books that Thomas kept between 1930 and 1934, years that were critical in the development of his poetry, from ages 15 to 19, and reflect the themes and currents that would make up the mature poetry. Thomas regarded these notebook drafts as drafts only and would use them years later to make fresh poems. Many of them, however, can be read as separate poems of a youthful period. After 1941 the poet stopped working from them.

Constantine Fitzgibbon, in his excellent biography *The Life of Dylan Thomas,*[2] comments on the poet's style during the four-year period of the *Notebooks,* in which the work "... shows a progression towards a greater density of meaning as he twisted syntax, piled image upon image and juxtaposed unexpected adjectival nouns in his determination to produce maximum effects and the greater measure of poetic truth." This was also a period of experimentation, and thus the reader will note a variety of lyric forms in the chapter and will encounter some obscurities that resulted from early experimentation.

In the notebooks, the interested student can discover the influences on Thomas in a less digested form than in the final poems or in later poems. Furthermore, these drafts reveal how early materials, sometimes raw and very different from final products of experience, depend on first inspirations for first construction, though the final construction, form, and inspiration communicated may be very different from the early work.

There is a definite movement in the body of these poems, Fitzgibbons continues, from a "confessional and hortatory free verse … to a more regular, packed stanza.…" The unglossed image abounds, and readers of the poetry written after 1941 will notice that those poems are clearer as they are shorter. Such a late poem as "In My Craft or Sullen Art" reveals not only the concerns of these earlier drafts and finished poems but also a technique, a love for words, a sense of music that is always clear and inspiriting no matter the darknesses.

Collected Poems is not arranged chronologically. This chapter, therefore, varies from the general procedure of this book and follows, instead, Thomas's own ordering. Thus, the final versions, the A versions, are not dated, but are printed as they appear in the *Collected Poems.* The B versions are notated with date of composition and number as found in the *Notebooks.* Also, because of Thomas's extensive practice of reworking his drafts, we have varied from the established system of the book in another way. There is no indication in the *Notebooks* which word or words the poet preferred. Therefore, unlike in the preceding chapters, both words in brackets and words in footnotes represent variants.

B

[*The nchback in the Park*]

The hunchback in the park,
A solitary mister
Propped between trees and water,

Going daft for fifty seven years,
Is [getting]³ dafter,   5
A cripple children call at,
Half-laughing, by no other name than mister,
They shout hey mister
Running when he has heard them clearly
Past lake and rockery   10
On out of sight.

There is a thing he makes when quiet comes
To the young nurses with the children
And the three veteran swans,

Makes a thing inside the hanging head,   15
[A]⁴ figure without fault
And sees it on the gravel paths
Or walking on the water.

The figure's frozen all the winter
Until the summer melts it down   20
To make a figure without fault.
[It is a poem and it is a woman figure.]

Mister, the children call, hey mister,
And the hunchback in the park
Sees the [wild/molten] figure on the water,   25
Misty, now mister,
[Calling 'Hey Mister']
Hears it's woman's voice;
Mister, it calls, hey mister,
And the hunchback smiles.

                                              May 9, 1932

1930–1932 Notebook LVVV. NOTE: The apostrophe in line 26 in the word "it's" is found in Thomas's notebook version.

A   *The Hunchback in the Park*

Final   The hunchback in the park
Version   A solitary mister
                 Propped between trees and water
                 From the opening of the garden lock
                 That lets the trees and water enter   5
                 Until the Sunday sombre bell at dark

                 Eating bread from a newspaper
                 Drinking water from the chained cup
                 That the children filled with gravel
                 In the fountain basin where I sailed my ship   10
                 Slept at night in a dog kennel
                 But nobody chained him up.

                 Like the park birds he came early

Like the water he sat down
And Mister they called Hey mister   15
The truant boys from the town
Running when he had heard them clearly
On out of sound

Past lake and rockery
Laughing when he shook his paper
Hunchbacked in mockery   20
Through the loud zoo of the willow groves
Dodging the park keeper
With his stick that picked up leaves.

And the old dog sleeper
Alone between nurses and swans   25
While the boys among willows
Made the tigers jump out of their eyes
To roar on rockery stones
And the groves were blue with sailors

Made all day until bell time   30
A woman figure without fault
Straight as a young elm
Straight and tall from his crooked bones
That she might stand in the night
After the locks and chains   35

All night in the unmade park
After the railings and shrubberies
The birds the grass the trees the lake
And the wild boys innocent as strawberries
Had followed the hunchback   40
To his kennel in the dark.

1. Both poems communicate a certain sadness about life. The final
version, however, with its added ambiguities, note line 4 and follow-
ing, presents a richer development of the central emotion. Discuss.

2. Discuss the various details of each version, namely lines A7 and B4.
How do these separate details or images constitute an attitude?

3. The "dog kennel" image is developed in A so that by the last stanza it becomes symbolic of a grave. Is there any such development of image, metaphor, or symbol in the notebook draft?

4. Do you like the last line of B? Why? The A poem ends on an entirely different note. Compare the two endings in terms of the poem's eventual tone, rhythm, and general movement.

5. The hunchback dreams as do the children. His dream makes up a larger portion of the earlier draft than of the final version. Discuss the dream and its role in both versions.

C

*[If I
Were
Tickled by
the Rub of
Love]*

Pass through twelve stages, reach the fifth
By retrograde moving from near death,
And puberty recoils at callow youth
Knowing such stuff as will confuse
That phantom in the blood, used to misuse,   5
Red rims, a little learning, and calf sense.
In carpet slippers, with a broken crutch,
Retrogress from pitch to pitch,
Leave the oncoming shadow at the door,
Leave it your odd shoes.   10
Let the scales fall from rheumy eyes,
And, stepping back through the medium of abuse,
Excess or otherwise, regain your fire.
Craft a monkey gland, old man, at fools' advice.

Shall it be male or female? say the cells,   15
The womb deliberates, spits forth manchild
To break or to be broken by the world,
A body cursed already by heredity.
The hundred-tainted lies in the cold and cools.

A one legged man ascending steps   20
Looks down upon him with regrets
That whips and stools and cistern sex
Have yet to add to that that mother strips
Upon her knee and shields from metal whisper
Of wind along the cot,   25
Sees cool get cold and childmind darker

As time on time sea ribbon rounds
Parched shires in dry lands.

The hundred-tainted must pulse and grow,
Victims of sires' vices breed heirs   30
To herring smelling fevers,
By way of ditch and gap arrive full stop.

Old man, would you arrive at pain,
Although new pain, by back lane,

Not dodging ruts but stepping through them,   35
Soaking old legs and veins,
And reach your youth again by them.

The child on lap is a nice child,
Has learnt, through cold, to love the heat,
On female knees takes a warm seat   40
And this is all there is to it:
The victim of grandfather's
Unwise desires, or even earlier's,
Has a hundred stigmas,
More chance to hand on   45
Unclean Round Robin,
And more to hear air engine,
May yet find wings as airman,
And parachute old scabs and branded spots.

April 23, 1933
February, 1933, Notebook XXVII

B   If I was tickled by the rub of love,
        A rocking girl who stole me for her side,
        Broke through her straws, breaking my bandaged string,
        If the red tickle as the cattle calve
        Still set to scratch a laughter from my lung,   5
        I would not fear the apple nor its flood
        Nor the bad blood of spring.
        Shall it be male or female? says the cells,
        And drop the plum like fire from the flesh.

If I was tickled by the hatching hair,   10
The winging bone that sprouted in the heels,
The itch of man upon the baby's thigh,
I would not fear the gallows nor the axe
Nor the crossed sticks of war.
[If from the first some mother of the wind   15
Gave suck to such a bud as forks my eye,
I would not fear the howling round the cots
As time on time the lean sea ribbons round
Parched shires in dry lands, and the rat's lot,
Nor all the herring smelling of the sea   20
Nor the death in the light.]
Shall it be male or female? say the fingers
Chalking the [jakes]⁵ with green [things of]⁶ [the brain]⁷
I would not fear the muscling-in of love
If I was tickled by the urchin hungers   25
Rehearsing heat upon a raw-edged nerve.
I would not fear the devil in the loin
Nor the outspoken grave.
If I was tickled by the lover's rub
That wipes away not crow's-foot nor the lock   30
Of sick old [age]⁸ up on the falling jaws:
Time and the crabs and the sweethearting crib
Would leave me cold as butter for the flies:
[The biting days would soften as I struck
Bells on the dead fools']⁹ toes.   35
This world is half the devil's and my own,
Daft with the drug that's smoking in a girl
And curling round the bud that forks her eye.
An old man's shank one-marrowed with my bone,
And all the herrings smelling in the sea,   40
I sit and watch the worm beneath my nail
Wearing the quick away.
And that's the rub, the only rub that tickles.
The knobbly ape that swings along his sex
From damp love-darkness and the nurse's twist   45
Can never raise the midnight of a chuckle,
Nor when he finds a beauty in the breast
Of lover, mother, lovers or his six
Feet in the rubbing dust.

And what's the rub? Death's feather on the nerve?   50
Your mouth, my love, the thistle in a kiss?
My Jack of Christ born thorny on the tree?
The words of death are dryer than his stiff,
My wordy wounds are printed with your hair.
I would be tickled by the rub that is: 55
Man be my metaphor.

April 30, 1934
August, 1933, Notebook XLI

A   *If I Were Tickled by the Rub of Love*

Final   If I were tickled by the rub of love,
Version   A rooking girl who stole me for her side,
                 Broke through her straws, breaking my bandaged string,
                 If the red tickle as the cattle calve
                 Still set to scratch a laughter from my lung,   5
                 I would not fear the apple or the flood
                 Nor the bad blood of spring.

                 Shall it be male or female? say the cells,
                 And drop the plum like fire from the flesh.
                 If I were tickled by the hatching hair,   10
                 The winging bone that sprouted in the heels,
                 The itch of man upon the baby's thigh,
                 I would not fear the gallows nor the axe
                 Nor the crossed sticks of war.

                 Shall it be male or female? say the fingers   15
                 That chalk the walls with green girls and their men.
                 I would not fear the muscling-in of love
                 If I were tickled by the urchin hungers
                 Rehearsing heat upon a raw-edged nerve.
                 I would not fear the devil in the loin   20
                 Nor the outspoken grave.

                 If I were tickled by the lovers' rub
                 That wipes away not crow's-foot nor the lock
                 Of sick old manhood on the fallen jaws,
                 Time and the crabs and the sweethearting crib   25

Would leave me cold as butter for the flies,
The sea of scums could drown me as it broke
Dead on the sweetheart's toes.

This world is half the devil's and my own,
Daft with the drug that's smoking in a girl   30
And curling round the bud that forks her eye.
An old man's shank one-marrowed with my bone,
And all the herrings smelling in the sea,
I sit and watch the worm beneath my nail
Wearing the quick away.   35

And that's the rub, the only rub that tickles.
The knobbly ape that swings along his sex
From damp love-darkness and the nurse's twist
Can never raise the midnight of a chuckle,
Nor when he finds a beauty in the breast   40
Of lover, mother, lovers, or his six
Feet in the rubbing dust.

And what's the rub? Death's feather on the nerve?
Your mouth, my love, the thistle in the kiss?
My Jack of Christ born thorny on the tree?   45
The words of death are dryer than his stiff,
My wordy wounds are printed with your hair.
I would be tickled by the rub that is:
Man be my metaphor.

1. The B version is very much like the final poem except for a few minor changes, which make the final poem more precise. The third stanza in B is excluded. What are your thoughts on this stanza? Does it contain ideas present already in the poem? Does it change anything other than the poem's structure?

2. The poem develops around a series of fears or anxieties. Does C, a poem vastly different from the other versions, clarify this thematic development in any way? The C poem contains lines that eventually are found in the final poem. Cite these lines and discuss their function in the two poems.

3. Discuss the early version and the finished poem from the point of view of dramatic design or structure.

4. Discuss literary allusions in poetry generally and in this poem specifically, for example, "Aye, there's the rub" from *Hamlet*.

<table>
<tr><td>

B

*Special-
ly When
the
October
Wind*]

</td><td>

Especially when the November wind
With frosty fingers punishes my hair,
Or, beaten on by the straight beams of the sun,
I walk abroad, feeling my youth like fire
Burning weak blood and body up,
Does the brain reel, drunk on the raw
Spirits of words, and the heart sicken
Of arid syllables grouped and regrouped with care,
Of the chosen task that lies upon
My belly like a cold stone.

By the sea's side hearing the cries of gulls,
In winter fields hearing a sheep cough
That wakes out of tubercular oblivion
Into a wet world, my heart rebels
Against the chain of words,
Now hard as iron and now soft as clouds,
While weighted trees lift asking arms far off.
Shut in a tower of words, I mark
Men in the distance walk like trees
And talking as the four winds talk,
Children in parks and children's homes
Speaking on fingers and thumbs,
And think, as drummed on by the sun,
How good it is to feel the November air
And be no words' prisoner.

To view the changing world behind
A pot of ferns, lifting the sunblind
See gilded people walking on hindlegs
Along the pavement where a blind man begs
Hopefully, helplessly, feeling the sun's wings,
To trim a window garden with a shears,
To read front pages, fall asleep,

</td><td>

5

10

15

20

25

30

</td></tr>
</table>

Undreaming, on a linen lap
This, when the heart goes sick
And ears are threatened in the spring of dawn   35
By the triumphant accents of the cock,
Is more to be longed for in the end
Than, chained by syllables at hand and foot,
Wagging a wild tongue at the clock,
Deploring death, and raising roofs   40
Of words to keep unharmed
By time's approach in a fell wind
The bits and pieces of dissected loves.

A   *Especially When the October Wind*

Final   Especially when the October wind
Version   With frosty fingers punishes my hair,
                   Caught by the crabbing sun I walk on fire
                   And cast a shadow crab upon the land,
                   By the sea's side, hearing the noise of birds,   5

                   Hearing the raven cough in winter sticks,
                   My busy heart who shudders as she talks
                   Sheds the syllabic blood and drains her words.

                   Shut, too, in a tower of words, I mark
                   On the horizon walking like the trees
                   The wordy shapes of women, and the rows
                   Of the star-gestured children in the park.
                   Some let me make you of the vowelled beeches,
                   Some of the oaken voices, from the roots
                   Of many a thorny shire tell you notes,   15
                   Some let me make you of the water's speeches.

                   Behind a pot of ferns the wagging clock
                   Tells me the hour's word, the neural meaning
                   Flies on the shafted desk, declaims the morning
                   And tells the windy weather in the cock.   20
                   Some let me make you of the meadow's signs;
                   The signal grass that tells me all I know

Breaks with the wormy winter through the eye.
Some let me tell you of the raven's sins.

Especially when the October wind   25
(Some let me make you of autumnal spells,
The spider-tongued, and the loud hill of Wales)
With fists of turnips punishes the land,
Some let me make you of the heartless words.
The heart is drained that, spelling in the scurry   30
Of chemic blood, warned of the coming fury.
By the sea's side hear the dark-vowelled birds.

1. It is necessary to read this poem aloud. Where in the poem does Thomas tell us this?

2. This poem, like a number of Thomas's other poems, is about the writing (or "making" or "telling") of poetry. The second stanza conveys a paradox of the imprisonment of the poet in his craft and his freedom to transform physical reality. In the earlier draft the stanza has an optimistic last line not in the final poem. How does the line strike you in light of the entire poem?

3. The romantic tone in lines 4 and 5 of version B are nowhere to be found, or felt, in the final version. Thomas has "made" his poem not only structurally tighter, but also more objectified in terms of the expression of his personal experience. At the same time, however, consider the change from "November" in B to "October" in A, the month of the poet's birth. Discuss the images in lines 9 and 10 of B. Although the imagery is clear, and also dramatic, Thomas obviously had second thoughts about using it. How is it at variance with the final development of imagery?

4. Comment on the change of gender in stanza 2.

5. Line B26 begins a narrative movement not to be felt at all in A. Are any of the materials or tones of this narrative finally transformed in the later poem?

6. The last stanza recalls the first through a number of poetic devices,

for example, rhymes and repetition of words, phrases, and images. What does Thomas accomplish through this conscious echoing? Does the earlier version have a similar design?

B

To E.P.

[*The
Force That
Through
the Green
Fuse Drives
the Flower*]

The force that through the green fuse drives the flower
Drives my green age; that blasts the roots of trees
Is my destroyer.
And I am dumb to tell the eaten rose
How at my sheet goes the same crooked worm,   5
And dumb to holla thunder to the skies
How at my cloth flies the same central storm.

The force that through the green fuse drives the flower
Drives my green age, that blasts the roots of trees
Is my destroyer.   10
And I am dumb to tell the crooked rose
My youth is bent by the same wintry fever.

The force that drives the water through the rocks
Drives my red blood; that dries the mouthing streams
Turns mine to wax.   15
And I am dumb to mouth unto my veins
How at the mountain spring the same mouth sucks.

The hand that whirls the water in the pool
Stirs the quicksand; that ropes the blowing wind
Hauls my shroud sail.   20

And I am dumb to tell the hanging man
How of my clay is made the hangman's lime.

The lips of time leech to the fountain head;
Love drips and gathers, but the fallen blood
Shall make her well;   25
And I am dumb to tell the aimless sun
[How time is all.]

And I am dumb to tell the lover's tomb
How at my sheet goes the same crooked worm.

October 12, 1933

August, 1933, Notebook XXIII

A   *The Force That Through the Green Fuse Drives the Flower*

Final
Version   The force that through the green fuse drives the flower
            Drives my green age; that blasts the roots of trees
            Is my destroyer.
            And I am dumb to tell the crooked rose
            My youth is bent by the same wintry fever.   5

            The force that drives the water through the rocks
            Drives my red blood; that dries the mouthing streams
            Turns mine to wax.
            And I am dumb to mouth unto my veins
            How at the mountain spring the same mouth sucks.   10

            The hand that whirls the water in the pool
            Stirs the quicksand; that ropes the blowing wind
            Hauls my shroud sail.
            And I am dumb to tell the hanging man
            How of my clay is made the hangman's lime.   15

            The lips of time leech to the fountain head;
            Love drips and gathers, but the fallen blood
            Shall calm her sores.
            And I am dumb to tell a weather's wind
            How time has ticked a heaven round the stars.   20

            And I am dumb to tell the lover's tomb
            How at my sheet goes the same crooked worm.

1. This poem is about the poet's youth and the natural forces working
on his sensibility and physical sense of life. Discuss the rhythm and
various patternings of sound in relation to the poem's central theme
or idea.

2. This is one of Thomas's most accessible poems. Yet its vast sugges-

tiveness and ambiguities provide the reader with endless possibilities for interpretation. Discuss the paradox of a clear, yet difficult image in this poem.

3. Discuss repetition—tonal and intellectual—in the poem, and discuss how these echoes or repetitions are shifted in order to carry various meanings.

4. Consider the image beginning at line 14 in the earlier version. What effect does its omission have in the later poem?

5. The rhythm of the poem is rising and falling (there is a short stop, a caesura, after each semicolon) as the central theme involves opposite poles of life and death, fruition and decay, mortality and immortality, and so on. Discuss this rhythm by citing the difference in line length and stress on individual words. Do the same with version B.

6. The poem ends with a two-line coda. The earlier version provides this conclusion as the fourth and fifth lines of the first stanza. How does this change affect the poem?

Notes

1. Ralph Maud, ed., *The Notebooks of Dylan Thomas* (New York: New Directions, 1967).
2. Constantine Fitzgibbon, *The Life of Dylan Thomas* (New York: Atlantic /Little Brown and Company, 1965).
3. going
4. creates a
5. walls
6. girls
7. their men
8. manhood
9. The sea of scums cold drown me as it broke / Dead on the sweethearts

P. K. PAGE

1916-

THE CANADIAN POET P. K. PAGE LIVES AND WRITES IN Victoria, British Columbia. Page's career as poet, novelist, painter, scriptwriter, and author of children's stories has spanned the larger part of the twentieth century. The critical acclaim regarding her work is daunting. Unstinting in its praise for her achievement, it invariably presents Page as a writer with a technique that is referred to as "dazzling." Rosemary Sullivan, essayist for *Canadian Literature*, writes that Page "reaches out for a reality larger than and beyond the visible world" with "such a remarkable verbal gift that the imagemaking process can become almost too seductive." The poems offered in this chapter, including examples of their revisions taken from the author's worksheets, demonstrate why Page continues to be so well received as a poet.

In "The Hidden Room," a free-verse poem that attempts to make us see "a room / disguised as a non-room / a secret space," Page is able to avoid all punctuation and at the same time offer an equivalent by way of rhythmically appropriate line breaks. Thus, in a series of tercets, are the syntactical toeholds so necessary to grasping the logic of a dream place that, like the punctuation, is both there and not there. The fact that the reader may "see only / a lumber room" and not a "prism" shortly becomes the view of the narrator who, in seeking it, finds that "it recedes." The mystical quality enhanced by the poem's grammatically seamless structure makes the "room" a dreamt reality. Ultimately, in the final draft, Page discarded her opening stanza, which explicitly locates the "room" in a dream.

"Single Traveller," originally titled "Ghazal," stands as a series of closed couplets. A varied but soothing pentameter is maintained throughout the poem. As in a ghazal, each stanza, or couplet, remains sufficiently distinct from both the next and the previous stanza. Each is presented as evidence of the poem's unifying theme (and rhyme) through the repetition of the word "companion." Here, within the structure of an exacting form, Page finds variant rhythms, rhythms that suit her individual topics, a "wasting world," "a trillium covered wood," "the street of love," a "squanderer of time." The graceful choice of rhythms enables us to submerge ourselves in the poetry, causing the reader to forget the poem's formality. It is as if the words themselves have found their own form.

"The New Bicycle" is similar to the "The Hidden Room" in that it relies on phrasing and sound to determine the poem's shape. "All the molecules in the house" (line 1) represent the "us" as in "it has changed us all" (last line). "House," "presence," "dials," "senses," "windows," "mantelpiece," "ourselves," "turquoise," all, in meaning and concreteness compel us to look for the vaster, more real effect that this bicycle is having on its new environment. If we stop to count these sibilant sounds we may mistakenly think that they are over-done. It is conceivable, however, that the author may have decided to take one or two out, possibly deeming them unsuitable or too notice-able to the ear.

The two "glosas" included in this chapter, "Hologram" and "The Gold Sun," poems that demonstrate considerable technical control, testify to Page's own revisiting of her past. As she describes in her fore-word to her book, *Hologram*,[1] "it occurred to me that now, towards the end of my life, it would be appropriate to use [the glosa] as a way of paying homage to those poets whose work I fell in love with in my formative years. I would pick four lines [*cabeza*] from Marvell, Blake, Donne…and, as it were, 'marry' them. And so I retraced the steps of my early reading…" Page's book contains fourteen glosas. Printed here, along with composites based on the author's drafts of each poem, are the first two of the fourteen. Page's skill at, and feeling for, this late fourteenth-century form used by the poets of the Spanish Court speaks for itself.

The final poem by Page included here is "Lily on the Patio." Like "The New Bicycle," the poem focuses on bringing a non-human object into a particular environment. Despite its own set of very different and unquestionably fine attributes, it becomes, nonetheless, a highly valued interloper that is in some sense almost superhuman.

B   *The Hidden Room*

[*Note: 1st stanza becomes the last stanza and then is dropped in the final draft.*]

composite
of early   I dreamed it last night
versions   Have dreamed it many times before
showing   or dreamed I dreamed it
variants in
brackets   I have come here since I was born [Have been coming] [of coming]
                never at my will
                only when it permits me

                Like the Bodleian like the Web [or the Internet]
                like Borges' aleph
                it contains it all [embodies all]

                It is in a house
                that is deeply hidden in my head
                It is mine and not mine

                yet if I seek it [The more I seek it]
                it recedes [the more it recedes]
                down [inscrutable] corridors [of amnesia] [anaesthesia]
                                [down the corridors of ether]

                Each single version
                is like and not like
                all the others

                a hidden place
                in cellar or in attic
                matrix of evil and good

                a room
                disguised as a non-room
                a secret space

                I am showing it to you
                fearful you may not
                guess its importance

that you will see it only as   [that you will see only]
a lumber room
a child's bolt hole

will not [realize] know it is eternal   [will not know]
a magic square   [it is a prism a magic square]
a prism   [the number nine]
the number nine

[Note: Originally part of the 1ˢᵗ stanza in earlier drafts, these three lines and the two that follow penultimately become the final stanza before they are discarded altogether.]

I dreamed it last night
have dreamed it many times before
or dreamed I dreamed it

each dream is like and not like
all the others

A   *The Hidden Room*

Final
version
                                I have been coming here since I was born
                                never at my will
                                only when it permits me

                                Like the Bodleian like the Web
                                like Borges' aleph
                                it embodies all

                                It is in a house
                                that is deeply hidden in my head
                                It is mine and not mine

                                yet if I seek it
                                it recedes
                                down corridors of ether

                                Each single version
                                is like and unlike
                                all the others

a hidden place
in cellar or attic
matrix of evil and good

a room
disguised as a non-room
a secret space

I am showing it to you
fearful you may not
guess its importance

that you will see only
a lumber room
a child's bolt hole

Will not know it as prism
a magic square
the number nine

1. Perhaps in some way seduced by the "number nine," the author seems concerned with how often she must use "it" when referring to "the hidden room." Does she remedy this for purposes of "streamlining," or might there be other reasons? Explain.

2. In the final version, stanza 4, line 3, Page leaps from "inscrutable...amnesia ... to "ether." Describe the effect she has achieved.

3. How is the final version of this poem changed by discarding the opening stanza? Was this a drastic change, or was it simply necessary? Discuss this point.

B

A
composite
of
early
versions
showing
variants in
brackets

[*Ghazal*][*The Companion*][*Single Traveller*]

What is this love that [has been] is my life's Companion?
Shape[face]-changer, sometimes faceless, this companion.

Single traveller, I wander a wasting world
awaiting the much anticipated Companion.

A trillium covered wood one April day
served [me] as a nearly [perfect] consummate companion.

A horse, two dogs, some [half-a-dozen] cats, [a blue macaw]
each in its [time] turn [becoming] [has been]
    became a [true] [sole] loyal companion.

Behind the loved embrace, a face of light —
demon or angel[?] — lures me from my companion.

The street of love is neither wide nor narrow.
Its width depends on me and my companion.

Am I too bound and blinded by coarse wrappings
ever to know true love as my companion?

O [Page] [Poet], [poor] squanderer of time and talents,
why do you [search for love as] [seek out love for] your Companion?

A

Single Traveller

Final
Version

What is this love that is my life's Companion?
Shape-changer, sometimes faceless, this companion.

Single traveller, I wander a wasting world
awaiting the much anticipated Companion.

A trillium covered wood one April day
served as a nearly consummate companion.

A horse, two dogs, some cats, a blue macaw
each in its turn became a loyal companion.

Behind the loved embrace, a face of light —
demon or angel? — lures me from my companion.

The street of love is neither wide nor narrow.
Its width depends on me and my companion.

Am I too bound and blinded by coarse wrappings
ever to know true love as my companion?

O Poet, squanderer of time and talents,
why do you search for love as your Companion?

1. Although Page has rejected her working title, "Ghazal," "Single Traveller," as a poem, still retains the mood of a ghazal, namely, the sense of mild distancing that exists between stanzas. Explain why the author settles on a different title for this poem.

2. Is retaining a tighter line (stanza 3, line 2) a required constraint in the case of this specific poem? Compare the "feel" of this line to line 2 of the first stanza.

3. Describe the difficulty inherent in choosing "search for love as" over "seek out love for" in the last line of this poem.

B   *The New Bicycle*

A com-
posite of   All the molecules in the house
early   readjust on its arrival,
versions   make way for its shining presence
showing   its bright dials,
iants in   and after it has settled
brackets   and the light
                  has explored its surfaces
                  — and the night —
                  they [settle] themselves again
                  in [a composed] order.

One senses the change at once
without knowing what one senses.
Has somebody cleaned the windows
used a [new] soap
or [are there bowls] of flowers
on the mantelpiece? –
for the air makes another shape
it is thinner or denser,
[has] a new design
[invisibly] stamped upon it.

How we all adapt ourselves
to the bicycle
aglow in the furnace room,
turquoise where turquoise
has never before been seen,
its chrome gleaming
on gears and pedals,
its spokes glistening.
Lightly resting on the incised
rubber of its airy tires
it has changed us all.

The New Bicycle

A

All the molecules in the house
readjust on its arrival,
make way for its shining presence
its bright dials,
and after it has settled
and the light
has explored its surfaces
– and the night –
they compose themselves again
in another order.

One senses the change at once
without knowing what one senses.
Has somebody cleaned the windows
used different soap

or is there a bowl of flowers
on the mantelpiece? –
for the air makes another shape
it is thinner or denser,
a new design
is invisibly stamped upon it.

How we all adapt ourselves
to the bicycle
aglow in the furnace room,
turquoise where turquoise
has never before been seen,
its chrome gleaming
on gears and pedals,
its spokes glistening.
Lightly resting on the incised
rubber of its airy tires
it has changed us all.

1. Since the difference between these two drafts seems very slight, does the tweaking of these lines in any way seem unwarranted?

2. Are there other lines in the final poem that might improve with more "adjusting?" Or must the artist finally put down the brush?

B   [*Holograph*] [*The Hologram*]

[*Holo-*   [Four lines—George Seferis]
  gram]

It was astonishing, larger than anyone could see
A com- Than anyone could imagine, but we strained to see it
posite of It was Kafka's benighted castle in a dream of wonder,
early   Nightmare transmuted, black become golden,
drafts   buttresses disappearing in the cloud and azure
a new geometry of interlocking octangles
and we, watching it, interlocked in a new dimension –
which neither your heart nor mine could have possibly invented:
a multiplying imprint, yet our vision was single
as all that morning we looked at the citadel from every angle. But
that was later, after we had made the passage

from the faint light of the morning star and a pale moon
to unscrupulous noonday with its major chords –
battalions marching across an Escher landscape
For us, at first, there was no hint of multiple images
no hint of anything that wasn't misty
and mysterious—shifting layers and lengths of chiffon
leading us inward/downward/upward, all
directions at once, a synesthesia as, methodically [observing we began
from the side in the shadow and the sea. meticulously]
Brave of us to begin in darkness. or was it wisdom
that made us so prepare ourselves for that radiance
little by little? A Jurassic age must pass before even colour
could enter the scene—dawn's greys being so infinite
and infinitely subtle—transparencies, opacities.
And then we sensed it together—the tremulous foreshock
of what lay ahead of us—what could not be imagined,
possibly not even dreamed, a new range of experience.
And, unbelievable, that which revealed itself as earthquake
was green, without brilliance, breast of a slain peacock.

We wept at the sight. To our eyes it was vivid—
It entered us like a spear. When joy is great enough
how distinguish it from pain?) and after the fugal greys

[But to our eyes that green was vivid and pierced us like a spear]

and the near-invisible shafts of no-colour that had stained us,
how could our eyes grow accustomed to such a spectrum?
And yet in a flash, from infra-red to ultra-violet,
we saw the hologram glittering above us
in glistening air we could enter like swallows
And then the whole citadel, rainbowed, exquisite, [immediate]
received us like time that has no break in it.

Hologram

All that morning we looked at the citadel from every angle.
We began from the side in the shadow, where the sea,
Green without brilliance, —— breast of a slain peacock,
Received us like time that has no break in it.

The King of Asine, George Seferis

It was astonishing, larger by far than we could imagine,
larger than sight itself but still we strained to see it.
It was Kafka's castle in a dream of wonder,
nightmare transmuted, black become golden,
buttresses disappearing in the cloud and azure:
a new geometry of interlocking octangles
and we, watching it, interlocked in a strange dimension ——
that neither your heart nor mine could have invented ——
of multiple images, complex as angels.
All that morning we looked at the citadel from every angle.

But that was later, after we had made the passage
from the faint light of morning star and pale moon
to unscrupulous noonday with its major chords ——
battalions marching across an Escher landscape.
For us, at first, there was no hint of clarity,
no hint of anything that wasn't misty ——
synaesthetic layers and lengths of space-time
leading us inward, downward, upward, as ——
from all directions at once —— observing closely,
we began from the side in the shadow and the sea.

Brave of us to begin in darkness. or was it wisdom
that made us so prepare ourselves for that radiance
little by little? A Jurassic age must pass before even colour
could enter the scene —— dawn's greys being so infinite
and infinitely subtle —— transparencies, opacities.
And then we sensed it together —— the tremulous foreshock
of what lay ahead: what could not be imagined,
possibly not even dreamed, a new range of experience.
And —— unbelievably —— what revealed itself as earthquake
was green, without brilliance, breast of a slain peacock.

But to the cones of our eyes that green was shining
and pierced us like a spear. (When joy is great enough
how distinguish it from pain?) And after the fugal greys
and the near-invisible shafts of no-colour that had stained us,
how could our eyes adjust to so full a spectrum?
And yet in a flash, from infra-red to ultra-violet,
we saw the hologram glittering above us
glistening in air we could suddenly enter like swallows
as the whole citadel, rainbowed, immediate,
received us like time that has no break in it.

1. "A marriage" between two authors, the "glosa" form, strictly speaking, only requires the rhyming of lines 6, 9, and 10. This rule, however, does not preclude other instances of rhyming. Can you account for another pattern of end-rhyming in stanza 1 that happens as a direct result of revision? Describe the value of this deliberately added rhyme. Do you find that this happens in the other stanzas as well?

2. Page often appears to be trying out a longer line before she, in fact, shortens it. Look for specific examples of this kind of revision in other areas of the poem. Consider stanza 1, line 8.

3. The end-rhyme, "closely," stanza 2, line 9, required a major decision on the part of the author. Can you explain this statement? Is it a valid one?

B   [Four lines—Wallace Stevens]

[The Gold   Sky whitened by a snow on which no swan
Sun]   is visible, and no least feather falling
         could possibly Or impossibly be seen,
A com-   sky whitened like the blank page of a book,
posite of   no letters forming into words unless
early   written in paleness—a pallidity
versions   faint as the little rising moons on nails—
showing   and so, forgettable and so, forgot.
variants in   While eyes the blue of lapis lazuli [Blue eyes dark as lapis lazuli]
brackets   *trace the gold sun about the whitened sky*

         You'll see the very thing no matter what.

                    [Let's see the very thing and nothing else]
Though it may blind you, what else will suffice?
                    [Though it may blind us...]
To smoke a glass or use a periscope
will give you other than the thing itself—[the very thing]
or more, or elements too various.
So let the fabulous photographer
catch Phaeton in his lens and think he is
the thing, not recognizing all the else [the very thing, not knowing
all the else]
he is become. But you will see it clear
without evasion by a single metaphor.

And yet, like a spun coin in the sky
                    [Let's see it with the hottest fire of sight]
that golden body, moving, yet at rest
in its outflinging course across the great
parabola of space, is sovereign. [parabola of space. This sovereign.]
So take my hand and hold it while you look
lest sun's appearance in its fieryness
strike terror in your bones, for gold alone
        [for gold is not]
a simple thing. Gold is the light [to be disposed of gold is not]
that makes sky's whiteness [How clear the sun of all its otherness]
Look at it in its essential barrenness.

Make a prime number of it, pure, and know
it indivisible and hold it so
in the white sky behind your lapis eyes.
Push aside everything that isn't sun
the way a sculptor works his stone,
the way a mystic masters the mystique
of making more by focussing on one
until at length, all images burn out [are gone]
except the sun, the very thing, deific, [the thing itself]
and say this, this is the centre that I seek.

The Gold Sun

Trace the gold sun about the whitened sky
Without evasion by a single metaphor.
Look at it in its essential barrenness
And say this, this is the centre that I seek.

Credences of Summer, Wallace Stevens

Sky whitened by a snow on which no swan
is visible, and no least feather falling
could possibly or impossibly be seen,
sky whitened like the blank page of a book,
no letters forming into words unless
written in paleness — a pallidity
faint as the little rising moons on nails —
and so, forgettable and so, forgot.
Blue eyes dark as lapis lazuli
trace the gold sun about the whitened sky

You'll see the thing itself no matter what.
Though it may blind you, what else will suffice?
To smoke a glass or use a periscope
will give you other than the very thing,
or more, or elements too various.
So let the fabulous photographer
catch Phaeton in his lens and think he is
the thing itself, not knowing all the else
he is become. But you will see it clear
without evasion by a single metaphor.

How strip the sun of all comparisons?
That spinning coin — moving, yet at rest
in its outflinging course across the great
parabola of space — is Phoebus,
sovereign: heroic principle,
the heat and light of us. And gold — no less
a metaphor than sun — is not the least
less multiple and married. Therefore how
rid the gold sun of all its otherness?
Look at it in its essential barrenness.

Make a prime number of it, pure, and know
it indivisible and hold it so
in the white sky behind your lapis eyes.
Push aside everything that isn't sun
the way a sculptor works his stone,
the way a mystic masters the mystique
of making more by focussing on one
until at length, all images are gone
except the sun, the thing itself, deific,
and say this, this is the centre that I seek.

1. Wallace Stevens was very concerned with "things as they are," or reality as "the thing itself." Describe the author's effort, or process, in stanza 2 as she works toward identifying Stevens' concern. Does this in some way illustrate a "marrying" of the two poets, Stevens and Page?

2. Compare the two versions presented here by considering the transformation that is taking place in the third stanza. Does the author get at the issue of metaphor versus "the thing itself" in a more satisfying way in the final version? Describe what you see happening here.

3. Consider the "glosa" form and then consider the author's need to achieve a formality that is worthy of it. Find examples that illustrate her success.

B   *Lily*

[*Lily on* It's like a person on the patio [It's like a slender person in a pot]
he Patio] one you would never meet [on a quirk] [as tall as I am in my shoes]
            [tall, hydra-headed with the presence of] [perfumed, parasolled, a
A com-   presence
posite of a triffid or a vegetable giraffe imperious ... Dispassionate.
early   objective, curial , mute, Genderless. Mute.]
versions
showing   Tall as the beanstalk. But no Jack am I [It's like the beanstalk, but...]
ariants in or Jill, to climb its spikey leaves to heaven.
brackets And where the sun shines through it
            who can tell if it is green
            chartreuse, or yellow.

It swings like a yacht at anchor and [a breeze] [scented too—]
an imperceptible breeze [blows this way]
some silken movement of the air [Sweet as a funeral] [yet you]
sleeves of kimonos loose [do not smell it, you're engrossed]

to waft its inner essence on us where
in our gross human flesh we stupefy
—a bare brown foot away—as silently
            [while silently—a bare brown foot away-]
open-mouthed enamelled trumpets bray. [its open-mouthed …]
Silence is where it leads. Its phantom gift
is voicelessness. Those swinging scented shafts [sheer voicelessness…]
beamed from its lighthouse and oblivious
of noisy all of us

pass over us and through us [are like neutrinos touching us our
reach us eventually, whether we know it or without our knowing]
whether we don't. They touch us as
nutrinos touch us, doing who knows what [Doing who knows what]
as they pass through us? [as they pass through us?]
Question: Who knows what? [Answer: Who knows what.]

A   *Lily on the Patio*

Final
version   It's like a slender person in a pot
           as tall as I am in my heels, a presence
           perfumed, parasolled, imperious.
           Dispassionate. Neuter. Mute.

           A budding Beanstalk — but no Jack am I
           nor Jill, to climb its spiky leaves to heaven.
           And where the sun shines through it who can tell
           its colour. Is it green chartreuse? Or yellow?

           Swings like a yacht at anchor in some sweet
           and imperceptible breeze,
           some silken rearrangement of the air
             — sleeves of kimonos loose —

to waft its inner essence on us
where in our gross human flesh we stupefy
while silently — a bare brown foot away —
its open-mouthed enamelled trumpets bray.

Silence is where it leads. Its phantom gift —
sheer voicelessness. Those swinging scented shafts
beamed from its lighthouse and oblivious
of noisy all of us

are like neutrinos touching us without our knowing.
Doing who knows what
as they pass through us?
Answer: *Who* knows what.

1. The composite of early drafts done here, while not entirely consistent in its flow, nonetheless serves to illustrate the many options that Page has set out for herself. Are there images here that you prefer, even though they are not used in the published poem?

2. In the composite, the analogous description of "lily" feels wonderfully quirky. Yet the author chooses instead—in the final version—to go for a more direct and narrowing comparison of the flower with herself. Still, "Lily" is a person "on the Patio," as in the title. Describe your reaction to where Page is heading with the opening stanza.

3. Who is the author ultimately addressing in this poem, a single "you" or an "us"?

Note

1. P.K. Page, *Hologram: A Book of Glosas* (London, Ont.: Brick books, 1994).

PHILIP LARKIN

1922–1985

ALREADY AN ACCLAIMED NOVELIST BY 1947 AND, LATER, the author of a book on Jazz (*All What Jazz*[1]), Philip Larkin's achievement as a poet—regardless of any confining reputation he may now have as one of the witty or sardonic members of the Movement[2] in England during the early 1950s—is unquestionably far-reaching. This would be the case if only for Larkin's clearly accomplished and successful attempt at continuing in the tradition of a tuneful and personally felt poetic realism. Profoundly influenced by Thomas Hardy, Larkin dismisses the romantic ambitions of his own early, less mature work and shifts away—in the mid-1940s—from the influence of Yeats: this, at a point when, by his own admission, he is considering giving up altogether on the "business" of poetry. The triumph of this shift in style is attested to by the obvious personal, and rooted-in-physical-reality, quality of the poems in his second collection, *The Less Deceived* (1955), published ten years after his more Yeatsian first book of poems, *The North Ship*. The Larkin poems (and their versions) offered here are representative of the latter influence only. Thus, they range in publication date from 1950 to 1980. They are, nonetheless, profoundly lyrical despite their seemingly tough-minded approach.

In "At Grass," completed in January 1950, Larkin intends to see and feel much more than a romantically perfected pairing of two retired racehorses now being let out to pasture. For the drafting of this poem, Larkin develops alternative stanzas that illuminate with tenacious detail the main events, talk, and publicity that are naturally part and parcel of any racehorse's career. Ultimately, he reduces nine stanzas to five. While the poem's lines are very much concerned with the effects of passing time and with the juxtaposition of memories, what we are left with, in fact, is a vivid picture of the horses standing "at ease," unscrutinized (except by the poet), or galloping "for what must be joy," met only by "the groom, and the groom's boy..." in the evening. Throughout the fiercely disciplined, yet nostalgic, feel of the poem, the reader "can hardly pick them out" as they stand "anonymous" and "faded" in "the unmolesting meadow[s]." Yet, a true horse, one that has done it all, now unobtrusively paired–"The other seeming to look on"—is what one finally, and only, sees.

"Deception," like "At Grass" in that both were inspired by external primary sources—the one from a compilation of Henry Mayhew's letters to the *London Morning Chronicle* (1849-50), the other from a television documentary—is also rigorously imagined. At the same time, this poem reveals Larkin's personal sense of an exacting detail that best tells of the agony inherent in the story of a rape, and of the wish to explain that agony without inadvertently dismissing it. The two versions of "Deception" presented in this chapter show only a fraction of the actual revision involved. The earlier version is merely a composite of earlier drafts and does not show the anchoring of the actual setting for the poem that Larkin seems to have needed before even beginning the second stanza. Curiously, as is evidenced by many of the poems in the workbooks, Larkin held to his opening line throughout the drafting process, which in this poem—and again as in "At Grass"—was considerable. Done at a time when he may have still felt himself being pulled by the urge to rely on "romantic" inspiration, Larkin's intense revising of "Deception"—three drafts for the first stanza and six drafts for the second—perhaps indicates his ability to resist that urge. Importantly, although the poem is dated "20/2/50," signalling that it is ready to be typed out, yet another version of the final stanza, one containing several additional changes that will, in fact, be used in the published version, is noted much later in the workbooks. This unmarked version, then, immediately follows a poem dated November 4, 1950.

"Reasons for Attendance," completed in December of 1953, is one of the Larkin poems associated with "The Movement." Apart from its obvious autobiographical referencing of Larkin's direct involvement with the art of jazz, it also represents the first time that Larkin inserts an ironical character, or speaker, for purposes of self-parody. The use of this device, from this point on, becomes typical of Larkin and may be noted here as having undoubtedly influenced the later, less formal, poetry of Robert Lowell. The poem itself is concerned with the "outsider" status of a self-conscious speaker, who finds himself drawn "to the lighted glass" by the "loud and authoritative" sound of a trumpet. He observes the dancers, all younger than himself, all the while presenting his own bemused case of psychic dissonance: "Why be out here? / But then, why be in there?" Again, although earlier drafting is included with this poem, a composite draft is utilized to indicate significant choices made by the poet.

Part of Larkin's method—one that makes viewing his revising process more accessible—was his scrupulous maintenance of eight workbooks between 1943 and 1980. A.T. Tolley, in *Larkin at Work*[3] (1997), presents a comprehensive analysis of many of Larkin's more manageable drafts. Tolley's analysis, concerning itself primarily with methodology rather than interpretation, reveals the time and effort taken by Larkin, the steps and leaps, the returns to earlier lines, especially to the first line, and, overall, it depicts the self-discipline required by Larkin "to get it right." Tolley also clarifies whether or not the "final version" exists in the Notebooks or has come about through alterations of a "fair copy" (usually in ink rather than in pencil) that has been transcribed onto a typewritten page. In some instances, as with "At Grass," there is "no final 'good version'" in the notebooks.

Several of the poems reproduced here were done quickly, taking up only a page or two in the workbook. Brevity of time and effort taken to compose does not preclude the success or real achievement of a poem. "Coming" (1950), "Days" (1953), and "How" (1970) are, in their individual ways, examples of just this point. The other choices for this chapter, however, like most of Larkin's major work, show considerable space being taken up in the workbooks. Not all of the drafting can or need be shown here. Specifically, then, and for the purposes of this chapter, the published (or A) version of the poem is given first, followed by earlier drafts that become increasingly more finalized. In some cases, an earlier draft may be a composite draft only, one that hints at significant shifts in the poem while retaining the appearance of the published version. Throughout these versions, brackets are used to indicate word choices ultimately rejected by Larkin in the workbooks.

A

Final
version

The eye can hardly pick them out
From the cold shade they shelter in,
Till wind distresses tail and mane;
Then one crops grass, and moves about
—The other seeming to look on—   5
And stands anonymous again.

Yet fifteen years ago, perhaps
Two dozen distances sufficed
To fable them: faint afternoons
Of Cups and Stakes and Handicaps,   10
Whereby their names were artificed
To inlay faded, classic Junes—

Silks at the start: against the sky
Numbers and parasols: outside,
Squadrons of empty cars, and heat,   15
And littered grass: then the long cry
Hanging unhushed till it subside
To stop-press columns on the street.

Do memories plague their ears like flies?
They shake their heads. Dusk brims the shadows.   20
Summer by summer all stole away,
The starting-gates, the crowds and cries—
All but the unmolesting meadows.
Almanacked, their names live; they

Have slipped their names, and stand at ease,   25
Or gallop for what must be joy;
And not a fieldglass sees them home,
Or curious stop-watch prophesies:
Only the groom, and the groom's boy,
With bridles in the evening come.   30

C

Earliest
version

> The eye can hardly pick them out
> From the cold shade they [select] shelter in—
> [To shelter in] Till wind distresses tail and mane:
> Then, on the far side of the field,
> We see them standing, nose to nose
>
> Fifteen years ago, they were
> More famous than most men, pursued
> By Cameras, field-glasses and cars,
> Ham-sandwiches, and newspapers:
> Their [every] morning gallops [was] were reviewed
> [In a hundred noisy] By lunchtime in the City bars.
> Spied on from bushes cheered from stands
>
> Broke three people in one day,
> The two between them: every race
> Created small disturbances
> A pawned coat, an advance of pay
> A hundred humiliations trace
> Back to their pure-bred energies.
> Do memories plague their [manes] ears like flies?
> They shake their heads. [The cloth of fame] The dusk comes on.
> Summer by summer, [it all dissolved] all wore away
> [Stripping from their backs fell back] away
> The starting gates, [and] the crowds and cries
> [Except as names, they were quite forgotten and none]
> All but their almanacked names, were all gone, are gone
> Imagines them

B *Drafted version with all nine stanzas: stanzas 2, 3, 6, and 7 were not published: line*
changes in the published version are indicated to the right.

At Grass

> The eye can hardly pick them out
> From the cold shade they shelter in,
> Till wind distresses tail and mane;
> Then one crops grass, and moves about;
> The other seeming to look on.

The sky blows dark with new Spring rain. / And stands anonymous
again /

And now no London newspaper
Pries round their paddock solitude.
They are as other horses are.
Yet, fifteen years ago, both were
More famous than most men, pursued
By camera, field-glasses and car.

In City dining-rooms in clubs
And barber's-shops and billiard halls,
Their flippant names were burrs that stuck
To gossip; and in back-street pubs
Their tinted pictures on the walls
Embodied every earthly luck.

Through thirty-three and-four, perhaps / Yet fifteen years ago,
perhaps
Two dozen distances sufficed
To fable them, far afternoon / faint afternoons
Of Cups and Stakes and Handicaps,
Whereby their names were artificed
To inlay faded, classic Junes.

Silks at the start: against the sky
Numbers and parasols: outside,
Squadrons of empty cars, and heat,
And littered grass; then the long cry
Hanging unhushed till it subside
To sports editions in the street. / To stop-press columns on the street

But money rode them, led them in,
Curry-combed their croups and flanks;
Every canter, swerve or sweat
Money measured; every win
Was endorsed at different banks.
Guiltlessly they galloped, yet

Broke three people in one day,
The two of them, and every race
They ran brought small disturbances—
One pawns his coat, on cannot pay:
[Strange such seediness to trace]
Back to such splendid energies.

Do memories plague their ears like flies?
They shake their heads. Dusk brims the shadows.
Summer by summer all ebbed away. / all stole away
— The starting-gates, the crowds and cries
All but the unmolesting meadows.
Almanacked, their names live; they

Have slipped their names, and stand at ease,
Or gallop for what must be joy;
No field glasses pursue them home.
　　　　　/ And not a field-glass sees them home
Stopwatches make no prophecies. /
　　　　　Or curious stop watch prophesies /
Only the groom, or the groom's boy,
　　　　　/ and the groom's boy
With bridles in the evening come.

1. Larkin very often remained loyal to the first line of a poem from start to finish in the drafting process. Discuss why this practice might make sense, especially in "At Grass." Is he deliberately striving for a series of muted rhymes?

2. Why are "they" not revealed to be race horses in the opening stanza We only discover that the "they" in the first stanza refers to race horse in the middle of stanza two. How is your reading experience affected by this delay in essential information?

3. Are the final stanza choices appropriate? Explain. Note: alternates for stanzas 1 and 3 are not published. Since they are perfectly expressed stanzas in themselves, why is their exclusion deemed necessary?

4. Larkin clearly establishes a distance between the narrator and the horses themselves. What effect is suggested by the line "Or gallop for

what must be joy" in the final stanza? Is there a connection between this phrase and other phrases in the poem such as "The other seeming to look on" in stanza 1, or "They shake their heads" in stanza 5?

5. In the early drafting of stanza 5, the "cloth of fame" seems relevant to the phrase "stripping from their backs fell back." In the final drafting what has "slipped" are "their names." Is this a large leap of faith made by the author? How does the theme of "names" work its way through the poem? Is it related to "anonymous" in the first stanza?

A   *Deceptions*

Final   "Of course I was drugged, and so heavily I did not regain my con-
version   sciousness till the next morning. I was horrified to discover that I had
been ruined, and for some days I was inconsolable, and cried like a
child to be killed or sent back to my aunt." Mayhew, *London Labour and the
London Poor* [1851]

        Even so distant, I can taste the grief,
        Bitter and sharp with stalks, he made you gulp.
        The sun's occasional print, the brisk brief
        Worry of wheels along the street outside
        Where bridal London bows the other way,   5
        And light, unanswerable and tall and wide,
        Forbids the scar to heal, and drives
        Shame out of hiding. All the unhurried day
        Your mind lay open like a drawer of knives.

        Slums, years, have buried you. I would not dare   10
        Console you if I could. What can be said,
        Except that suffering is exact, but where
        Desire takes charge, readings will grow erratic?
        For you would hardly care
        That you were less deceived, out on that bed,   15
        Than he was, stumbling up the breathless stair
        To burst into fulfilment's desolate attic.

Even so distant I can taste the grief,
Bitter and sharp with stalks, he made you gulp:
The heartless patterns of sun, the brisk brief
Worry of wheels along the street outside—
Where virgin London streaming the other way.   5
And light unanswerable and tall and wide
Gives nowhere to secrete the scar, no shame
For yours to hide against. No cover shrives.
Your memories glittering like a box of knives.

Across the slum of years I would not dare   10
Console you if I could. What can be said,
Except that suffering scalds deceit, and
Illusion scatters, pain is most emphatic?
For you would hardly care
That you were nearer truth, stretched on that bed,   15
Than he was, stumbling up the eager stair
To burst into fulfilment's desolate attic.

The origin of this poem, a quotation, was written down by the poet in his workbook before beginning the initial draft. The final shape of the poem is already apparent in the early draft of the first stanza. Of note: the first lines drafted for the second stanza, "I marvel he should sweat so up the stairs | To burst into fulfillment's desolate attic," ultimately are revised and used, instead, to conclude the poem.

1. Consider the transformation (line 5) from "virgin London streaming" to a "bridal London" that "bows." Is the word "Shame" (line 8) more soundly anchored, or isolated, in terms of its disconnection from the "bridal" image? If retained, would "virgin" and "streaming" add too much light to the final version of this stanza? Is line 9 changed for the same reason? Discuss the poet's use of light in the first stanza.

2. How has the first stanza been slowed down, or brought to a more secure sense of conclusion, by the final changes in lines 8 and 9?

3. The first line of stanza 2 becomes two sentences. Discuss the effect of this change.

4. In line 3 of the second stanza, the poet rejects the metaphor "suffering scalds deceit." What do you think of the change of language as a consequence of this choice?

5. The rhetorical questioning represented by lines 11-13 is retained in the final version. Is this effective? Discuss the evolution, or transformation, of this question.

6. Compare, in the final lines, "nearer truth" with "less deceived," "out" with "stretched," and "breathless" with "eager."

Coming

A

Final
version

On longer evenings,
Light, chill and yellow,
Bathes the serene
Foreheads of houses.
A thrush sings,   5
Laurel-surrounded
In the deep bare garden,
Its fresh-peeled voice
Astonishing the brickwork.
It will be spring soon,   10
It will be spring soon-
And I, whose childhood
Is a forgotten boredom,
Feel like a child
Who comes on a scene   15
Of adult reconciling,
And can understand nothing
But the unusual laughter,
And starts to be happy.

C

Earliest
draft for
"Coming"
showing
working
title:
"ebruary"

[In the evening
In the evening, in February,
It is light to leave work
On longer evenings light is cold and yellow]
On longer evenings,
Light, chill and yellow
Bathes the serene
Foreheads of houses.
Laurel-shielded, in
The cold wet garden,
[The] A thrush sings,
Astonishing the brickwork.
With a fresh-peeled song.
[A new sound, fresh peeled]

(*Drafting ends here*)

B

ultimate
draft

On longer evenings,
Light, chill and yellow,
Bathes the serene
Foreheads of houses,
A thrush sings,
Laurel-[shielded in] surrounded
In
The bare deep garden,
Its fresh-peeled voice
Astonishing the brickwork.
It will be spring soon,
It will be spring soon,
And I, whose childhood
Is a forgotten boredom,
Feel like a child
Who comes on
[Coming upon] a scene
Of adult [reconciliation] reconciling
And [understands] can understand nothing
But [the] the unusual laughter
And [begins] starts to be happy.

"Coming," written in the same month as "Deceptions," is an example of a poem done quickly and with minimal drafting, although the second draft shows a significant rearranging of what was begun in the first draft.

1. What does Larkin do with the first line of the poem that enables him to continue?

2. Is the repositioning of the "A thrush sings" a major change, one that helps to justify the changed title of the final version?

3. Does "bare deep garden" significantly change the mood of the second version? What specific difference does the reordering of these words make?

4. The notion of a child coming upon the scene appears only in the second draft. Discuss this development in terms of how it affects the entire poem.

A   *Reasons for Attendance*

Final   The trumpet's voice, loud and authoritative,
version   Draws me a moment to the lighted glass
               To watch the dancers—all under twenty-five—
               Shifting intently, face to flushed face,
               Solemnly on the beat of happiness.   5

               —Or so I fancy, sensing the smoke and sweat,
               The wonderful feel of girls. Why be out here?
               But then, why be in there? Sex, yes, but what
               Is sex? Surely, to think the lion's share
               Of happiness is found by couples—sheer   10

               Inaccuracy, as far as I'm concerned.
               What calls me is that lifted, rough-tongued bell
               (Art, if you like) whose individual sound
               Insists I too am individual.
               It speaks; I hear; others may hear as well,   15

               But not for me, nor I for them; and so
               With happiness. Therefore I stay outside,
               Believing this; and they maul to and fro,

Believing that; and both are satisfied,
If no one has misjudged himself. Or lied.   20

<table>
<tr><td>C</td><td>Passing the lighted hall</td></tr>
</table>

C

Passing the lighted hall
A trumpet speaking, loud and authoritative

Early
drafts
that seek
direction
and tone

Draws me aside up to the lighted pane
I listen a moment. Jazz? No, fooled again.
A trumpet's voice, loud and authoritative,
[Diverted me towards]Drew me a moment to the lighted glass
[By which I saw the dancers shuffling pass]
To see the crowd—all under twenty-five—
[Shifting in a composite embrace]
Shifting intently, face to flushed face

The noise, the smell of smoke, cosmetics, sweat,
The feel of girls — Why was I outside?
Why were they inside? Sex, of course, but what
Is sex?

B

composite
draft
based on
earlier
drafts

A trumpet's voice [speaking], loud and authoritative
Drew me a moment to the lighted glass [pane]
To see the crowd— all under twenty-five—
[Shifting intently, face against face]
Solidly on the beat of happiness
Or so it seemed. Think of the smoke, the sweat,
The wonderful feel of girls. Why stay out here [outside]
But why are [were] they inside? Sex, yes, but what
Is sex? Surely, to think the largest [biggest] share
Of [good in life] happiness is found by couples—sheer

[absurdity] Inaccuracy, as far as I'm concerned
What called me here was that rough-languaged bell
(Art, if you like) [spilling bright sound] whose individual sound
Insists I too am individual.
[Pleasing me]It speaks, I hear; others may hear as well,

But not for me, nor I for them; and so
With happiness. Therefore, I stay outside,
Believing that [me better off]; and both are satisfied
If no one has misjudged himself. Or lied.

1. Discuss the process that the author might be undergoing as he begins the early drafting for the first two stanzas. At what point does he appear to be establishing the movement and possibly the point of view of the poem?

2. In two of the three early drafts, Larkin utilizes the past tense. Considering both the later (composite) version and the final version, explain the necessity of reverting to the present tense.

3. The notion of "shifting" is borrowed from the earliest drafting of the second stanza. "Shifting in a composite embrace" becomes "Shifting intently, face to flushed face" in the opening stanza. Is this alteration in some way related to the changing of "To see the crowd" back into "To watch the dancers"? Discuss other dynamics in the drafting of this poem in terms of whether they offer greater clarity or definition.

4. In stanza 1, is "solemnly" a more effective word-choice than "solidly"? Might this one word change the way this entire stanza feels?

5. Acceptance of the self-ironical speaker is crucial to many of Philip Larkin's mature poems. Which final word-choice offers this alleged outsider more dignity or realism for the stance that he takes?

6. Clichés are the enemy of good poetry. Larkin uses "lion's share." How does he get away with this?

A

How

*Final
version*

How high they build hospitals!
Lighted cliffs, against dawns
Of days people will die on.
I can see one from here.

How cold winter keeps   5
And long, ignoring
Our need now for kindness.
Spring has got into the wrong year.

How few people are,
Held apart by acres
Of housing, and children
With their shallow violent eyes.

B   *"How"*

How high they build hospitals!
Lighted cliffs against mornings
When there's always somebody dying
I can see one from here.

How long winters are
And how cold, ignoring
That you can't stand it for ever.
Spring is late, like a train.

How few people are
And how separated
By housing estates of children
With their shallow violent eyes

C

How high they build hospitals!
Lighted cliffs against dawns
Of days people will die on
I see one from here.

How cold winter keeps
And long, ignoring
Our need of kind climates
Giving is held back, somewhere

How few people are
Separated by acres
Of housing, and children
With violent shallow eyes.

1. Larkin, in effect, has three distinct versions of "How," though only
one actually appears in the workbook. Larkin did considerable cor-
recting on the typescript version, and further work was done else-

where for the published version. Note that lines 7 and 8 are quite different from version to version. Can you spot other less obvious differences?

2. Which words or phrases remain untouched within all three drafts?

3. "How" is, of course, a keyword to this poem, and in the earliest draft it is used with greater frequency. Describe the effect of having this extra usage of "how" removed in the later versions.

4. Does reinserting "can" into line 4 of the final poem feel significant?

5. What is the advantage of breaking up line 11, "By housing estates of children" (workbook version)?

6. From our limited perspective, has "valid rawness" of imagery and feeling been sacrificed in the name of poetic refinement anywhere in the revising process of this poem?

A   *Days*

Final   What are days for?
version   Days are where we live.
                 They come, they wake us
                 Time and time over.
                 They are to be happy in: 5
                 Where can we live but days?

                 Ah, solving that question
                 Brings the priest and the doctor
                 In their long coats
                 Running over the fields.   10

C   What are days for?
                 Days are to wake in
Early   To discover our dear loves
draft   Over and Over
                 They are to be happy in
                 There is nowhere to live but in days.

Why do nights come?
Nights are to [stay] hide in
When we have no loves
Or they have gone over
When [we] days have sickened us
Nights are to pretend in.

B

*Draft
two years
later*

What are days for?
Days are where we live.
Are to be happy in
Over and over:
[once we have woken up] When once they wake us
[There is nowhere to live but days] [Let us once wakeup]
[Days are all we have.] [There] is
[We can have nowhere else.]
And so [Why do] nights come
What are days for?
Days are where we live,
And to be happy in
Over and over.
They come, they wake us
[When Once they / wake us]
Where [have we to live]
[We have nowhere to live]
can we live but days?
[And so / the nights come]
What are days for?
Days are where we live
They come, they wake us,
Time and time[Over and] over.
They are to be happy in:
Where can we live but days?
And [seeking] to seek where they join
Brings the priest and doctor
On their long coats running over the fields.

1. The two workbook drafts for "Days" appear as two years apart. Which image, or question, clearly gets dismissed in the later draft?

2. Is stanza 2 of the final poem visible anywhere in the initial draft?

3. Describe the one-line transformation that, for you, most immediately gives the final poem greater simplicity and depth of feeling.

Notes

1. Philip Larkin, *All What Jazz: A Record Diary, 1961-1971* (New York: Farrar, Straus & Giroux, 1985) B.J. Leggett, *Larkin's Blues: Jazz, Popular Music and Poetry* (Baton Rouge: Louisiana State University Press, 1999).
2. "The Movement"—label for a group of English Poets in the 1950s (Amis, Larkin, Wain, Davie, Gunn) who valued wit and traditionalism and were distrustful of poetic grandeur.
3. A.T. Tolley, *Larkin At Work: A study of Larkin's mode of composition as seen in his workbooks* (Hull: The University of Hull Press, 1997).

SYLVIA PLATH

1932–1963

IN THE LIST OF POSSIBLE LABELS, OR TERMS, THAT MIGHT BE USE-
ful for describing the work of Sylvia Plath, the poet, "confession-
al" stands at the top. While not necessarily the most accurate
term any more, it did at one time represent a purposeful catego-
ry. In the mid-1950s, Plath's familiarity with Robert Lowell's work and
with the work of other "psychological-stress poets" of her time (Ann
Sexton, Theodore Roethke, John Berryman)—all who were in some
way legitimately dealing with post-World War II "angst"—would
have quite naturally affected her willingness to take on personal, and
extremely painful, material using imagery of the grotesque sort. This
does not mean, however, that she was not also influenced by the
more conservative, and formalistically concerned, Movement poets
of Britain, also of the mid-1950s, among them Philip Larkin, their
leader and the most famous (Plath's poetry, at times, will also turn a
down-to-earth realistic phrase).

Although Plath was vitally engaged in trying out traditional poetic
forms, the disturbing fact of her suicide might easily, though not
accurately, lend credence to the belief that she was, at least partially, a
rebellious "victim" striking out on her own. Her circumstances, those
reflected (or "deflected") to some degree in the portion of her work
now commonly referred to as "The Ariel Poems," and the risk she
may have taken to portray them, are often blamed for her death. This
has caused many critics[1] to say that a fair assessment of Plath's mas-
tery or control as an artist is not yet possible. Critics also agree that
finding a category that accommodates Sylvia Plath's work is a difficult
task. Some will arguably prove that Plath's poems are not confession-
al at all. Are Plath's poems, themselves, along with their author, in
fact, suicidal? Can this question be fairly asked or answered? Often
deemed, in part, to be murderous, ruthless, or obsessed, the Ariel
Poems have gained a popularity, and notoriety, that is ongoing today,
nearly forty years after her death. The real question is, of course, can
we dispense with all of the notoriety and, instead, actually enjoy and
benefit from reading her work? The answer is not an unequivocal yes.

The poems selected for this chapter are from among those composed by Sylvia Plath in the last year of her life. Susan R. Van Dyne, in her book, *Revising Life: Sylvia Plath's Ariel Poems,*[2] describes Plath's new habit of carefully dating her work as having begun with these poems. She also recounts Plath's method of writing and revising these specific poems—"twenty-five in less than a month" in the fall of 1962—on the backs of previous manuscripts, specifically, a typed version of *The Bell Jar;* a manuscript of Ted Hughes' famous poem, "The Thought-Fox"; a typed manuscript of an unpublished play by Hughes, *The Calm;* and on used and unused Smith College memo paper. In addition, Plath's very last poems were written on the reverse side of manuscripts from the previous fall's successfully published poems. Many of these manuscripts are now in the Sylvia Plath Collection, Smith College Library Rare Book Room. Van Dyne points to Plath's consistent need to revise the scripts of her life and to her skill at interweaving previous texts with current texts.

As presented here, the poems range in composition date from August 1962 to February 1963. This is a period when Plath was often feeling bereft and completely on her own following her separation from Ted Hughes. Plath's journal for this time stretch was destroyed by Hughes for the sake of the children. Many of the poems are highly imagistic, skillful renderings of personal struggle that, despite their intense subjectivity, attempt to embody rather than conceal Plath's personal sense of loss, anger and betrayal. "The white fists of old / Letters and their death rattle," seen in the opening of "Burning the Letters," though deft, cannot hide the sense of antagonism and threat felt by the speaker toward the ex-lover now being viewed retrospectively for the first time. Others among the poems, such as "Lady Lazarus" and "Ariel," offer the hope of dominance, control, or transcendence in the endless male/female power struggle as personally experienced by Plath in her marriage. "Medusa" takes on the mother figure, utilizing an adroit mire of mythological shapings interspersed with very contemporary sounding attacks—"I didn't call you. / I didn't call you at all." "There is nothing between us"—and fails. "Words" and "Edge" both deal on some level with the issue of maternity / authorship.

Revision, as it is seen in the draft juxtapositions used in this chapter to indicate many of Plath's choices or decisions, is often major, yet, equally often, it may be seen as slight. The leaps toward a better direction or more economically satisfying image are not always obvious. The poems represented require a more detailed accounting of the revising process than is possible in this chapter. It is hoped that enough information is included. The reader should be able to reach his or her own conclusions about Plath's involvement in her process. Brackets seen to the right of (or placed about phrases within) the published version of a poem always indicate an earlier version or choice for that specific area of the poem.

A   *Burning the Letters*

Final   I made a fire; being tired
version   Of the white fists of old
            Letters and their death rattle
            When I came too close to the wastebasket.
            What did they know that I didn't?   5
            Grain by grain, they unrolled
            Sands where a dream of clear water
            Grinned like a getaway car.
            I am not subtle
            Love, love, and well, I was tired   10
            Of cardboard cartons the color of cement or a dog pack
            Holding in its hate
            Dully, under a pack of men in red jackets,
            And the eyes and times of the postmarks.

            This fire may lick and fawn, but it is merciless: 15
            A glass case
            My fingers would enter although
            They melt and sag, they are told
            Do not touch.
            And here is an end to the writing,   20
            The spry hooks that bend and cringe, and the smiles, the smiles.
            And at least it will be a good place now, the attic.
            At least I won't be strung just under the surface,
            Dumb fish
            With one tin eye,   25
            Watching for glints,
            Riding my Arctic
            Between this wish and that wish.

            So I poke at the carbon birds in my housedress.
            They are more beautiful than my bodiless owl,   30

They console me—
Rising and flying, but blinded.
They would flutter off, black and glittering, they would be coal
        angels
Only they have nothing to say to anybody.
I have seen to that.   35
With the butt of a rake
I flake up papers that breathe like people,
I fan them out
Between the yellow lettuces and the German cabbage
Involved in its weird blue dreams,   40
Involved as a foetus.
And a name with black edges

Wilts at my foot,
Sinuous orchis
In a nest of root-hairs and boredom—   45
Pale eyes, patent-leather gutturals!
Warm rain greases my hair, extinguishes nothing.
My veins glow like trees.
The dogs are tearing a fox. This is what it is like—
A red burst and a cry   50
That splits from its ripped bag and does not stop
With the dead eye
And the stuffed expression, but goes on
Dyeing the air,
Telling the particles of the clouds, the leaves, the water   55
What immortality is. That it is immortal.

B   *Burning the Letters*

Composite   I made a fire; being tired
of earlier   Of the white fists of old
drafts   Letters and their death rattle
When I came too close to the wastebasket.
What did they know that I didn't?
Grain by grain, they unrolled
Sands where a dream of clear water
Grinned like a getaway car.

I am not subtle
Love, love, and well, I was tired
Of cardboard cartons the color of cement or a dog pack
Holding in its hate
[The hounds I saw had the] [yellow eyes] [of the mad]
[Peeled upon forms of so much lovelessness].
Dully, under a pack of men in red jackets,
[With no chins and womenish whinnies]

This fire may lick and fawn, but it is merciless.
It is a glass case.
It flickers between me and everything I look at.
"Do not touch."
My fingers would reach through to you, but are bent back.
And here is your handwriting, the spyhooks, the lies.
I got tired of looking
And there was nobody for me to know or go to.
So I burned the letters & the dust puffs and the old hair.
At least it will be clean in the attic.
At least I won't hang underneath it, dumb as a fish,
My tin eye waiting for glints and a signal,
Riding the cold, pure Arctic
That was the space between your speaking, your thinking of me.

So I poke at the carbon birds in my housedress
Rising and flying, but blinded and with no message.
Only they have no words to say to anybody.
I have seen to that—
The mouth of this house is shut [up]. With the butt of a rake
I open the white wads that would save themselves.
[Spirit] Word after [Spirit] [gives itself up] word is lit!
They darken like Joan of Arc, the heart is a cinder?
And the name of the girl flies out.
[4 lines   [Now] a man [is alighting] with black edges
  from   Wilts at my foot [it is your writing]
   the   [A notorious] Sinuous Orchis
 ˪ draft]   In its nest of root hairs and boredom.]
As the rain greases my hair, but extinguishes nothing.
My veins glow like trees.

The dogs are tearing a fox, my love. This is what it is like—
The [red flash] burst heart and the cry
That splits from its ripped bag and does not stop
With the dead eye
And the stuffed expression, but goes on
Dyeing the air,
Telling the particles of the clouds, the leaves, the water
What immortality is. That it is immortal.

Drafted on the back of a manuscript originally used for Ted Hughes's poems, one of the drafts done on the reverse side of "The Thought-Fox," a landmark poem in her husband's career, this poem represents Plath's earliest attempt at capturing her feelings of rage and the need for revenge following her legal separation from Hughes.

1. Among descriptions in the earlier drafts that are suppressed in the final draft is that of the "men in red jackets" who have "no chins and womenish whinnies." Describe the effect of removing this emasculating image. Likewise, why is the "dog pack" reduced to "Holding in its hate?"

2. Other pieces of personal or intimate information are withheld or seemingly de-intensified. In stanza 2, "My fingers would reach through to you" becomes "My fingers would enter." "And here is your handwriting" becomes "here is an end to the writing." At the end of this stanza, "between your speaking, your thinking of me" becomes "between this wish and that." What is Plath's chief strategy here? Discuss.

3. In stanza 3 of the final draft, "The name of the girl flies out" is translated as "a name with black edges," while "Joan of Arc" and "my love," are removed altogether. What other examples of "masking" or "suppressing" are apparent in the final draft. Discuss this attempt to portray a greater control over subjectivity. Does it defeat or enhance the conceit of the poem?

4. Again, in stanza 3, does "The dogs are tearing a fox" feel even more like a non-sequitur without the tag, "my love?" Explain.

5. Which draft exacts a greater sense of revenge? Which draft portrays the speaker as more vulnerable? Support your view.

A

*Final
version
juxtaposed
with lines
from
earlier
drafts*

I have done it again.
One year in every ten
I manage it

A sort of walking miracle, my skin
Bright as a Nazi lampshade,   5
My right foot

A paperweight, [Peel off the napkin]
My face a featureless, fine   [Love, enemy.]
Jew linen.   [Do I terrify?]

Peel off the napkin   [Yes Herr Professor]   10
O my enemy.   [I is I]
Do I terrify? —   [Can you deny]

The nose, the eye pits, the full set of teeth?
The sour breath
Will vanish in a day.   15

Soon, soon the flesh
The grave cave ate will be
At home on me

And I a smiling woman.
I am only thirty.   20
And like the cat I have nine times to die.

This is Number Three.
What a trash
To annihilate each decade.

What a million filaments.   25
The peanut-crunching crowd
Shoves in to see

Them unwrap me hand and foot——
The big strip tease.

Gentlemen, ladies   30
These are my hands
My knees.
I may be skin and bone,

Nevertheless, I am the same, identical woman.
The first time it happened I was ten.   35
It was an accident.

The second time I meant
To last it out and not come back at all.
I rocked shut

As a seashell.   40
They had to call and call
And pick the worms off me like sticky pearls.

Dying
Is an art, like everything else.
I do it exceptionally well.   45

I do it so it feels like hell.
I do it so it feels real.
I guess you could say I've a call.   [I guess I'm a natural]

It's easy enough to do it in a cell.
It's easy enough to do it and stay put.   50
It's the theatrical

Comeback in broad day
To the same place, the same face, the same brute
Amused shout:

'A miracle!'
That knocks me out.   55
There is a charge

For the eyeing of my scars, there is a charge [For fingering my scars]
For the hearing of my heart——   [For stethoscoping my heart]

It really goes.   [It really goes!]   60

And there is a charge, a very large charge
For a word or a touch   [For a night in my bed, or a touch]
Or a bit of blood

Or a piece of my hair or my clothes.
So, so, Herr Doktor.   65
So, Herr Enemy.   [So, Herr enemy] [So, love, so enemy]

I am your opus,   [I burn & turn]
I am your valuable,   [You age, & I am new.]
The pure gold baby [I am the baby / on / your anvil, / I eat fire.]

That melts to a shriek.   70
I turn and burn.   [I burn & turn and have no need of you.]
Do not think I underestimate [You say I am dangerous]
        your great concern.

Ash, ash—   [Out of that ash]
You poke and stir.   [You poked]   75
Flesh, bone, there is nothing there— [Till it lay in a hush]
                                   [Without cough or stir]

A cake of soap,   [I rise with my red hair]
A wedding ring,
A gold filling.

Herr God, Herr Lucifer   80
Beware
Beware.

Out of the ash
I rise with my red hair   [I rise,] [I eat the air]
And I eat men like air.   [Each time I rise, I rise a virgin]   85

The juxtapositions for this poem are based on a six-page draft done over a period of six days, culminating in the final version. The necessity for replacing or altering some of the lines becomes more apparent if we consider that Plath is attempting to discard or conceal any explicit suggestion that there are two actual lovers, as antagonistic as they may be.

All of the changes shown are significant in terms of having achieved this. More significantly, three of the six pages of revision are devoted to reshaping the ending, making it consistent with the steadily increasing sense of mastery or self-determination that we are hearing in the narrator's voice.

1. Word choices that indicate literal, or physical, intimacy between the antagonists are carefully revised to bring out larger themes or forces at work—e.g., the Holocaust, feminist empowerment, artistic performance. Does this strategy help or hinder the now understated dynamic of two actual, albeit antagonistic, lovers?

2. What effect does the omission of the word "love" in the final version have on the poem—on *your* experience with the poem?

3. In relation to the speaker's projected audience (beginning in stanza nine), why is "I guess you could say I've a call" so crucial as a revision? Who, or what, is the audience from this point on in the poem?

4. In stanza 20, "fingering" and "stethoscoping" are replaced by "eyeing" and "hearing." Is this an effective change?

5. The result of many of the changes is that we see a more fiercely determined and in-control narrator. Discuss "And I a smiling woman" (stanza 7) in light of this statement.

6. Discuss the transformation from "I eat fire" to "I eat the air" to "I eat men like air."

A   *Medusa [Working Title: "Mum: Medusa"]*

Final   Off that landspit of stony mouth-plugs,
version   Eyes rolled by white sticks,
juxtaposed Ears cupping the sea's incoherences,
with lines You house your unnerving head—God-ball,
from   Lens of mercies,   5
earlier
drafts   Your stooges
            Plying their wild cells in my keel's shadow,
            Pushing by like hearts,

Red stigmata at the very center,
Riding the rip tide to the nearest point of departure,   10

Dragging their Jesus hair.
Did I escape, I wonder?
My mind winds to you
Old barnacled umbilicus, Atlantic cable,
Keeping itself, it seems, in a state of miraculous repair.   15

In any case, you are always there,
Tremulous breath at the end of my line,
Curve of water upleaping   [Curve of bright water unleaping]
To my water rod, dazzling and grateful, [To my water-finder rod]
Touching and sucking.   [O silver tentacle!]   20

I didn't call you.
I didn't call you at all.
Nevertheless, nevertheless
You steamed to me over the sea,
Fat and red, a placenta   25

Paralysing the kicking lovers.
Cobra light
Squeezing the breath from the blood bells
Of the fuchsia. I could draw no breath,
Dead and moneyless, Dead and moneyless   30
                    [I watched that loony white Martyr's smile]
Overexposed, like an X-ray.   [That Martyr's smile]
Who do you think you are?   [That loony pivot!]
A Communion wafer? Blubbery Mary? [That stellar jelly-head]
I shall take no bite of your body, [A million little suckers loving me]
Bottle in which I live,   [Wh(at)o do you think you are?]   35

Ghastly Vatican. [There is simply nothing I want to be in touch with]
I am sick to death of hot salt.   [No mercy, no mercy]
Green as eunuchs, your wishes [I am sick of hot salt]
Hiss at my sins.   [I am sick to death of the kisses]
Off, off, eely tentacle!   40

There is nothing between us. [Wh(at)o do you think you are?]
                              [A Communion wafer? Blubbery Mary?]
                              [I am no pieta.]
                              [I refuse to be.]
                              [Pulse by, pulse by!]
                              [I shall take no bite of your body]

"Medusa" is considered the companion poem to Plath's "Daddy," composed four days earlier. Its title figure, suggested by both the jelly-fish and the Gorgon, threatens the author who, at the same time, feels guilt and fear over losing the love of the real-life mother.

1. In stanzas 7 through 10, what is the effect—despite leaving "Blubbery Mary" in—of removing "That loony white Martyr's smile," or the "smile" altogether?

2. Do translations from the earlier lines in some way present a more Gothic aesthetic? Compare. Discuss.

3. Compare "There is simply nothing I want to be in touch with" to the final line in the final draft. Is the final line equivocal, even paradoxical, or is it a literal rendering of distance between mother and daughter?

A   *Ariel*

Final   Stasis in darkness.
version   Then the substanceless blue
compared   Pour of tor and distances.
with first
and third   God's lioness,   [God's lioness also, how one we grow]
drafts   How one we grow,   [Crude mover whom I move & burn to love]   5
               Pivot of heels and knees! — The furrow

               Splits and passes, sister to
               The brown arc
               Of the neck I cannot catch,

Nigger-eye   10
Berries cast dark
Hooks——

Black sweet blood mouthfuls,
Shadows.
Something else   [Something else]   15

Hauls me through air,   [[I foam], O [I] flakes from my heels, [I]]
Thighs, hair; Foam [in]to white wheat, a glitter of seas.
Flakes from my heels.

White   [Hands, hearts, dead men]
Godiva, I unpeel—   [Dead men]   20
Dead hands, dead stringencies. [Hands, hearts, peel off]
                         [In a season of burning, I]
And now I   [am Godiva]
Foam to wheat, a glitter of seas. [On fire, my hair, my one resort]
The child's cry

Melts in the wall.   [Melts in the wall]   25
And I   [O bright beast, I]
Am the arrow,   [am the arrow, the dew that flies]

The dew that flies   [Suicidal, at one with the drive]
Suicidal, at one with the drive   [Into the red]
Into the red   [Eye, the cauldron of morning]   30

Eye, the cauldron of morning.

                         [[I rise, I rise now]]
                         [[I am] [the arrow] [I am] the [rain] dew that flies]
                         [Into the sun's]
                         [In the cauldron of morning]
                         [One white melt, upflung]
                         [To the lover, the plunging]
                         [Hooves I am, that over and over.]

"Ariel" is one of Plath's Birthday Poems. The Lady Godiva legend is retold as a striptease. As with "Stings" and "Lady Lazarus," the protagonist once again clearly achieves the sense of self-mastery.

In it, speaker and horse (Ariel) become one. Plath strives toward short lines that form complete sentences.

1. In the transition from first draft to final draft, what purpose is served by replacing "Crude mover whom I move & burn to love" with "Pivot of heels and knees!...?

2. In the published version of "Ariel," the author delays using "Foam to wheat, a glitter of seas" until after the speaker's striptease. She also rejects the image of Godiva "on fire," [her] hair, [her] one resort." "Peel off" becomes "I unpeel," followed by "Dead hands, dead stringencies. / And now I / Foam to wheat..." Interpret this process.

3. Does this poem become more streamlined, or gain velocity in any way, as a result of the choices Plath is making? Explain.

A	*Edge [Nuns in Snow]*	

Final		[Here they come]
version		[The Edge]
juxtaposed		[[Down there the] [dead] [terrible]
with the		[woman is perfected]
first draft	The woman is perfected	
	Her dead	[Her dead]

Body wears the smile of accomplishment,
The illusion of a Greek necessity

Flows in the scrolls of her toga,   5
Her bare

Feet seem to be saying:
We have come so far, it is over.
                                        [Now nothing can happen]
Each dead child coiled, a white serpent,[We stiffen in
One at each little   the air like beacons]   10
                                        [At the road's end]
Pitcher of milk, now empty.   [She is taking them with her]
She has folded   [One at each little]

Them back into her body as petals
Of a rose close when the garden

Stiffens and odors bleed   15
From the sweet, deep throats of the night flower.

The moon has nothing to be sad about,
Staring from her hood of bone.

She is used to this sort of thing.
Her blacks crackle and drag.   20

1. Despite an implied bond between mother and child in "Edge," the
feeling of objectified intimacy, death, and cold space is pervasive. Still,
there is a heightened sense of ambivalence about this seeming fact.
What is created goes back into the creator (author) and is sealed there.
Does deleting what would have been the second line of stanza 5, "She
is taking them with her," add to this effect? Discuss.

2. Do the other deletions from this area of the poem feel justified? Can
you say why?

A   *Words*

Final   Axes
version   After whose stroke the wood rings,
juxtaposed   And the echoes!
with   Echoes traveling
first-draft   Off from the center like horses.
choices   [Peasants and beggars]
                 The sap   [Encounter them on the road]
                 Wells like tears, like the   [Dry and proud,
                 Water striving   in a lather of sweat]
                 To re-establish its mirror
                 Over the rock

                 That drops and turns,
                 A white skull,
                 Eaten by weedy greens.
                 Years later I

Encounter them on the road——

Words dry and riderless,	[Words dry, proud
The indefatigable hoof-taps.	[and riderless]
While	
From the bottom of the pool, fixed stars	[From the
Govern a life.	[bottom of the pool,]
	[fixed stars]
	[constellations]
	[Of pebbles govern]

1. Paradoxically, "words" do not literally figure in this poem until the final stanza, where they are viewed as "dry and riderless." Only at this point does the "I" begin to question their evolution. The distance between what they represented when first sounded, "rings" and "echoes," and what they are now, those "indefatigable hoof-taps," feels vast and problematic. Discuss the significance of delaying their re-discovery. Why has Plath discarded the three lines intended for the second stanza: "Beggars and peasants / Encounter them on the road / Dry and proud, in a lather of sweat"? Discuss.

Notes

1. Linda Wagner-Martin, *Sylvia Plath: A Literary Life* (New York: St. Martin's, 1999); Paul Alexander, *Rough Magic: A Biography of Sylvia Plath* (New York: Da Capo Press, 1999); Anne Stevenson, Lucas Myers and Dido Merwin, *Bitter Fame: A Life of Sylvia Plath* (Boston: Houghton Mifflin Company, 1998); Janet Malcom, *The Silent Woman: Sylvia Plath and Ted Hughes* (New York: Vintage Books, 1995).
2. Susan R. Van Dyne, *Revising Life: Sylvia Plath's Ariel Poems* (Chaple Hill & London: The University of North Carolina Press, 1993).

STEPHEN WATSON

1954–

THIS CHAPTER IS UNIQUE IN THAT THE MATERIAL, ALL from *Return of the Moon: Versions from the /Xam* by Stephen Watson, was constructed from oral transcriptions of a now extinct tribe that lived in the Cape Colony, South Africa. Watson recently translated the original words, which were taken down by European linguists during the nineteenth century. Therefore, even though the printed (or final) poems are not revisions of any existing poetry, Watson's translations into poetry are themselves the product of numerous revisions. The finished poem appears first, followed by the "original transcript," followed by earlier drafts, or "tryouts," chosen to represent the most interesting changes. In other words, we see the evolution of a finished contemporary poem shaped out of the raw material of very distant lives.

Stephen Watson teaches English at the University of Cape Town. His poetry collections include *Poems 1977-1982* (1983), *In This City* (1986), *Return of the Moon* (1991), *Presence of the Earth: New Poems* (1995), and *The Other City: Selected Poems* (2000). He has also published two collections of prose, *Selected Essays, 1980-1990* (1990) and *A Writer's Diary* (1997).

Watson discovered more than 12,000 pages of transcripts made by W.H. Bleek and Lucy Lloyd who had learned the /Xam language (now extinct). Over a five-year period in the 1870s, they copied down the stories and songs of some of the last remaining members of the /Xam group, one of the several Bushman clans, all of them the oldest continuing cultures in the country. Watson has reinvented the spoken record taken down more than a century ago, and possibly has removed much of the attitude and disposition of the original transcribers and speakers—the new words must speak for themselves. Nonetheless, the poems offer complex rendering: we are shown the preservation of remnants of the Bushmen's speech and culture along with the social and aesthetic consciousness of a contemporary South African.

Watson calls the Bleek and Lloyd transcriptions "one of the world's most remarkable ethnographic records." These transcribers were in the process of learning the very difficult click language of the /Xam and actually prevented the unjust imprisonment of the last three /Xam tribesmen by pressing them into service. They were just in time to save whatever knowledge now remains of a rich—and rich in poetry—culture. In his introduction to *Return of the Moon*, Watson provides information about these three last remaining /Xam Bushmen and about Bleek and Lloyd's arduous process of creating the original transcription of the oral record. The challenge for Watson was somehow to transmit a faraway sensibility, knowing at the outset that the words had already been transformed by the original transcribers, and also to create poems that might interest contemporary readers.

Watson comments on his process as follows:

> Throughout these translations the chief goal (and indeed justification for my practice) has been dictated by the central problem posed by the material itself: the fact that it is dead, doubly dead. Apart from the isolated attention of anthropologists and other academic specialists, the astonishing riches contained in the Bleek and Lloyd collection might as well not exist. Accordingly, I have worked to bring the words of the narrators to life once more, and in such a way that they might continue to speak to us who are alive in the last decade of the twentieth century. Although a few of the translations as they appear here are so close as to be almost literal renderings, my goal has inevitably meant that a good number of the poems are "imitations" rather than exact word-for-word versions. The /Xam believed that the dead spoke to the living. Without in any way believing that I, as translator, could speak with the tongues of the dead in turn, I have tried to hear the voice of Bleek and Lloyd's three main informants—//Kabbo, /Han=kasso, and Dia!kwain—and create poems which work in the English language. As such, these translations are really extensions of several voices, languages and sensibilities....

Prefacing his helpful "notes to the poems" which offer the religious and cultural contexts of many of the translations, Watson states: "The phonetic symbols //, !, /, and =, represent the various clicks in the /Xam language. I have retained them for the visually estranging effect they create, as a reminder of the 'foreignness' of the world of the

/KABBO / THE BOW-STRING / /KABBO THE BOW-STRING OF THE RAIN

RAINMAKING WITH A BOW STRING.

/Kammu he used to strike the bow-string

& the clouds came out while we [others] slept.

And the people awoke in the cloud [surrounded by cloud,]

that had shut in the place [while the people were sleeping.]

And the people awoke when the clouds/had shut out the sun

And the rain made a ... [bow]

it rained there, rained while the sun set.

Day broke while it rained there,

& the sun again, the sunset

& the rain in the ..... the rain broke.

And it altogether broke

while it did not again rain.

We were sleeping.

He sat taking up the bow, while we were sleeping.

And we, we heard the bow-string [in dream?]

as he was striking it there.   We can still hear ...?

[a sommer]/Kammu struck the bow at my & the clouds came out. [in the dark, before daybreak ...

He, who'd been sleeping   awoke in the cloud,

cloud had surrounded the place where we slept.

We awoke to find cloud had shut out the sun. [the sun dimmed by cloud]

And the rain began, raining while the sun set. [It was still

It [would be] was still raining when the next day broke. [The next day broke in rain ...

It would rain right through to the sunset [for days & two sunset).

before it would cease ...

While we were sleeping, /Kammu would [at time] take up his bow,

[making] [rhythm]/ taking up his dream, plucking his bow string [in a rhythm]

producing the rhythm which murmured the clouds/rain

And we, hearing it in our sleep, being the string and [the tone] (of the string,)

we would sleep or wake in the cloud.

playing the bow resting till we wake in the cloud.

in a day beginning with rain ___.

Focus on the bow-string among the rain.

/Xam. If they were actually pronounced, they would in most cases disturb the metre of the poems.

Of the six poems selected from *Return of the Moon*, "The Rain-Sorcerer," "Rainmaking with a Bow-String," and "Sorcerers Are Like Lions," were narrated by /Han≠Kasso; "Presentiments" was narrated by Dia!kwain; "The Abandoned Old Woman" and "The Lost Tobacco Pouch: a Song" were narrated by //Kabbo.

A   *Rainmaking with a Bow-String*

> While we were sleeping, /Kaunu would sit.
> He struck his bow-string, cloud coming out.
> He plucked out a rhythm that summoned the cloud,
> and we woke in the cloud, the sun shut out.
>
> We would hear a far twanging, coming from cloud.
> We would wake to find we were sleeping in cloud.
> And a rain would begin, lasting into the sunset;
> the rain would pour down through two sunsets.
>
> While we were sleeping, /Kaunu sat there, awake.
> He made the rain fall by striking his bow-string.
> And we woke in the clouds, a sound in the clouds,
> cloud pouring out of the sound of a bow-string.

Original Transcript   Kaunu, A Rainmaker. / Kaunu he used to strike the bowstring, and the clouds came out, while we others slept; and the people awoke while the clouds had shut in the place while the people were sleeping. And the people awoke when the clouds had shut out the sun.

And the rain made a cloak (of rain), it rained there, poured down while the sun set. Day broke while it rained there, and the sun again the sun set and the rain in the... the rain broke. And it altogether broke while it did not again rain. We were sleeping; he sat taking up his bow, while we were sleeping. And we... we heard the bow-string as he was striking it there.

/Kaun/The Bow-String
Kauna and the Bow-String & The Rain/
Rain-Making with a Bow-String

/Kaunu he used to strike the bow-string
and the clouds came out while we [others] slept.
And the people awoke in the cloud [surrounded by cloud]
that had shut in the place [while the people were sleeping.]
And the people awoke when the clouds/had shut out the sun
And the rain made a ... [bow?]
it rained there, rained while the sun set.
Day broke while it rained there,
and the sun again, the sunset
and the rain in the ..... the rain broke.
And it altogether broke
while it did not again rain.

We were sleeping.
He sat taking up the bow, while we were sleeping.
And we, [...] we heard the bow-string [in dream?]
as he was striking it there. [We can still hear ... ?]

We would hear the bow-string while we were sleeping.
/Kaunu [a sorcerer] struck the bow-string and the clouds came
          out [in the dark, before daybreak ...]
We, who'd been sleeping, awoke in the cloud,
cloud had surrounded the place where we slept.
We awoke to find cloud had shut out the sun. [the sun obscured
          by cloud]
And the rain began, raining while the sun set. [It was still ...]
It was [would be] still raining when the next day broke.
[The next day broke in rain ...]
It would rain right through to the [next day's] sunset
[for two days and two sunsets] before it would cease ...
While we were sleeping, /Kaunu would take up his bow,
[sit there]taking up his bow,
plucking his bow-string [in a rhythm]
[making][playing] [rhythm]
producing the song which summoned the clouds/rain.

And we, hearing it in our sleep, hearing the thin sound/
of the twang of the string,
we would sleep on and wake in the cloud,
playing the bow-string till we woke in the cloud,
in a day beginning with rain—

B

*Penulti-
mate draft*

We awoke to find cloud had shut out the sun.
We would awake to find we were sleeping in cloud,
that a mist surrounded the place where we slept.
/Kaunu struck his bow-string, and cloud came out.
A rain would [then] begin, lasting into the sunset.
Because /Kaunu plucked his bow, and cloud came out.
A rain would not stop till the next day's sunset.
Because /Kuanu plucked a song while we had slept.
While we were sleeping, /Kaunu would sit there,
plucking the rhythm that summoned the rain,
striking his bow-string till we woke in cloud,
our place in the cloud, [and] day beginning with rain.

Author's Note: the sound of the bow-string, coming through cloud /
the sound of the string, making the cloud/ coming out of the cloud

*Poetry used in the service of religion and ritual is the language of power. Tribal peoples
from India to Africa to the Americas believed that the poet possessed magic words that
could bring good fortune to the hunt, cure the ill, or save the crops from drought by call-
ing for rain. A number of the /Xam poems point to this transformative power of ritual
poetry. The vast collections of chants and spells, generally very rhythmical, repetitious,
and formal, are as much the reservoirs of people's aspirations and fears as is the literary
poetry studied in traditional English classes "Rainmaking With A Bow-String" is about
one of those magical language musicians.*

1. Certain words and phrases recur throughout this poem of meta-
morphosis in which the bowstring, when touched by /Kaunu, releases
rain from the clouds. Discuss the use of repetition in the original
transcript, the early draft, and the final version. How does the place-
ment of key words, which are repeated, influence the final form and
impact of this poem?

2. What is the value or the effectiveness of translating the prose tran-
script into set quatrains? Looking at the rather formless earlier drafts,

what can you say about the poet's motivation toward the final
form?

3. Note how in the first stanza the lines are rearranged, with /Kaunu
moving from line 4 in the early draft to line 1 in the final version. Why
would the poet make such a change? Are there other similar position-
al changes worth discussing?

4. The diction of "cloud coming out" in line 2 is odd. Are there other
such odd locutions that contribute to the voice or special quality of
the poem?

5. The "early draft" is considerably longer than the "penultimate
draft." Discuss what has been dropped.

A   *The Lost Tobacco Pouch: A Song*

Because I,//Kabbo, have lost my tobacco pouch,
because a dog has run off with it in the night,
and awoke in the dark, wandering round in the dark,
I can find it nowhere, yes nowhere, I sing:
Famine it is,
tobacco-hunger it is,
famine is here!

Because there was nothing to do but lie down,
because I could do nothing, not even sleep,
and getting up early, even wandering around early,
I could still find it nowhere, I sing, and must sing:

Famine it is,
tobacco-hunger it is,
famine is here!

//Kabbo's song on the loss of his tobacco pouch (It was stolen by a hungry dog, named "blom", which belonged to !gou!nui.) [Dictated by /han=kasso—January 1878]

> Famine[1] it is,
> Famine it is,
> Famine is here.
> Famine it is,
> Famine it is,
> Famine is here.

C

Composite
based
on early
drafts

[have no more tobacco]
Because [I] he, Kabbo, could no longer smoke,
[stolen] [the pouch] [night]
because a dog named "Blou"[2] had come in the dark.

The Lost Tobacco Pouch: A Song

[I][he] [now, no longer]
Because, Kabbo, could not smoke,
because a dog in the night/dark [had come in the night ..]
     [I] [got up]
and he arose in the night, missing his pouch/
aware it was lost,
[I] [wandered around/about in the dark]
Kabbo rose in the night [dark], and sang out:

> [O,] Famine it is.
> Tobacco-hunger it is,
> famine is here.

[I] [could do nothing better]
Because he had to lie down again,
[I] [do nothing, not even]
because he could not (now) smoke,
[seeking for the pouch]
because we went out early, looking everywhere
because it was [nowhere] not to be found, [I] he [Kabbo] sang:

[O,] Famine it is.
Tobacco-hunger it is;
O famine is here.

B

Pen-
ultimate
draft

[he] [have no more tobacco]
Because I Kabbo, could no longer smoke
[had]
Because a dog has stolen pouch in the night,
[I] [in the night] [aware it was gone]
Because Because I Kabbo, could no longer smoke
Kabbo got up having (?) it gone
[I went]
Kabbo wandered about in the dark, and he sang:

Famine it is,
tobacco-hunger it is,
famine is here!

Because he could do nothing but lie down again,
because he could do nothing else, not even smoke,
because he went out early, seeking the lost pouch,
and finding it nowhere, he was forced to sing out:

Famine it is,
tobacco-hunger it is,
famine is here!

Author's note: Many commentators have drawn attention to the /Xam fondness for tobacco. Dorothea Bleek and A.M. Cronin-Duggin, for instance, write: "Barter with Hottentot and Bantu tribes has long been carried on by the Bushmen. Besides utensils and iron for knives and arrowheads, tobacco has been the object of greatest demand. In exchange Bushmen give game and skins, but they adore smoking and as they grow no tobacco, must obtain that from others. Everyone smokes, even the children."[3] /Xam songs, as Hewett has said, "tend to be brief, unelaborated statements, repeated several times."[4]

1. The penultimate draft of this cry of despair over the lost tobacco shows the poet's indecision over who should be singing this song. The

final version settles on a first person—I, Kabbo. Note the absence of first person in the original transcript. Discuss how the choice of pronoun is important both for the poet and the reader.

2. The phrase "tobacco-hunger" as an equivalent for the word "famine" is used by Watson as part of the refrain or the song's chorus. It is not so used in the original transcript except in parentheses. What can you say about this word?

A   *Sorcerers Are Like Lions*

If a person, good looking, suddenly falls ill,
and seeming to improve, suddenly grows sicker,
sorcerers have seized him: he dies seized.

Sorcerers are like lions, their eyes like lions.

And when the dogs at night, restless, keep barking,
sorcerers are coming to work their bewitchment:
it means they're coming close to shoot a sick man.

Sorcerers are like lions, their eyes like lions.

Though the thing is unseen which strikes the sick man,
though invisible arrows are the ones they fire,
these arrows are fatal: they can lay a man dead.

Sorcerers are like lions, their eyes like lions.

Although others try healing, removing harm's things,
a sorcerer still shoots him under their noses.
And thus his heart fails: his heart falls down.

Sorcerers are like lions, their eyes like lions.

Original transcript Sorcerers Are Like Lions. Their eyes are alike. When a person is good looking than that person falls ill, and dies. They seize him, therefore the person dies because they are seizing him. Then the people say, that man is ill again; he seems to get better and then he gets ill again. Then the man dies, because they keep coming up to bewitch him. Therefore the dogs do not sleep but keep on barking at the sorcerers who are coming to shoot the person who is ill. Then, though the thing is new which strikes the man, he dies of it. The arrow is new with which they shoot him. They shoot killing; they lay the person dead. That happens when people are snoring[5] the man although they are asking things out of him, he is very ill. He does not look as if they had taken anything out of him, for the sorcerers shoot at him under people's noses.[6] Then his heart falls although they are snoring him his heart falls down.

D   Sorcerers are like lions. [Their eyes are like lions.]
    Their eyes are alike.

First   [handsome]
draft   //When a person is good-looking then that person falls ill [and
dies]. [the Sorcerers] They seize him and the person dies [because
they are seizing him.]
Then the people say, that man is ill again;
he seems to get better and then he gets ill again.

//Then the man dies, because they keep coming up to bewitch him.
Therefore the dogs do not sleep but keep on barking
at the sorcerers who are coming to shoot the person who is ill.
        [come in the dark.]

//Then, though the thing is new which strikes the man,
        he dies of it.
The arrow is new with which they shoot him.
        [to kill?]
They shoot killing; they lay the person dead.

//This happens when people are snoring[7] the man.
Although they are taking things out of him, he remains [very] ill.
He does not look as if they had taken anything out of him,
for the sorcerers shoot at him under the people's noses.
//Even though they are snoring him, his heart falls,
his heart falls down, [he is dead]

Refrain: "Sorcerers are like lions, their eyes are like lions."

C   Sorcerers are like lions, their eyes [are] like lions.

Second
draft
1. When a person is handsome, [and] he [suddenly] falls ill and dies,
Sorcerers [like lions] have seized him, and seized he dies.
And people say, he who seemed to get better
       is ill again.
Repeat [He seems to get better, then gets ill again.]
       [keep coming up to bewitch him]

2. [The man dies because the sorcerers have bewitched him.]
And so the dogs do not sleep but keep barking
[at the sorcerers like lions, at their lion's eyes.]
who come in the dark to shoot the sick man.

3. The arrow might be new with which they shoot him.
But sorcerers are like lions, their eyes like lions.
Their arrows kill; they lay a person dead.

4. And the sorcerers shoot him under other people's noses.
Even though they are snoring (him), sorcerer's are like lions,
[their eyes like lions]
his heart falls, his ...
       [others]
Even though people snore him, the arrows still hit,
and the person's heart falls, his heart falls down
because sorcerers are like lions, their eyes like lions.

B   Sorcerers are like lions, their eyes are like lions'.

Penulti-
mate draft
When a person is handsome and suddenly falls ill,
and he who seemed to get better falls ill and dies,
Sorcerers are like lions have seized him—he dies.

And so the dogs do not sleep but keep barking
at the sorcerers like lions, at their lions' eyes,
who come in the dark to shoot the sick man.

The arrow might be new with which they shoot him.
But sorcerers are like lions, their eyes like lions',
Their arrow kills; they lay a person dead.

Even though people snore him, the arrows still hit,
and the person's heart fails, his heart falls down
because sorcerers are like lions, eyed like lions.

1. This poem recalls the spells or incantations used by shamans to per-
form some transforming act, here from illness to death. But in this
poem the sorcerer is more active than simply casting a spell. Or,
might all the action—the shooting—be considered as metaphor for a
spell?

2. The sorcerers are portrayed as an inexorable force, machine-like and
beyond human restraint. They are powerful and invisible, yet are they
felt by the reader as evil or simply as part of the life process, no more
guilty than lions?

3. There are interesting elements, words, and ideas in the original
transcript that Watson does not use. Make your own version of this
poem employing some of the missing pieces.

4. There is more repetition and balance in the final version of this
poem than in any of the drafts. Discuss how this finished, fluid poem
makes its subject matter come alive more than the prose transcript,
which includes more actual information.

A   *Presentiments*

A presentiment
is that thing which we fear
when something is happening,
near or far, at some other place.

A presentiment is like
a dream which we dream.

Sometime
when we are alone,
our body starts up, shaken—
it seems as if, to the body,
something was there
which the body feared.

And we pass it,
we who are /Xam,
because our body is telling us:
there is danger at that place.

A presentiment is that thing which we feel when something is
happening at another place. A presentiment is like a dream
which we dream. Sometimes when we are alone, our body
starts—some place, it seems as if (our body), something were
there which our body feared. We pass it because our body is
telling us there is danger at that place.

B

First draft

A presentiment
is that thing which we feel
when something is happening,
[far or near]
way off, at some other place.

A presentiment is like
a dream which we dream.

Sometime
when we are alone,
our body starts up, shaken [our nerves alerted]—
it seems as if, to the body,
something was there
which the body feared.

And we pass it,
because our body is telling us:
there is danger at that place.

1. Here the author notes that the poem was "simply adapted" from
the original transcript. What is it about this prose transcript that
invites a poet merely to break up the lines to create a poem?

2. There are fewer changes here between the draft and the final poem
than in most of Watson's revisions. Of the few changes, which do you
think are most beneficial to the final version?

3. Why did the writer add/include the line in the last stanza "we who are /Xam," when it does not in fact appear in the original transcript?

4. There is a slight rhythmical awkwardness in certain parts of this poem. For instance, in the lines "it seems as if, to the body,/ something was there/ which the body feared." the phrase "to the body" is a case in point. Why do you think the writer intruded such phrases when the rest of the poem is rhythmically even and relatively smooth?

A   *The Rain That is Male*

The rain that is male is an angry rain.
It brings with it lightning loud like our fear.
It brings water storming, making smoke out of dust.

And we, we beat our navels with our rigid fists.
We, we press a hand, flat to the navel.
We snap our fingers at the angry, male rain.

And we stand outside in the force of the water,
we stand out in the open, close to its thunder,
we snap our fingers and chant while it falls:

"Rain, be gone quickly! Fall but be gone!
Rain, turn away! Turn back from this place!
Rain, take your anger, be gone from our place!"

For we want the other, the rain that is female,
the one that falls softly, soaking into the ground,
the one we can welcome, feeding the plains—
So bushes sprout green, springbok come galloping.[8]

Original
transcript   And they strike their (?) navels with their fists, and they press
their fingers at the rain,... And they speak to the rain, and they
speak, they say, "thou shall falling turn back, that thou mayest
falling pass along to yonder place. For thou doest (art) not a lit-
tle lighten (lightening); for it seems if thou art very angry."

D   When the rain is angry, (along with thunder and lightning)
the Bushman stand opposite to it (?)

First draft   (Note in right-hand margin: The rain that is male is an angry rain,
beats down on the earth,
raising the dust, accompanied by
thunder-heads, ("waters of the
thunder-heads")

And they strike their navels with their fists
and they press their hand on their navels
and they snap their fingers at the rain.

And they speak to the rain, they say:
"You shall falling turn back,
that may(est) falling pass along to yonder place.
For thou dost (art) not a little lightning);
for it seems as if thou art angry,
Male rain—not female rain" etc.

C   1. The rain that is male is an angry rain.
It comes down thundering [storming], making dust smoke

Second   [it makes the dust smoke/smoke out of dust?]
draft   It brings with it lightning, [loud like our fear.]
       [thunder, our fear]

      [tightened]
2. And we, we beat our navels with our clenched [rigid] fists.
We, we pass a hand, hard to our navels.
We snap our fingers at the angry, male rain.

      [full flood]
3. And, we stand outside in the force of the water.
We, we plead with the rain, we call to it:
We snap our fingers, calling to the male rain:
"Rain, male rain, you will falling turn back."

      [repent]
4. Rain, male rain, turn back, fall far off [over there].
       vent yourself [deleted], in falling
       spill your anger, falling turn back!

5. [End] We long for the rain that is female,
soaking, falling gently, that brings life,
        feeding it deeply

        feeding water to the grasses
                that feed.

Additional Note:
"You bring the lightning, cleaving the sky.
You bring lightning's anger, scorching the earth.
Now we want the other, the rain that is female
        [the welcome of well-watered plains!]
Falling softly, soaking softly, feeding water to the plains"!!

B

Pen-
◄ltimate
draft

The rain that is male is an angry rain.
It brings with it lightning loud like our fear.
It brings water storming, making smoke out of dust.

And we, we beat our navels with our rigid fists.
We, we press a hand, flat to the navel.
We snap our fingers at the angry, male rain.

And we stand outside in the [wild flood] force of the water,
        [storm water]
we stand out in the open, close to its thunder,
we snap our fingers and chant while it falls:

"Rain, be gone quickly! Fall but be gone!
Rain, turn away! Turn back from this place!
[Fall but be gone; fall but turn back from this place]
Rain, turn back [go away] fall elsewhere, fall far off!"

The rain that is male is an angry rain.
It brings with it lightning, cleaving the sky.
It brings with it thunder, shaking our hearts.

"For [now] we want the other, the rain that is female,
the one that falls softly, feeding the plains
        [soaking into the ground]
        [feeding deep the ground]

the one we can welcome, from which we /Xam drink
So bushes sprout green, springbok come galloping."

1. Here the final poem contains much that is either not in the original transcript or only hinted at there. Discuss the features of the finished poem that seem to develop independent of the transcript.

2. Note that in the original transcript there is no gender designation for the different forces of rain. It is understood that in /Xam mythology the hard but useless rain (for it wouldn't be absorbed in the needy earth) was called male and the replenishing rain was called female. Can you recall other examples in poetry you have read where the natural elements are identified by gender?

3. The voice of this chant-like poem is the voice of the tribe; it is a ritualized presentation of a people's anxiety regarding natural disasters and their desire for fertility to "come galloping." Inside this poem is a more direct and simple chant used for its ritual power. Discuss this stanza (the 4th) in terms of the entire poem.

4. Discuss the draft workings and how the various word choices were narrowed down to the final version.

A   *The Abandoned Old Woman*

Our mother, old, unable to walk,
lay there, incapable,
alone in her old grass and reed hut.

Before we, her sons,
were obliged to leave her behind,
we blocked up her hut's sides,
closing the openings used as a door,
making use of the struts
from the other huts we were leaving,
but leaving the roof open, exposed to the sky,
so she could still feel
some warmth from the sun.

We had made a small fire.
We had gathered for her
as much dry wood as we could.

It was none of our fault;
we were all of us starving.
No-one could help it,
that we had to leave her behind.
We were all of us starving,
and she, an old woman,
she was too weak to go with us,
to seek food at some other place.

The old Woman, [who was] unable to walk lay in an old deserted
hut. Before her sons left her, they had closed the circle [sides] of
the hut, as well as the door opening, with sticks from the others
huts, leaving the top of the hut open, so that she should feel the
sun's warmth. They had left a fire for her and had fetched more
dry wood. [They were obliged to leave her behind, as they were
all starving and she was too weak to go with them to seek food at
some other place.]

Old Woman Left in Her Hut [*working title*]

An old woman, incapable, unable to walk,
[sickening fast]
lay there abandoned, alone,
[rundown, ramshackle, grass and clay/stick]
in her old, tumbledown hut.

[all of]
Before her sons
        [behind]
were forced to leave her,
they blocked up the sides of the hut
        [was used as a]
closing the opening that was its door,
        [using]
taking sticks leftover from the other huts,

                    [a hole in]
(but) leaving its roof,
open to sky,
so she could still feel
some warmth from the sun.

                    [left, laid]
They had made a small fire;
          [especially]
for her they had gathered
[together] [as much] [large] [as possible]
a pile of dry wood.

[But they could not help it]
          [were obliged/forced]
For they simply had
to leave her: they were
all of them starving;
and she, an old woman, she
          [just]   [now]
was too weak to go with them,
to seek food at yet another place.

B

Penulti-
mate draft

An old woman, incapable
unable to walk,
lay there, abandoned,
alone in her old grass and sticks hut [Bushwoman's].

Before [all of] her sons,
were forced to leave her behind,
they blocked up the hut sides,
closing and opening that [was] used as a door,
taking sticks leftover from the other huts, [soon to be left]
but leaving its roof holed, exposed to the sky,
so she could still feel
some warmth from the sun.

They had made a small fire.
They had gathered for her
as much dry wood as we could.

[But they could not help it;]
For they simply had
to leave her behind: they were
all of them starving;
and she, an old woman, she
was too weak to go with them, [now] us,
to seek food at some other place.

1. The poem is both heartbreaking and brave—how an impossible circumstance, starvation, and the real need to sacrifice a member of the family or of the tribe for the general good are faced. The tone of the narration reveals much about the tribe's attitude toward life and death. Discuss.

2. How do the simplicity and understated style of both the original transcript and the poem contribute to the poem's overall effectiveness?

3. The opening phrase of the final poem is "Our mother." This is a major change from the draft. Discuss this and other changes that were made during the poetic process.

Notes

1. Famine ("tobacco-hunger") is meant here — he did not smoke, because a dog had come in the night (and) carried off from him his pouch. And he arose in the night, he missed his pouch. And he arose in the night, he missed his pouch. And then he again lay down, while he did not smoke. And we were early seeking for the pouch. We did not find the pouch.
2. Afrikaans for "Blue"
3. Dorothea Bleek and A.M. Cronin-Duggin, *The Bushman Tribes of Southern Africa* (Kimberley: Alexander McGregor Memorial Museum, 1942) 5.
4. Roger Hewett, *Structure, Meaning and Ritual in the Narratives of the Southern San* (Hambury: H. Buske, 1986) 54.

5. Hewett, *Structure, Meaning and Ritual* 293: "If the curing failed to work, this was accounted for in a number of ways. In some cases the snoring was believed to have a delayed effect but if the illness went away and returned after a short while, this was put down to the work of malignant !giten [sorcerers] who had been firing invisible arrows at the patient. If the patient showed no signs of immediate recovery, or even died during treatment, this was attributed to malignant !giten firing arrows in the same way...."

6. Hewett, *Structure, Meaning and Ritual* 295: "!Giten were believed to possess the bodies of certain animals through which they were able to know of events which they themselves did not actually witness—the animals doing the seeing for them. They were also believed to bewitch those who came near them, even people who approached them from behind their line of vision, and were thought to be able to kill illness and death at a glance. They were believed to be particularly hostile to good-looking people whom they would kill if they got the chance, and they were also thought to prowl about at night and attack people."

7. Snoring: the English equivalent is exorcising.

8. Note: & the rain obeys the man. Text refers to "his" rain goes there: are these men sorcerers?

THREE POETS

1. ROBERT FROST

1874–1963

ROBERT FROST WAS AMONG THE FOREMOST AMERICAN poets to emerge in the first half of the twentieth century. This four-time winner of the Pulitzer Prize is noted for his use of natural speech rhythms and has often been called the voice of New England, whether in dialogue or meditation. Frost's voice can be casual or wise or both simultaneously. In terms of technique, Frost set traditional meters against natural speech rhythms; in this way he was able to portray a variety of tones, ironies, and human dispositions.

Frost was a poet of nature and of place. The place usually is rural New England, and his conception of nature is as complex as any serious poet's, pitting a dark and sometimes cynical vision against an urge to affirm religious truths and nature's bounty. His wry humor is a salutory ballast against the dark or haunted vision.

Such famous poems as "Stopping by Woods on a Snowy Evening" and "The Road Not Taken" are too often praised for their charming sentiments, or worse, their messages. The poet frequently complained that readers tended to "pressure" his poems into messages. One possible reason for this need to interpret Frost's poems is their sense of mystery. No doubt, Frost may be considered a "thinking trap," but he is best read for his close-up observations about people or nature, which mostly occur in the longer narratives. These life-like characters take over and command our rapt attention.

Frost often mixes serious themes with vivid or light tones as in "Fire and Ice," "Provide Provide," and the poem printed here, "Design." Mystery replaces ecstasy, and the mystery here runs as deep as the reader will allow. The original title of this Petrarchan sonnet was "[A Study] In White." It was sent in a letter to the poet's friend, Miss Ward. Lawrence Thompson, the author of the indispensable three-volume biography of Frost,[1] feels that "the revisions sharpen the ironies without changing the central meaning."[2] This is certain, but the poem is also strengthened with each word change, from "dented" to "dimpled" in the first line, to all the changed words in the last line.

Thompson notes that "Design" might be seen as a companion piece for his later "study in whiteness," called "Wrong to the Light" before it was entitled "For Once, Then Something."[3] This poem is often singled out as an example of the poet's more negative side. Like Blake's "The Tyger," Frost's poem questions the troubling design of the universe where beauty and "blight" seem to coexist on a canvas apparently void of beneficent order or freedom of choice. The flower has nothing to do with its color any more than the spider has choice over its appetite. The final version of this tightly constructed, highly ambiguous poem grew out of a fairly clumsy draft composed 24 years earlier. It is a testament to revision at its miraculous best.

Frost in this poem may be taking on those who complacently accept "the argument from design" as proof of the existence of God. According to Thompson, Frost was in sympathy with William James, who wrote: "Pragmatically, then, the abstract word 'design' is a blank cartridge. It carries no consequences, it does no execution." This is not to say Frost was a non-believer, for Thompson points out how Frost longed for positive religious belief: "… he preferred to manipulate the notion [that the Designer must be evil] in a detached way to tease and mock those whose religious beliefs seemed to him to be sentimental."[4]

The poem "Design," in its final version, mixes the elements of disgust, fear, awe, and delight, just as does nature in its design. In the first stanza we see death, horror, and a grim, amoral picture of the universe. The second stanza is full of profound questions regarding purpose in the world. This is one of the poems that prompted the great critic and poet Randall Jarrell to identify Frost's poems as "unsparingly truthful." Jarrell also noted Frost's "subtlety and exactness; such classical understatement and restraint make the reader feel that he is not in a book but in a world." Some see in "Design" a "cold finality"— another critic called it a "conclusively merciless poem." Instead, one might see it as a triumph of form and language and an example of the poet's drive toward a most difficult truth.

B

*Earlier
version*

In White
A dented spider like a snowdrop white
On a white Heal-all, holding up a moth
Like a white piece of lifeless satin cloth—
Saw ever curious eye so strange a sight?—
Portent in little, assorted death and blight
Like ingredients of a witches' broth?—
The beady spider, the flower like a froth,
And the moth carried like a paper kite.

What had that flower to do with being white,
The blue Brunella every child's delight.
What brought the kindred spider to that height?
(Make we no thesis of the miller's
            [i.e., miller-moth's] plight.)
What but design of darkness and of night?
Design, design! Do I use the word aright?

A

*Final
version*

Design

I found a dimpled spider, fat and white,
On a white heal-all, holding up a moth
Like a white piece of rigid satin cloth-
Assorted characters of death and blight
Mixed ready to begin the morning right,
Like the ingredients of a witches' broth-
A snow-drop spider, a flower like a froth
And dead wings carried like a paper kite.

What had that flower to do with being white,
The wayside blue and innocent heal-all?
What brought the kindred spider to that height,
Then steered the white moth thither in the night?
What but design of darkness to appall?—
If design govern in a thing so small.

1. "In White" is not a finished poem. What is it about the finished poem that leads you to declare it as superior? Certain key words and phrases (along with their connotations) have been changed and the changes might seem minor—for example, "dented" became "dim-

pled," and in line 3 "lifeless" became "rigid." But these changes are major in establishing clarity, concision and a particular tone here. Discuss how these (and other) single word alterations affect tone and meaning.

2. The 4th line of the early draft is particularly clumsy with its inverted poetic language: "Saw ever curious eye so strange a sight." This becomes the unaffected and truly frightening line "Assorted characters of death and blight." Do you see other examples of Frost's evolution towards clarity and grace?

3. From the start, Frost is working in the sonnet form. Even though the early draft sounds unfinished, the poet has already found his form. How does form assist the poet in delivering and developing his poem?

4. Is Jarrell's assessment of "Design" as a "conclusively merciless poem" equally true for both versions?

Notes

1. Lawrence Thompson, *Robert Frost* , 3 vols. (New York: Holt, Rinehart and Winston, 1966, 1970, 1976)
2. Lawrence Thompson, *Robert Frost: The Early Years 1874-1915* (New York: Holt, Rinehart and Winston, 1966) 582.
3. Lawrence Thompson, *Robert Frost: The Years of Triumph, 1915-1938* (New York: Holt, Rinehart and Winston, 1970) 600.
4. Thompson, *Robert Frost: The Early Years* 388.

2. WILLIAM CARLOS WILLIAMS

1883-1963

WILLIAM CARLOS WILLIAMS IS ONE OF THE MOST deservedly acclaimed poets of the twentieth century. Astonishingly, he spent his life working as a family doctor and obstetrician in Patterson, N.J., while creating a body of work that includes fiction, drama, criticism, and, most powerfully, poetry. He was a second-generation American and a member of a group of artists who flourished and defined modern art between the two World Wars. Many, including T.S. Eliot and Williams's friend Ezra Pound, left the U.S. by the 1920s, never to return, while Williams remained in Patterson.

Though Williams's poems are concrete, specific, and often childlike in their apparent simplicity, their influence on recent generations of poets, the current one not excluded, is inestimable. The reader unfamiliar with this major poet's work might well begin with the rich sampling of both poetry and prose offered by *The William Carlos Reader,* edited with an introduction by M.L. Rosenthal.[1] The *Collected Poems* exists in two volumes edited by A.Walton Litz and Christopher Mac-Gowan (1986); however, there is also the most recent *Selected Poems* (1985), edited by the British poet Charles Tomlinson, or the earlier *Selected Poems* (1949), edited by the American poet and critic Randall Jarrell. Williams's *Autobiography* (1951) and *I Wanted to Write a Poem* (1958) are both full of information and insight into his creative process.

It is possible to characterize many of Williams's poems as snapshots either of small objects—a tree, a wheelbarrow, or a person just sitting or standing about. His famous slogan "no ideas but in things" has perhaps encouraged a facile characterization that his poems are unmeditated upon still lives. But his great enterprise, his humanism, lies in the suggestion, as M.L. Rosenthal puts it, "that everything has [significance]; not that eye and object alone make the poem, but that these, together with ear and intellect and formal movement, shape a poem through their convergence. Conception, empathy, compassion, and technique become functions of the same thing."

Williams came of age as an artist during the flowering of Modernism in the U.S. and Europe. Although he remained a poet of locality, one who captured local speech as well as observation, his works nonetheless have a broad and lasting appeal. He wrote in his *Autobiography*: "Not to talk in vague categories but to write particularly, as a physician working, upon a patient, upon the thing before him, in the particular to discover the universal...." Believing that "only the moment is real," he attempted to capture visions from nature, a nature subject to an often grim and careless urban reality.

In Williams's *Selected Poems,* appearing on back-to-back pages are two versions of "The Locust Tree in Flower." Originally the longer version was published in *Poems* (1933), and the shorter version appeared in *An Early Martyr and Other Poems* (1935). Two years apart, they are almost as different from each other as Marianne Moore's two versions of "Poetry" below and, as with Moore, both versions may be regarded as final versions. Williams himself printed the two together in the *Collected Earlier Poems* (1951) and in *More Power, Report of the Newark Public Library, 1946-1952* (Fall-Winter 1952). That later publication included this comment: "I didn't think this gave a picture of the locust flower, so I had to cut it down... I literally cut out unessential lines." Shorter usually means more concise: the one word per line in the second version aims at this tightness. But Williams chose to print both versions. Like the cubist painters, and so many others involved in experimental writing, Williams offers studies or takes or improvisations on a topic, no one take necessarily more important than the other.

The second set, "Young Woman at a Window," offers a slightly different story. While the *Collected Poems* prints both versions on a single page, a note states: "WCW printed these two versions together in *The Westminster Magazine* (Autumn, 1934) but subsequently reprinted only [the shorter version]." Still, the issue presented by these two sets of poems is not how either found its final form. Instead, the idea of "final form" is being explored by the poet. Two final versions suggest a paradox in aesthetics—a work can have multiple outcomes that all feel inevitable. Perhaps we might contemplate whether or how the length of a poem influences its emotional resonance. Might a smaller poem provide greater emotional depth? Whatever the answers, the versions require the reader, in Williams' words, to "concentrate as much as he can."

Version 1	Version 2
The Locust Tree in Flower	*The Locust Tree in Flower*
Among	Among
the leaves	of
bright	green
green	stiff
of wrist-thick	old
tree	bright
and old	broken
stiff broken	branch
branch	come
ferncool	white
swaying	sweet
loosely strung—	May
come May	again
again	
white blossom	
clusters	
hide	
to spill	
their sweets	
almost	
unnoticed	
down	
and quickly	
fall	

Version 1	Version 2
Young Woman at a Window	*Young Woman at a Window*
While she sits	She sits with
there	tears on

with tears on	her cheek
her cheek	her cheek on
her cheek on	her hand
her hand	the child
this little child	in her lap
who robs her	his nose
knows nothing of	pressed
His theft	to the glass
but rubs his	
nose	

1. The word "again" is crucial in both versions. Discuss its placement in both.

2. Neither version has any punctuation. What value or effectiveness has this omission?

3. What do you think Williams is doing with the odd use of the preposition "of" in the second version?

4. This poet was always aiming at concision and linguistic precision. Shorter usually means more concise: the one word per line in the second version aims at this concision. Is the poem successful in terms of this issue.

5. In the second version it's May that is "sweet." In the first version the word is pluralized and has a wider range of possible associations. Discuss this comparison.

6. Discuss motion in both these versions.

Note

1. M.L. Rosenthal, ed. *The William Carlos Reader* (New York: New Directions, 1966).

3. ROBERT LOWELL

1917–1977

R OBERT LOWELL IS REGARDED BY MANY TO BE AMERICA'S last major poet, that is, an artist who receives the unstinting admiration of the largest segment of the poetry-reading public. Since his death in 1977, there has been a cornucopia of books about Lowell's life and art. Ian Hamilton's *Robert Lowell, A Biography* (1982), was the first full life and Paul Mariani's *Lost Puritan, A Life of Robert Lowell* (1994), the most recent. Additionally there are Katharine Wallingford's *Robert Lowell's Language of the Self* (1988) and *Robert Lowell and Life Studies: Revising the Self,* by Terri Witek (1993), both especially informative regarding Lowell's methods and motivations for poetic revision.[1]

After winning the Pulitzer Prize for his second book of poems, *Lord Weary's Castle* (1946), Lowell published more than a dozen collections of poetry and translations. *Life Studies* (1959) includes a sequence of poems about family life, domestic and marital matters, as well as separate, but thematically and stylistically related, poems about his emotional tribulations. In a review of this book for the *Nation* magazine (Sept. 10, 1959), M.L. Rosenthal coined the phrase "confessional poetry," an idea that eventually became somewhat distorted. Rather than thinking of confessional poetry as mere subjective outpouring, Rosenthal would have us understand it as more of "an outgrowth of the social criticism that has marked almost the whole sweep of poetry in this century. Thus Lowell's poems carry the burden of the age within them .... The private life embodies the national life." This psychic strain is clearly felt in both "Man and Wife," and "To Speak of Woe That is in Marriage," two poems in *Life Studies* that began as one.

Paul Mariani, in his biography, notes that upon returning to Boston after a reading tour in 1957 in the company of Alan Ginsberg and other "beat" writers, Lowell "began writing lines like these from an early draft of 'Man and Wife'":

On warm spring nights ... we can hear the outcry,

If our windows are open wide,

I can hear the South End,
The razor's edge
Of Bastan's negro culture. They as we
Refine past culture's possibility,
Fear homicide,
Grow horny with alcohol, take the pledge ...

But he put the poem aside and didn't return to it until he had immersed himself in contemporary poetry written in the colloquial free-verse style, such as that practised by Ford Madox Ford, William Carlos Williams, and his own student, W.D. Snodgrass. "Man and Wife," originally called "Holy Matrimony," and its break-off poem "To Speak of Woe...," were written during a fertile four-month period during which he wrote eleven of the poems that make up the heart of *Life Studies,* including the famous "Skunk Hour." Ian Hamilton prints the draft in his biography and notes that although unfinished, it has a genuine political background and that the "old-fashioned tirade" section became the basis for "To Speak of Woe..." which is distanced by being presented in the third person.

At last the trees are green on Marlborough Street,
Blossoms on our Saucer Magnolia ignite
For their feverish five days white ....
Last night I held your hands, Petite,
Subtlest of all God's creatures, still pure nerve, Still purer
        nerve than I,
Who, hand on glass,
And heart in mouth,
Outdrank the Rhavs once in the heat
Of Greenwich Village, and sat at your feet—
Too boiled and shy
And poker-faced to make a pass,
While the shrill verve
Of your invective scorched the old South.

On warm spring night [sic] though, we can hear the outcry,
If our windows are open wide,
I can hear the South End,
The razor's edge
Of Boston's negro culture. They as we
Refine past culture's possibility,

Fear homocide [sic],
Grow horny with alcohol, take the pledge ...
At forty why pretend
It's just the others, not ourselves, who die?
And now you turn your back,
Sleepless, you hold
Your pillow to your hollows like a child,
And once again,
The merciless Racinian tirade
Breaks like the Atlantic on my head.

"It's the injustice ... you are so unjust-
There's nothing accommodating, nice or kind—

But *What can I do for you?* What can I do for you,
Shambling into our bed at two
With all the monotonous sourness of your lust,
A tusked heart, an alcoholic's mind,
And blind, blind, blind
Drunk! Have pity! My worst evil
Is living at your level.
My mind
Moves like a water-spider ....

The legs stick and break in your slough.
Why prolong our excruciation now?

What is your purpose? Each night now I tie
Ten dollar

Hamilton adds that "the draft ends here, but the line finally (in 'To Speak of Woe...') reads":

Each night now I tie
ten dollars and his car key to my thigh ....

The first version of the poem "Water" appeared in Lowell's *For The Union Dead* (1964), the book that extended the poetic principles set in motion in his earlier volume, *Life Studies*. Using personal experience as the basis of his work, the literal "I" moved center-stage. Lowell significantly revised "Water" for his 1967 collection, *Notebook.* In that book, "Water" is the first of four poems for Elizabeth Bishop, a poet who was a long time friend of Lowell's. Aside from the form, the most obvious difference among the versions is that the sonnet names the specific town in Maine, Stonington, along with a specific date attached to the title. It seems that the poet wanted to clarify and specify the experience he earlier explored in a more casual manner. A third version appeared in Lowell's late book, *History* (1973). In a prefatory note, Lowell defends his penchant for revising:

> About 80 of the poems in *History* are new, the rest are taken from my last published poem, *Notebook* begun six years ago. All the poems have been changed, some heavily. I have plotted. My old title, *Notebook,* was more accurate than I wished, i.e. the composition was jumbled. I hope this jumble or jungle is cleared—that I have cut the waste marble from the figure.

Not all will agree that versions two and three of "Water" are superior poems; Katharine Wallingford argues that these revisions feel to her like repetitions and that in this case the obsessive revision process led Lowell to an inferior poem. The change of tense to the present, in the final version, bothers Wallingford the most, for it changes the entire tone and theme of nostalgia in the first and second versions. Leaving aside the value judgements sparked by these three different published pieces, they decisively provide insight into the technical decisions an artist makes, how an individual wrestles, aesthetically and morally, with the materials of his or her experience.

Later
version

For Elizabeth Bishop (twenty-five years)

I Water

At Stonington each morning boatloads of hands
Cruise off for the granite quarry on the island,
Leaving dozens of bleak white frame houses stuck
Like oyster shells on the hill of rock. Remember?
We sit on the slab of rock. From this distance in time,
It seems the color of iris, rotting and turning purpler,
But it is only the usual gray rock
Turning fresh green when drenched by the sea....

The sea flaked the rock at our feet, kept lapping the matchstick
Mazes of weirs where fish for bait were trapped.
You dreamed you were a mermaid clinging to a wharfpile,
Trying to pull the barnacles with your hands.
We wish our two souls might return like gulls to the rock.
In the end, the water was too cold for us.

Four Poems for Elizabeth Bishop

*Later
version*

I Water 1948

Stonington: each morning boatloads of hands
cruised off for the granite quarry on an island;
they left dozens of bleak white frame houses stuck
like oyster shells on the hill of rock. Remember?
We sat on the slab of rock. From this distance in time,
it seems the color of iris, rotting and turning purpler,
but it was only the usual gray rock
turning fresh green when drenched by the sea.
The sea flaked the rock at our feet, kept lapping the matchstick
mazes of weirs where the fish for bait were trapped.
You dreamed you were a mermaid clinging to a wharfpile,
trying to pull off the barnacles with your hands.
We wished our two souls might return like gulls to the rock.
In the end, the water was too cold for us.

*Earlier
version*

Water

It was a Maine lobster town
each morning boatloads of hands
pushed off for granite
quarries on the islands,

and left dozens of bleak
white frame houses stuck
like oyster shells
on a hill of rock,

and below us, the sea lapped
the raw little match-stick

mazes of a weir,
where the fish for bait were trapped.

Remember? We sat on a slab of rock.
From this distance in time,
it seems the color
of iris, rotting and turning purpler,

but it was only
the usual gray rock
turning the usual green
when drenched by the sea.

The sea drenched the rock
at our feet all day,
and kept tearing away
flake after flake.

One night you dreamed
you were a mermaid clinging to a wharf-pile,
and trying to pull
off the barnacles with your hands.

We wished our two souls
might return like gulls
to the rock. In the end,
the water was too cold for us.

1. Comment on how the two different poetic forms strike you. The first poem is made up of quatrains and the second is a loosely constructed (note the lack of rhymes) sonnet.

2. The one word followed by the question mark, "Remember?" is a key to this apostrophe (a poem addressed to a person absent from the reader's view). In the first version it appears in line 13; in the later version, it's in line 4. How does this change in placement affect your perception of the poem?

3. The poet Elizabeth Bishop is the person addressed here, but we only discover this in the second version. Does this in any way influence your understanding of the poem?

4. There are other apparently small changes, e.g. "usual green" becomes "fresh change," and the word "drenched" is used twice in adjacent lines (20-21) in the first version, while in the later poem it's used but once. What other little changes interest you and which poem do you prefer and why?

Note

1. Ian Hamilton, *Robert Lowell, A Biography* (New York: Random House, 1982); Paul Mariani, *Lost Puritan, A Life of Robert Lowell* (New York: W.W. Norton, 1994); Katharine Wallingford, *Robert Lowell's Language of the Self* (Chapel Hill, NC: University of North Carolina Press, 1988); and Terri Witek, *Robert Lowell and Life Studies: Revising the Self* (Columbia, MO: University of Missouri Press, 1993).

JOHN KEATS

1795-1821

BECAUSE OF THE INTENSITY AND BREVITY OF THEIR LIVES, as well as the style and content of their poetry, a number of English poets have been given by succeeding generations the title "Romantic." Romanticism, as a philosophical and literary movement, is generally associated with the rise and exaltation of individualism, radical political thought, creative freedom, and reaction against neoclassical dictates of objectivity, clarity, and imitation. These might be exemplified, particularly in poetry, by many qualities, for example, heightened sensibility, extravagant imagination, references to both the self and nature, use of old verse forms, and fascination with the remote or primitive. The poet, by definition, seemed to embody many of these characteristics.

John Keats is one of a number of English Romantic poets who died young. In the *Oxford History of English Literature,* Ian Jack quotes a fellow student of Keats: "Poetry was ... the zenith of all his aspirations: the only thing worth the attention of superior minds: so he thought: all other pursuits were mean and tame.... The greatest men in the world were poets and to rank among them was the chief object of his ambition."[1]

Before dedicating his life to poetry, Keats pursued a course directed toward medicine. In 1815, he was working in the London Hospital, but by September 1816, he had given up medicine for poetry.

His belief or developing philosophical attitude toward poetry is elusive. His letters are rich with references to poetry, but the terms he employs defy systematic definition. Keats says that through apprehension of the beautiful, man is able to connect with "the highest reality" or "essences" of the physical universe. This in turn leads to profound happiness. Truth is tied up with perception of the beautiful—"a truth of sensation." We are led to a philosophy of impression and feelings rather than a systematic ordering and analysis of empirical or spiritual knowledge. However, as the reader of Keats' great odes already knows, there is a depth of thought, a reflectiveness, that transcends mere loveliness or sensation of feeling.

Keats' first volume of *Poems* appeared in 1817 to few and unenthusiastic reviews. The early poems already show a concentration on sensual imagery not always rooted in the real world. Although this might be termed "poetry of escape," for example, escape into Spenser's world of faerie, a land far from the mundane realm of medical studies, Keats is rarely fanciful. Even in his early poetry there is the mark of authenticity, a concern for life as it is now.

Endymion, an ambitious work of great length, appeared in 1818 and shows the influence of Shakespeare's style, diction, and imagery. While the poem does exhibit many of the excesses of Romantic effusiveness, a "soft lusciousness of style," here Keats was attempting to move toward what he regarded as the "impersonality of Shakespeare," or what Matthew Arnold about fifty years later would call "disinterestedness." Keats liked the way in which Shakespeare stepped back from and refused to enter the lives of his characters. In a short time Keats moved toward this objectivity in art. In *Endymion,* as in the poems to follow, the persistent influence of the English Renaissance is felt. *Endymion* was attacked by the critical press, and Keats was beginning to grow accustomed to the viciousness of critics.

Most of Keats' great poetry was written between September 1818 and September 1819. The product of this short period is *Lamia, Isabella, The Eve of St. Agnes,* and *Other Poems* (1820), which has been called the greatest single volume of English poetry of the nineteenth century. Through this volume in particular, Keats became the greatest influence of his age on the following period in poetry, an influence epitomized by his effect on Robert Browning.

The Eve of St. Agnes is a tale of youthful, romantic love set against a background of family feud, revelry, tempest, and bitter cold. This poem, which many feel to be Keats' crowning achievement, is based on popular superstitions with echoes of Gothic Romances, Shakespeare's plays, and folk tales reverberating throughout its stanzas.

While the poem rests on the popular legend about St. Agnes' Eve, Keats went to Spenser, the most elaborate of Elizabethans, for his stanza, music, lavish adornment of narrative, sensuous imagery, and medieval matter. The Spenserian stanza has nine lines rhyming abab-bcbcc; the first eight lines are iambic pentameter, the last line an Alexandrine, a verse line with six iambic feet. The stanza itself is most suited for this narrative; it is processional in its movement and offers opportunities for richer effects of vowel music and sensuous luxury. The use of color and architectural detail are embellishments, to be sure, but, also, these elements epitomize states of mind and emotional levels reached by the characters in the poem.

The Eve of St. Agnes is built on many antitheses that demonstrate an internal drama going on beyond the simple drama of the lovers. Patterns of warmth and cold, color and colorlessness, tumultuous sound and silence are continually interwoven.

The beauties of this poem are revealed by a close examination of its language rather than by the kind of structural analysis to which much modern poetry lends itself. For a close study of the poem we are indebted to M.R. Ridley's *Keats' Craftsmanship: A Study in Poetic Development.*[2] Ridley records the genesis of the poem from about January 18, 1819. He collates the four written copies of the poem with the final version printed in 1820. However, there remain a few editorial problems. Ridley himself admits that in scattered instances (namely stanzas 36 and 37) there is uncertainty as to the precise wording. Each editor has his own idea as to authenticity.

Unlike the preceding chapters, this one contains only one poem, *The Eve of St. Agnes.* Because it is a relatively long poem, and the number of alterations are many, the poem stands alone as a chapter. This chapter presents only an A version with the early variations and later deletions indicated in the poem. Here again, as in the Auden chapter, the bracketed words are earlier variants that were replaced in the final version by the underlined words. However, a number of stanzas went through extensive reworking, and not all minor changes are included here. Therefore, where interesting variants occur the commentary draws the reader's attention to these changes. We see the material developing and also get an inkling of how Keats' mind worked through these changes.

In this chapter the questions and commentary are numbered according to the stanza to which they refer.

Final version with variants in brackets

The Eve of St. Agnes

I

St. Agnes' Eve—Ah, bitter <u>chill</u> [cold] it was!
The owl, for all his feathers, was a-cold;
The hare limped trembling through the frozen grass,
And silent <u>was</u> [were] the flock in woolly fold:

Numb were the Beadsman's fingers, while he told
His rosary, and while his frosted breath,
Like pious incense <u>from</u> [in] a censer old,
Seemed taking flight for heaven, without a death,
Past the sweet Virgin's picture, while his prayer he saith.

2

His prayer he saith, this patient, holy man;
Then takes his lamp, and riseth from his knees,
And back returneth, meagre, barefoot, wan,
Along the chapel aisle by slow degrees:
The sculptured dead, on each side, seem to freeze,
Emprisoned in black, purgatorial rails:
Knights, ladies, praying in dumb orat'ries,
He passeth by; and this weak spirit fails
To think how they may ache in icy hoods and mails.

3a

But there are ears may hear sweet melodies,
And there are eyes to brighten festivals,
And there are feet for nimble minstrelsies,
And many a lip that for the red wine calls—
Follow, then follow to the illumin'd halls,
Follow me youth—and leave the Eremite—
Give him a tear—then trophied banneral
And many a brilliant tasseling of light
Shall droop from arched ways this high Baronial night.

3

Northward he turneth through a little door,
And scarce three steps, ere Music's golden tongue
Flattered to tears this aged man and poor;
But no—already had his deathbell rung:
The joys of all his life were said and sung:
His was harsh penance on St. Agnes' Eve:
Another way he <u>went</u>, [turn'd;] and soon among

Rough [Black] ashes sat he for his soul's reprieve,
And all night kept awake, for sinner's sake [souls] to grieve.

4

That ancient Beadsman heard the prelude soft;
And so it chanced, for many a door was wide,
From hurry to and fro. Soon, up—[and now] aloft,
The Silver, snarling trumpets 'gan to chide:
High-lampcd [The level] chambers, ready with their pride,
Were glowing [Seem'd anxious] to receive a thousand guests:
The carved angels, ever eager-eyed,
Stared, where upon their heads the cornice rests,
        With hair blown back, and wings put cross-wise
            on their breasts.

Stanza 1: The changes in stanza I may have been typographical correc-
tions on the type proofs. Do you see, as Keats obviously saw, the need
to correct these few words in this stanza? Characterize these changes.

Stanza 3a: Stanza 4 introduces the reader to a festive scene, the place
of the opening action. 3a makes this introduction more gradual and
more elaborate. The omission of the stanza gets us into the action
more swiftly and with less pretense of narrative accuracy. There is no
need for a narrative poem to provide each step of the story. Often dra-
matic tension is created by omission of detail. Discuss.

Stanza 3: The omission of "turn'd" in line 7 is interesting for it is clear-
ly a more dramatic word than his preferred "went." What virtue does
this gained simplicity have in the context of the developing narrative?
in the stanza itself? "Turn'd" would be an echo from the first line. Is
such an echo unfortunate? What effect is lost? What is gained? Discuss
similarly the change in the last line from "souls" to "sake."

Stanza 4: Comment on the changes in lines 3 and 5. Both changes
heighten drama and texture, yet they work in very different ways.

The "chambers" in line 5 are ready to receive guests. Whether they
"glow" or "seem anxious" depends upon the kind of personification
the poet chooses. Which personification seems more reasonable?

Many kinds of personification are used in poetry and the best is not always the most fanciful or extravagant. The entire question of poetic decorum is at issue here. Also, the two choices presented differ in that one presents an image, while the other is difficult to picture in the mind.

5a

At length <u>burst</u> [step] in the argent <u>revelry</u>, [revelers]
With plume, tiara, and all rich array,
Ah what are they? the idle pulse scarce stirs,
The muse should never make the spirit gay;
Away, bright dulness, laughing fools away,—
And let me tell of one sweet lady there
Whose heart had brooded, all that wintry day,
On love, and winged St. Agnes' saintly care,
As she had heard old <u>dames</u> [Dames] full many times declare.

5

At length burst in the argent revelry,
With plume, tiara, and all rich array,
Numerous as shadows haunting faerily
The brain, new stuffed, in youth, with triumphs gay
Of old romance. These let us wish away,
And turn, Sole-thoughted, to one Lady there,
Whose heart had brooded, all that wintry day,
On love, and winged St. Agnes' saintly care,
As she had heard old dames full many times declare.

6a

'Twas said her future lord would there appear
Offering as sacrifice—all in the dream—
Delicious food even to her lips brought near:
Viands and wine and fruit and sugar'd cream,
To touch her palate with the fine extreme
Or relish: then soft music heard; and then
More pleasures followed in a dizzy stream

Palpable almost: then to wake again
Warm in the virgin morn, no weeping Magdalen.

6

They told her how, upon St. Agnes' Eve,
Young virgins might have visions of delight.
And soft adorings <u>from</u> [of] their loves receive
Upon the honeyed middle of the night,
If ceremonies due they did aright;
As, supperless to bed they must retire,
And <u>couch</u> [lay] supine their beauties, lily white;
Nor look behind, nor sideways, but require
Of Heaven with upward eyes for all that they desire.

7

Full of this whim was thoughtful Madeline:
The music, yearning like a God in pain,
[Touch'd not her heart] <u>She scarcely heard</u>: her maiden eyes
       divine,
Fixed on the floor, saw many a sweeping train
Pass by—she heeded not at all: in vain
Came many a tiptoe, amorous cavalier,
And back retired; not cooled by high disdain,
But she saw not: her heart was otherwhere:
She sighed for Agnes' dreams, the sweetest of the year.

8

She danced along with vague, <u>regardless eyes</u>, [uneager look]
Anxious her lips, her breathing quick and short:[3]
The hallowed hour was near at hand: <u>she sighs</u> [—and]
Amid the <u>timbrels</u>, [Timbrels] and the thronged resort
Of <u>whisperers</u> [Whisperers] in anger, or in sport;
'Mid looks of <u>love</u>, [Love] defiance, hate, and scorn,
<u>Hoodwinked with faery</u> [She was hoodwink'd with] fancy; all
       amort,

Save to St. Agnes and her <u>lambs</u> [Lambs] unshorn,
And all the bliss to be before tomorrow morn.

Stanza 5: This stanza has been entirely recast. Discuss the changes, especially in lines 3–6, in terms of developing action, rhyme scheme, and total effect.

Stanza 6: Here we have the ritual detail of the superstition about St. Agnes' Eve told to us by the "old dames." In 6a other details are provided, most likely from a literary source other than that which provided the materials for 6. There is information in the omitted stanza (6a) essential to the entire structure of the poem. Questions are left in the reader's mind regarding Madeline's words upon waking (stanza 35). Answers may be provided out of the material in 6a. It has been suggested that the stanza was omitted because readers found it overly "sensual." Do you find the sensuality at odds with the development of language and imagery thus far in the poem?

Stanza 8: From this stanza forward Ridley examines Keats' own first draft. Up to this point, we have been working from the second draft manuscript as the preceding stanzas were lost in first draft state. The corrections here do not represent any single method of composition, that is, Keats crossed out a phrase and immediately put in another, as the printed text here would lead one to suspect. Rather, "… by corrections and interlinear insertions he got them into a condition which a compositor would have set as the second version." Treat these changes in the same way you have been doing throughout the text.
   Consider the changes in the first three lines. When does the suggestiveness in a phrase give way to mere vagueness?

9

So, purposing each moment to retire,
She lingered <u>still</u> [fearful who might]. Meantime, across the
         moors,
Had come young Porphyro, with heart <u>on fire</u> [afire]
For Madeline. <u>Beside</u> [Within] the <u>portal doors</u>, [Portal Doors]
Buttressed from moonlight, stands he, and implores
All saints to give him sight of Madeline,

But for one moment in the tedious hours,
That he might gaze and <u>worship all unseen;</u> [or speak, or
      kneel]
Perchance speak, kneel, touch, kiss—in sooth such things
      have been.

10

He ventures in: let no buzzed whisper tell:
All eyes be muffled, or a hundred swords
Will storm his heart, Love's fev'rous citadel:
For him, those chambers held barbarian hordes,
Hyena foemen, and hot-blooded lords,
Whose very dogs would execrations howl
Against his lineage: not one breast affords
Him any mercy, in that mansion foul,
Save one old beldame, weak in body and in soul.

11

Ah, happy chance, the agéd creature came,
[Tottering] <u>Shuffling</u> along with ivory-headed <u>wand</u>, [staff]
To where he stood, hid from the torch's flame,
Behind a <u>broad</u> [huge] hall-pillar, far beyond
The sound of merriment and chorus bland:
He startled her; but soon she knew his face,
And grasped his fingers in her palsied hand,
Saying, "Mercy, Porphyro! hie thee from this place:
They are all here tonight, the whole blood-thirsty race!

12

"Get hence! get hence! there's dwarfish Hildebrand;
He had a fever late, and in the fit
He curséd thee and thine, both house and land:
Then there's that old Lord Maurice, not a whit
More tame for his gray hairs-Alas me! flit!
Flit like a ghost away — Ah, Gossip dear,
We're safe enough; here in this arm-chair sit,

And tell me how"—"Good <u>Saints</u> [Gods]! not here, not here;
Follow me, child, [—hush hush] or else these stones will be
    thy bier."

Stanza 9: The action is moved along, after a feeling of stasis in the three previous stanzas, by the entrance of Porphyro. In an earlier version line 2 delayed the suspense even longer. The deletion of "fearful who might" is evidence that Keats desired the action to pick up. A different observation may be made at line 4. Here Keats leaves Porphyro "Beside" rather than , "Within" the doors to justify the following line realistically. The changes here also determine the reader's response to the nature of the hero. For example, in an earlier draft "piteous" preceded "... implore/All saints ..."

    Stanza 10: There were a number of changes in this stanza, both dramatic and metaphysical. The first three lines read:

He ventures in wrapped in a dark disguise

Let no Man see him, or a hundred Swords
Will storm his heart for all his amorous sighs
Comment on the revised opening.

Stanza 12: In the two changes consider the muting of tone. The hero is in danger. How is this handled and what effect does such toning down have on the entire development here?

13

He followed through a lowly archéd way,
Brushing the cobwebs with his lofty plume,
And as she mutter'd "Well-a—well-a-day!"
He found him in a little moonlight room,
Pale, <u>latticed, chill,</u> [casemented] and silent as a tomb.
"Now tell me where is Madeline," said he,
"O tell me, <u>Angela</u> [Goody], by the holy loom
Which none but <u>secret</u> [holy] sisterhood may see,
When they St. Agnes' wool <u>are weaving</u> [do weave full]
    piously."

14

"St. Agnes! Ah! it is St. Agnes' Eve—
Yet men will murder upon <u>holy days</u> [holidays]:
Thou must hold water in a witch's sieve,
And be liege-lord of all the Elves and Fays,
To venture so: <u>it fills me with</u> [in truth it doth] amaze
[Young Signor] <u>To see thee</u>, Porphyro!—St. Agnes' Eve!
God's help! my lady fair the conjuror plays
This very night: good angels her deceive!
But let me laugh awhile, I've mickle time to grieve."

15

Feebly she <u>laugheth</u> [laughd] in the [bright] languid moon
While Porphyro upon her face doth look,
Like <u>puzzled</u> [As doth an] urchin on an aged crone
Who keepeth closed a wond'rous riddle-book.
As spectacled she sits in chimney nook.
But soon his eyes grew brilliant, when she told
His lady's purpose; and he scarce could brook
Tears, at the thought of those enchantments cold,
And Madeline asleep <u>in lap of</u> [among those] legends old.

16

Sudden a thought came like a full-blown rose,
Flushing his <u>brow</u> [Young Cheek], and in his <u>painéd</u> [painful]
        heart
Made purple riot: then doth he propose
A stratagem, that makes the beldame start:
"A cruel man and impious thou art:
Sweet lady, let her pray, and sleep, and dream
Alone with her good angels, far apart
From wicked men like thee. Go, go [: by christ]!—I deem
Thou canst not surely be the same that thou didst seem."

Stanza 13: The stanza began differently: "He followed her along a pas-
sage dark." Discuss the two versions of the opening line. Characterize
the change in the last line. In line 5 we can see the vision clarifying

itself as Keats is describing not merely scenery but a state of being as well.

Stanza 15: Madeline's situation is described more specifically in the final last line than earlier. Discuss this. Are there any changes of a similar nature in this stanza?

Stanza 16: The changes recorded here have to do with literary taste and decorum. The first change in line 2, however, may be of different substance. The first line earlier read: "Sudden a thought more rosy than the rose/Flush'd . . ." Discuss this change in emphasis.

17

"I will not harm her, by all <u>saints I swear</u>, [the great St. Paul;]"
Quoth Porphyro: "O may I ne'er find grace
When my weak voice shall <u>whisper its last prayer</u>, [unto
    heaven call]
If one of her soft ringlets I displace,
Or look with ruffian passion in her face:
Good Angela, <u>believe me by these tears</u>; [thou hearest how I
    swear]
Or I will, even in a moment's space,
Awake, with horrid shout, my foemen's ears,
And beard them, though they be more fanged than wolves
    and bears."

18

"Ah! why <u>wilt thou</u> [will you] affright a feeble soul?
A poor, weak, palsy-stricken, churchyard thing,
Whose passing-bell may ere the <u>midnight</u> [morning] toll;
Whose prayers for thee, each morn and evening,
Were never missed." —Thus plaining, doth she bring
A gentler speech from burning Porphyro;
So <u>woeful</u> [gentle], and of such deep sorrowing,
That <u>Angela gives promise she will</u> [The old Beldam promises
    to] do
Whatever he shall wish, betide her weal or woe.

19

Which was, to <u>lead</u> [guide] him, in close secrecy,
Even to Madeline's chamber, and there hide
Him in a closet, <u>of such privacy</u> [if such one there be]
That he might see her beauty unespied,
And win perhaps that night a peerless bride,
While legioned faeries <u>paced the coverlet,</u> [round her pillow
     flew]
And pale enchantment held her sleepy-eyed.
<u>Never</u> [O when] on such a night have lovers met,
 Since Merlin paid <u>his Demon</u> [the demons] all the monstrous
     debt.

20

"It shall be as thou wishest," said the Dame:
"All cates and dainties shall be storéd there
Quickly on this feast-night: by the tambour frame
Her own lute thou wilt see: no time to spare,
For I am slow and feeble, and scarce dare
On such a catering trust my dizzy head.
<u>Wait here, my child, with patience</u> [But wait an hour passing];
     kneel in prayer
The while: Ah! thou must needs the lady wed,
Or may I never leave my grave among the dead."

Stanza 17: Note the care the poet takes with the question of swearing and by whom—one saint or many. What do such alterations suggest about the poet's conception of Porphyro and how does the developing action take shape from such considerations?

Stanza 19: The action of this stanza follows fast upon the one preceding. But an earlier development is revealed in the first attempt at an opening line: "Which was, as all who ever lov'd will guess." Comment on the two approaches to the action as it is eventually worked out. Do you recognize where certain changes have been made anticipating rhyming difficulties?

Stanza 20: This marks, in Professor Ridley's words, "almost the last moment of easy composition in the poem …" He continues: "But now, as the crisis of the action approaches, the fever of composition increases, and one can study with an excitement almost painful the workings of the creative spirit in the throes of creation." Discuss.

21

So saying, she hobbled off with busy fear.
The lover's endless minutes slowly passed;
The dame returned, and whispered in his ear
To follow her; with agéd eyes aghast
From fright of <u>dim espial</u> [any noise]. Safe at last,
Through <u>many a dusky</u> [lonely oaken] gallery, they gain
The maiden's chamber, silken, hushed, and chaste;
Where Porphyro took covert, pleased amain.
His poor guide hurried back with agues in her brain.

22

Her <u>falt'ring</u> [With fautling] hand upon the <u>balustrade</u>,
        [Ballustrad]
Old Angela was feeling for the <u>stair</u>, [Stair]
When Madeline, St. Agnes' charméd maid,
Rose, like a missioned spirit, [to her] unaware:
With silver [And with her] taper's light, and <u>pious</u> [gentle] care,
She turned, and <u>down</u> [led] the aged gossip <u>led</u> [down]
To <u>a safe</u> [the save] level matting. Now prepare,
Young Porphyro, <u>for gazing</u> [a-gazing] on that bed; [Bed]
She comes, she comes again, like ring-dove frayed and fled.

23

Out went the taper as she <u>hurried</u> [floated] in;
Its little smoke, in pa'llid moonshine, died;
She closed the door, she panted, all akin
To spirits of the air, and visions wide:
No uttered syllable, or, woe betide!
But to her heart, her heart was voluble,
Paining with eloquence her balmy side;
As though a tongueless nightingale should swell

Her throat in vain, and die, heart-stifled, in her dell.

24a

A Casement ach'd tripple archd and diamonded
With many coloured glass fronted the Moon
In midst <u>whereof</u> [of which] a shilded scutcheon shed
High blushing gules: upon she kneeled saintly down
And inly prayed for grace and heavenly boon
The blood red gules fell on her silver cross
And her white[st] hands devout

24

A casement high and triple-arched there was,
All <u>garlanded</u> [gardneded] with carven imag'ries
Of fruits, and flowers, and<u> bunches of knot-grass</u>, [sunny corn]
And diamonded with panes of quaint device,
Innumerable of stains and splendid <u>dyes</u>, [dies]
As are [is] the tiger-moth's <u>deep-damasked</u> [rich sunset] wings
And in the midst, 'mong <u>thousand</u> [man] heraldries,
And [dim] twilight saints, and dim emblazonings,
A shielded scutcheon blushed with <u>blood of queens and kings</u>.
    [Blood of Queens and Kings.]

Stanza 21: The earliest attempt at the first line reads like a prose state-
ment of what is to become poetry: "So saying she hobbl'd out busily."
And the simple but dramatic line 2 earlier read: "And we will pass the
Lover's endless hour." What role does poetic imagination play in the
refining of this material? Is the preferred version of line 5 much better
than the original? If yes, why?

Stanza 22: This stanza was to continue Porphyro's story—"There
secreted,"—but the poet changed his mind and got back to Angela.
An early draft of the opening lines reads:

Scarce had old Angela the staircase found
Ere Madeline, like an affrightened Bird
Flew past her.

What problems can you discern here? Discuss the other revisions in this stanza.

Stanza 23: The last line, the Alexandrine, is a foot too long in the first draft: "Her barren throat in vain and die heart stifled in her dell." The "in vain" was first deleted, then replaced for the final edition.

Stanza 24A: Discuss the fragment in light of the above.

Stanza 24: The stanza began "A Casement ach'd" and then Keats made his image more elaborate, richer. Since the emotional stress is minimal and the action is at rest (for this and the next stanza) the poet works with language as a painter works with brush strokes. Though the narrative is in stasis here, values take shape in these two stanzas. By noting the revisions, demonstrate how those values evolve.

25

Full on this <u>casement</u> [Casement] shone the wintry moon,
And threw <u>warm</u> [red, rich] gules on Madeline's fair <u>breast</u>,
    [face]
As down she <u>knelt</u> [kneel'd] for heaven's grace and boon;
<u>Rose-bloom fell on her</u> [Tinging her pious] hands, together
    prest,
And on her silver cross soft <u>amethyst</u>, [Amethyst]
And on her hair a glory, like a <u>saint</u>: [Saint's]
She seemed <u>a splendid angel, newly drest</u>, [like an <u>immortal</u>
    [silvery] angel drest,]
Save wings, for heaven:—<u>Porphyro</u> [Lionel] grew faint:
She knelt, <u>so</u> [too] pure a thing, so free from mortal taint.

26

<u>Anon</u> [But soon] his heart revives: her <u>vespers</u> [praying] <u>done,</u>
    [prayers said]
Of all its wreathed pearls her hair she <u>frees</u>; [strips]
Unclasps her <u>warmed</u> [bosom] jewels one by one;
Loosens her fragrant bodice; by degrees
Her <u>rich</u> [sweet] attire <u>creeps rustling</u> [falls light] to her knees:
Half-hidden, like a <u>mermaid in sea-weed</u>, [Syren of the Sea]
<u>Pensive awhile she dreams awake</u>, [She stands awhile in
    thought,] and sees

In fancy, fair St. Agnes in her bed,
But dares not look behind, or all the charm is <u>fled</u>. [dead]

27

Soon, trembling in her soft and chilly nest
<u>In sort of wakeful swoon,</u> [She lay, in sort of wakeful swoon
  perplext] <u>perplexed she lay,</u>
Until the poppied warmth of sleep oppressed
Her soothéd <u>limbs,</u> [Limbs] and <u>soul</u> [Soul] fatigued away;
Flown, like a thought, until the morrow-day;
Blissfully haven'd both from joy and pain;
<u>Clasped</u> [Shut] like a missal where swart <u>Paynims</u> [paynims]
  pray;
<u>Blinded alike from</u> [Dead to] <u>sunshine</u> [Sunshine] and from
  rain,
As though a rose should <u>shut,</u> [close] and be a bud again.

28

Stol'n to this paradise, and so entranced,
Porphyro gazed upon her empty dress,
And <u>listened</u> [listen] to her breathing, if it chanced
To wake into slumberous tenderness;
Which when he heard, that minute did he bless,
And breathed himself: then from the closet crept,
<u>Noiseless</u> [Silent] as <u>fear</u> [Fear] in a <u>wide</u> [wild] wilderness,
And over the <u>hushed</u> [silent] carpet, <u>silent,</u> [hushing] stept,
And 'tween the <u>curtains</u> [Curtains] peeped, <u>where,</u> [and] lo! —
  how fast she slept.

Stanza 25: What in the fragment becomes extended in the following stanza and to what effect? In other words, by abandoning the moon imagery and the picture of Madeline in stanza 24, Keats allows himself working room in stanza 25. Elaborate. The minor changes in line 7 create an interesting effect. Discuss.

Stanza 26: Earlier Keats began this delicate and mildly erotic passage with "she lays aside her veil," but we have nowhere seen her veil and the poet is sure not to introduce extraneous detail where none is

needed. So the stanza proceeds with the many starts and stops record-
ed above, indicating the complexity of the poetic process.

Line 4 went through painful workings:

> Loosens her bursting, her boddice from her
> her boddice lace string
> her boddice and her bosom bare
> her

The poet leaves off with an unfinished line. Later he writes:
"Loosens her fragrant bodice and doth bare/Her ..." but gets no fur-
ther. He begins again moving toward the final vision: "Loosens her
fragrant boddice: and down slips/Her sweet attire." For the further
alteration of these lines view the stanza. Can you account for these
revisions?

Stanza 27: Earlier the stanza began: "The charm fled not—she did not
look behind;/Soon trembling ...." Why do you think the poet deleted
this opening in favor of the less transitional line?

Stanza 28: Originally line 7 read: "Silent as Fear, and ? not with." Dis-
cuss the elaboration of this figure of speech, the simile of fear. The
question mark indicates Keats at work.

29

> Then [on] by the bed-side, where the faded <u>moon</u> [Moon]
> Made a <u>dim, silver</u> [an illumed] twilight, soft he set
> A table, <u>and, half anguished, threw thereon</u> [and with anguish
>   spread thereon]
> A <u>cloth</u> [Cloth] of woven crimson, gold, and jet:—
> O for some drowsy <u>Morphean</u> [morphean] amulet!
> The boisterous, midnight, festive clarion, [of the <u>Ball</u> [feast]]
> [Sounded though faint and far away]
> <u>The kettle-drum</u> [And kettle-drums] and far-heard clarinet,
> <u>Affray his</u> [Reach'd his scar'd] ears, though but <u>in dying</u> [with
>   faintest] tone:—
> The <u>hall</u> [Hall] door shuts again, and all the noise <u>is</u> [was] gone.

30

And [But] still she slept an azure-lidded sleep,
In blanchéd linen, smooth, and lavendered,
While he from forth the closet brought a heap
Of candied apple, quince, [fruits/sweets] and plum, and gourd;
With jellies soother than the creamy [dairy] curd,
And lucent syrups, tinct [smooth] with cinnamon;
[And sugar'd dates from that o'er Euphrates fard]
Manna and dates, in argosy [Brigantine] transferred
From Fez; and spicéd dainties, every one,
From silken [wealthy] [glutted] Samarcand to cedared Lebanon.
    [Lebanon]

31

These delicates he heaped with glowing hand
On golden dishes [salvers] and in baskets bright
Of wreathéd [twisted] silver: sumptuous they stand
In the retired quiet of the night,
Filling the chilly room with perfume light.—
"And now, my love [And now saith he], my seraph fair, awake!
Thou art my heaven, and I thine eremite:
Open thine eyes, for meek St. Agnes' sake,
Or I shall drowse beside thee, so my soul doth ache."

32

Thus whispering, his warm, unnervéd arm [s]
Sank in her pillow. Shaded was her dream [sleep] [dreams]
By the dusk curtains: 'twas a midnight charm [dreamless of
     alarms]
Impossible to melt as icéd stream:
The lustrous salvers in the moonlight gleam;
Broad golden fringe upon the carpet lies: [lies wealthy on the F]
It seemed he never, never could [can] redeem
From such a stedfast spell his lady's eyes;
So mused awhile, entoiled in wooféd phantasies.

Stanza 29: Line 3 originally read: "A table light, and stilly threw there-on." Discuss this line. Discuss Keats' handling of tense in this stanza. What has the question of tense to do with poetic values?

Stanza 30: Here we can observe the poet working with individual words to create the sensual effect of the feast. Discuss his choices.

Stanza 31: Line 4 earlier began: "Amid the quiet of St. Agnes' night,/And now saith he my seraph." This would have begun the action of the stanza two lines earlier. What is the nature of the delay here? Is this a delay the structure of the stanza seems to determine? Discuss the deleted phrase in line 6.

Stanza 32: Discuss the shift in rhythm and tense in the stanza.

33

Awakening up, he took her hollow lute—
Tumultuous,—and, in chords that tenderest be,
He played an ancient ditty, long since mute,
In Provence called, "La belle dame sans merci:"
Close to her ear touching [beheld] the melody;
Wherewith disturbed, she utter'd a soft moan:
He ceased—she panted quick [her breathing ceas'd]—and
        suddenly
Her blue affrayéd [half-frayed] eyes wide open shone:
Upon his knees he sank, pale as smooth-sculptured stone.

34

Her eyes were open, but she still beheld,
Now wide awake, the vision of her sleep:
There was a [some] painful change, that nigh expelled
The blisses of her dream so pure and deep
At which fair Madeline began to weep,
And moan forth witless [little] words with many a sigh;
While still her gaze on Porphyro would keep;
Who knelt, with joinéd hands and piteous eye, [with an aching
        brow]
Fearing to move or speak, she looked so dreamingly.

35

"Ah. Porphyro!" said she, "but even now
Thy voice was at sweet tremble in [by] mine ear,
Made tuneable with every sweetest vow;
And those sad [thy kind] eyes were spiritual and clear:
How changed thou art! how pallid, chill, and drear!
Give me that voice again, my Porphyro,
Those looks immortal, those complainings dear!
Oh, leave me not in this eternal woe,
For if thou diest, my Love, I know not where to go."

36

Beyond a mortal man impassioned far
At these voluptuous accents [words], he arose,
Ethereal, flushed, and like a throbbing star
Seen mid the sapphire heaven's deep repose;
Into her dream he melted, as the rose
Blendeth its odor [her/its perfume] with the violet,—
Solution sweet: meantime the frost wind blows
Like Love's alarum pattering the sharp sleet
Against the window panes [casement gloom]; St. Agnes' moon
      hath set.

Stanza 33: Discuss the change in line 7.

Stanza 34: "Little" in line 6 may be more interesting than "witless." Discuss.

Stanza 36: The action of the poem is now mounting to its climax. The poet begins with a false start: "Impassion'd far beyond a mortal man." Line 5 was a struggle: "With her bright dream he …" and then: "In her bright dream he…" "Window dark" was an earlier possibility for the final line. Comment.

37

'Tis dark: quick [still] pattereth the flaw-blown sleet.
"This is no dream, my bride, my Madeline!"

'Tis dark: the iced gusts still rave and beat:
"No dream, alas! alas! and woe is mine!
Porphyro will leave me here to fade and pine. [Ah] Cruel! what
       traitor could thee hither bring? I curse not, for my
       heart is lost in thine,
Though thou forsakest a deceivéd thing;—
A dove forlorn and lost [A silent mateless dove] with sick
       unprunéd wing."

38

"My Madeline! sweet dreamer! lovely bride!
Say, may I be for aye thy vassal blest?
Thy beauty's shield, heart-shaped and vermeil-dyed?
Ah, silver shrine, here [by thee] will I take my rest
After so many hours of toil and quest,
A famished pilgrim,—saved by miracle.
Though I have found, I will not [cannot] rob thy nest,
Saving of thy sweet self; if thou think'st well
To trust, fair Madeline, to no rude infidel.

39

"Hark! 'tis an elfin-storm from faery land,
Of haggard seeming, but a boon indeed: [my love, to us]
Arise—arise [my love]! the morning is at hand;—
The bloated wassailers will never heed,—
Let us away, my love, with happy speed;
There are no ears to hear, or eyes to see,—
Drowned all in Rhenish and the sleepy [drench of] mead:
Awake! arise! my love, and fearless be,
For o'er the southern moors I have a home for thee."

40

She hurried at his words, beset with fears,
For there were sleeping dragons all around, [About]
At glaring watch, perhaps [Or perhaps at glaring ...], with
       ready spears—
[well] Down the wide stairs a darkling way they found;
In all the house was heard no [not a] human sound.

A chain-drooped lamp was flickering <u>by each door</u>; [here and
    there]
The arras, <u>rich</u> [flutterd] with horseman, hawk, and hound,
Fluttered <u>in the besieging</u> [with cold] wind's uproar;
And the long carpets rose along the gusty floor.

Stanza 37: Line 8 was at one time conceived as line 9, the longer
Alexandrine: "Though thou should'st leave forsaken a deceived
thing." Ridley offers "wind" for "wing." What special purpose does
the longer line have in each stanza? Take up the question of the
Alexandrine in the context of this stanza.

Stanza 38: This stanza was to open: "My Madeline! The Dark is this
wintry night." Rather, it begins with an impassioned apostrophe
(address) to the heroine. Is there any need for the natural description
the deleted line begins to offer?

Line 6 has a complicated evolution: "With tearful features pale and
mournful Pilgrim's weeds." This line is one foot too long. Then it goes
through: "Pale featured and in mournful Pilgrims' weeds" to: "Pale
featured and in weeds of Pilgrimage."

Stanza 39: It is interesting that after line 5 Keats was about to introduce
a definite setting. He deleted "over the moors ..." What would this
early introduction produce in the stanza? The last two lines earlier
read: "Put on warm clouthing sweet, and fearless be/Over the bleak
Dartmoor I have a home for thee." There is a directness, a naturalness
of diction to the "put on warm clothing ..." that is omitted in the
final version. What different effects does such a change in language
produce? Is there an advantage to the less localized final reading?

Stanza 40: Line 6 went through many attempts before the final vision.
The simple ideas fixed in this vision established themselves:

> The Lamps were flickering death shades on the walls
> Without, the tempest kept a bellow roar
> The Lamps were flickering
> The Lamps were dying in
> But here and there a Lamp was flickering out

Discuss.

41

They glide, like phantoms, into the wide hall;
Like phantoms, to the iron porch they glide,
Where <u>lay</u> [slept] the Porter, in uneasy sprawl,
With a <u>huge</u> [large] empty <u>flagon</u> [beaker] by his side:
The wakeful bloodhound rose, and shook his hide,
But his <u>sagacious</u> [unangered] eye an inmate owns:
By one, and one, the <u>bolts full easy slide</u>:—[easy bolts
　　　　backslide]
<u>The chains lie silent on the footworn stones;</u> [Across the
　　　　pavement lie the heavy chains]
The key turns, and the door upon its hinges groans.

42

And they are gone: aye, ages long ago
These lovers fled <u>away into the storm</u>. [into a night of storms]
That night the Baron dreamt of many a woe,
And all his warrior-guests with <u>shade</u> [shades] and <u>form</u> [forms]
Of witch, and demon, and large coffin-worm,
Were long be-nightmared. Angela the old
Died palsy-twitched, with meagre face deform;
The Beadsman, after thousand aves told,
For aye unsought-for slept among his ashes cold.

Stanza 41: The stanza began "Like Spirits into the wide-paven hall/They glide, and to the iron porch in haste." In the final version Keats has created a repetition of the central verb. Beginning the stanza with this verb also heightens the movement of action.

Line 6 was originally: "And paced round Madeline all angerless." Discuss the evolution of this line and its changed effect.

Stanza 42: Discuss the difficulties with the word "night" in lines 2 and 3.

Notes

1. Ian Jacks, English Literature, 1815-1832: Scott, Byron and Keats. Vol 12: Oxford History of English Literature (Oxford: Oxford University Press, 1990).
2. M.R. Ridley, Keats' Craftsmanship: A Study in Poetic Development (New York: Russell & Russell, 1962).
3. A variant for line 2 reads: "Her anxious mouth full pulpd with rosy thoughts—"

MISCELLANY OF POETS

THIS LAST CHAPTER DIFFERS FROM THE PRECEDING ONES IN two ways. First, rather than containing the poetry of one major poet, it presents a variety of poets, including several contemporary poets, with a few examples of their work. Second, the reader will find here two or more versions of a poem and will proceed with his or her own comparative analysis, instead of being prompted by our comments and questions. At this point, the questioning method should be part of the reader's instinctive approach to poetry. Asking questions about specific changes is a good first step into larger questions and perceptions about poetry in general.

In no case are the poems offered here intended to represent what could be called the epitome of full achievement. These selections were not meant to be representative, but rather they were chosen for their utility in studying poetic revision.

WILLIAM SHAKESPEARE

1564-1616

THE *Sonnets* of William Shakespeare were published in 1609. The B version presented here is from that publication and the one most likely taken from Shakespeare's own manuscript. Alterations in punctuation and spelling came in a later edition. The "corrected" version, in this case the A version, is the one most readers have read and taken as the final form. Ultimately, the reader should not be overly concerned with which version comes closer to Shakespeare's original (the 1609 edition may have contained errors, and Shakespeare was not likely to have seen the proofs). The reader should, however, find it interesting to compare punctuation and spelling in terms of the total effect on the poem.

Th' expence of Spirit in a waste of shame
Is lust in action, and till action, lust
Is perjurd, murdrous, blouddy full of blame,
Sauage, extreame, rude, cruell, not to trust,
Inioyd no sooner but dispised straight,   5
Past reason hunted, and sooner had
Past reason hated as a swallowed bayt,
On purpose layd to make the taker mad.
Made In pursut and in possession so,
Had, hauing, and in quest, to haue extreame,   10
A blisses in proofe and proud and very wo,
Before a ioy proposed behind a dreame,
    All this the world well knowes yet none knowes well,
    To shun the heauen that leads men to this hell.

Sonnet 129

Th' expense of Spirit in a waste of shame
Is lust in action; and till action, lust
Is perjured, murderous, bloody, full of blame,
Savage, extreme, rude, cruel, not to trust;
Enjoy'd no sooner but despised straight;   5
Past reason hunted; and, no sooner had,
Past reason hated, as a swallow'd bait
On purpose laid to make the taker mad:
Mad in pursuit, and in possession so;
Had, having, and in quest to have, extreme;   10
A bliss in proof, and proved, a very woe;
Before, a joy proposed; behind, a dream.
    All this the world well knows; yet none knows well
    To shun the heaven that leads men to this hell.

MATTHEW ARNOLD

1822–1888

MATTHEW ARNOLD IS CONSIDERED ONE OF THE outstanding literary and social critics of the Victorian period in England. While his name may rank behind the two major Victorian poets, Browning and Tennyson, his achievement as a poet is certainly considerable. "Philomela" and "Dover Beach" number among the most anthologized of English poems. "Quiet Work" is an example of Arnold's earlier poetry.

Arnold published his first book of poems at the age of 26, and by the time he was 32, three volumes later, he was mostly finished writing poetry and was turning to prose criticism. Through his criticism he was to achieve the status of guide to his age. This quality of guide or sage is also present in the poetry.

B

y version

Quiet Work

Two lessons, Nature, let me learn of thee,
Two lessons that in every wind are blown;
Two blending duties, harmonis'd in one,
Though the loud world proclaim their enmity—

Of toil unsever'd from tranquility!   5
Of labour, that in one short hour outgrows
Man's noisy schemes, accomplish'd in repose,
Too great for haste, too high for rivalry!

Yes, while on earth a thousand discords ring,
Man's weak complainings mingling with his toil,   10
Still do thy sleepless ministers move on,
Their glorious course in silence perfecting;
Still working, chiding still our vain turmoil,
Labourers that shall not fail, when man is gone.

Additional alternatives:

1.3: two duties serv'd in one/kept in one [at one]

1.6: that in still advance outgrows/that in fruit by far outgoes [by far outgrows] [in lasting fruit outgrows]

1.7: Man's noisy feats [work]

1.10: Man's senseless uproar/Our senseless uproar mingling with our toil,/Man's senseless uproar mingling with his toil,

1.11: quiet ministers

A   *Quiet Work*

Final version
One lesson, Nature, let me learn of thee,
One lesson which in every wind is blown,
One lesson of two duties kept at one
Though the loud world proclaim their enmity—

Of toil unsever'd from tranquility!   5
Of labour, that in lasting fruit outgrows
Far noisier schemes, accomplish'd in repose,
Too great for haste, too high for rivalry!

Yes, while on earth a thousand discords ring
Man's fitful uproar mingling with his toil,   10
Still do thy sleepless ministers move on,
Their glorious tasks in silence perfecting;
Still working, blaming still our vain turmoil,
Labourers that shall not fail, when man is gone.

B   *Philomela*

Early version
Hark! ah, the nightingale—
The inken throated!
Hast thou not yet, poor bird
Been help'd by slipping years
At least to half forgetfulness   5

Of that old pain.
Can change of scene, and night,
And moonlight, & the dew,
And these frail acacia [blanch'd song-stirr'd] boughs
Thro whose frail [light] leaves, & showers   10
Of blossom'd clusters pale,
Thy voice in [by] gushes comes,
To thy torn heart and brain
Afford no balm?
Dost thou still behold   15
Here, through the moonlight on this English grass,
The unfriendly palace in the Thracian wild?
Dost thou still peruse
In the white acacia flowers
With hot cheeks and sear'd eyes   20
The too clear web, and thy dumb sister's shame?
Dost thou still reach
Thy husband, weak avenger, thro thyself?
Dost thou once more assay
Thy flight, and feel come over thee,   25
Poor fugitive, the feathery change
Once more, and once more seem to make resound
With love and hate, triumph and agony,
Lone Daulis, and the high Cephissian vale?
Hark, hark, Eugenia!   30
How thick the bursts come crowding through the leaves!
Once more—thou hearest?
Eternal passion!
Eternal pain!

A   *Philomela*

Final   Hark, ah, the nightingale—
version   The tawny-throated!
               Hark, from that moonlit cedar what a burst!
               What triumph! hark!—what pain!

               O wanderer from a Grecian shore,   5
               Still, after many years, in distant lands,
               Still nourishing in thy bewilder'd brain

That wild, unquench'd, deep-sunken, old-world pain—
Say, will it never heal?
And can this fragrant lawn   10
With its cool trees, and night,
And the sweet, tranquil Thames,
And moonshine, and the dew,
To thy rack'd heart and brain
Afford no balm?   15
Dost thou to-night behold,
Here, through the moonlight on this English grass,
The unfriendly palace in the Thracian wild?
Dost thou again peruse
With hot cheeks and sear'd eyes   20
The too clear web, and thy dumb sister's shame?
Dost thou once more assay
Thy flight, and feel come over thee,
Poor fugitive, the feathery change
Once more, and once more seem to make resound   25
With love and hate, triumph and agony,
Lone Daulis, and the high Cephissian vale?
Listen, Eugenia—
How thick the bursts come crowding through the leaves!
Again—thou hearest?   30
Eternal passion!

Eternal pain!

<table>
<tr><td>

A

</td><td>

Dover Beach

</td></tr>
</table>

Final
version
with
variants in
brackets

The sea is calm to-night.
The tide is full, the moon lies fair
Upon the straits;—on the French coast the light
Gleams [Shines] and is gone; the cliffs of England stand,
Glimmering and vast, out in the tranquil bay.   5
Come to the window, sweet [hush'd] is the night-air!
Only, from the long line of spray
Where the sea [ebb] meets the moon-blanch'd land,
Listen! you hear the grating roar
Of pebbles which the waves draw [suck] back, and fling,   10
At their return, up the high [steep/barr'd] strand,

Begin, and cease, [Cease and begin] and then again begin,
With tremulous [regular/mournful] cadence slow, and bring
The eternal note of sadness in.

Sophocles long ago   15
Heard it on the Aegean, and it brought
Into his mind the turbid [troubled] ebb and flow
Of human misery; we
Find also in the sound a thought,
Hearing it by this distant northern sea.   20

The Sea of Faith
Was once, too, at the full, and round earth's shore
Lay like the folds of a bright girdle [garment] furl'd.
But now I [we] only hear
Its melancholy, long, withdrawing roar,   25
Retreating, to the breath
Of the night-wind, down the vast edges drear
And naked shingles of the world.

Ah, love, let us be true
To one another! for the world, which seems   30
To lie before us like a land of dreams,
So various, so beautiful, so new,
Hath really neither joy, nor love, nor light,
Nor certitude, nor peace, nor help for pain;
And we are here as on a darkling plain   35
Swept with confused alarms of struggle and flight, [fight]
Where ignorant armies clash by night.

GERARD MANLEY HOPKINS

1844–1889

G ERARD MANLEY HOPKINS WAS A POET AND JESUIT priest. His poetry is charged with a religious, indeed, a mystical fervor. His ideas and feelings about the new kind of poetry he was writing in the 1870s and 1880s are recorded in his correspondence with his friend, and later his literary editor, Robert Bridges.

C

The Windhover[1]

Early
version

I caught this morning morning's minion, king
   Of daylight's dauphin, dapple-dawn-drawn Fal-
      con—he was riding
      [con, riding]
      [Rolling]
      Rolling level underneath him steady air, and striding
      Hung
      [:Hung]
[He hung] so and rung the rein of a wimpled wing
In an ecstacy; then off,: forth on swing,
   -As a skate's heel sweeps smooth on a bow
      -bend: the hurl and gliding
[Rebuffed the big : wind. My heart]
    in
    Rebuffed the big : wind. My heart in hiding
: Stirred for a bird—for the master of the thing!

Brute beauty and valour and act, O air, pride, plume,
   here
   Buckle! And the fire that breaks from thee then, a billion
[Times to]
: Times told lovelier, more dangerous, O my chevalier!

No wonder of it : sheer : plod makes plough down sillion
      : Shine, and blue-bleak embers, ah, my dear,
Fall, gall themselves, and gash : gold-vermilion.

<table>
<tr><td>B</td><td>I caught this morning morning's minion, king</td></tr>
</table>

B

*Later
version*

I caught this morning morning's minion, king
    Of daylight's dauphin, dapple-dawn-drawn Falcon,
        in his riding
    Of the rolling level underneath him steady air, and
striding :
O how he rung upon the rein of a wimpling wing
In his ecstacy! then off, : forth on swing,
    As a skate's heel sweeps smooth on a bow-bend:
        the hurl and gliding
    Rebuffed the big : wind. My heart in hiding
: Stirred for a bird—for the mastery of the thing!

A

*Final
version*

The Windhover:

I caught this morning morning's minion, king-
    dom of daylight's dauphin, dapple-dawn-drawn Falcon, in
        his riding
    Of the rolling level underneath him steady air, and striding
High there, how he rung upon the rein of a wimpling wing   5
In his ecstacy! then off, off forth on swing,
    As a skate's heel sweeps smooth on a bow-bend: the hurl
        and gliding
    Rebuffed the big wind. My heart in hiding
Stirred for a bird,—the achieve of, the mastery of the thing!

Brute beauty and valour and act, oh, air, pride, plume here   10
    Buckle! AND the fire that breaks from thee then, a billion
Times told lovelier, more dangerous, O my chevalier!

No wonder of it: shéer plód makes plough down sillion,
Shine, and blue-bleak embers, ah my dear,
    Fall, gall themselves, and gash gold-vermilion.

Note

1. A prose note by Hopkins read, "Sprung [Falling] paeonic rhythm,
sprung and outriding."

D.H. LAWRENCE

1885-1930

ALTHOUGH D.H. LAWRENCE'S REPUTATION RESTS ON his fiction more than on his poetry, the two are essentially related. He was a revolutionary artist and a moralist, who applied the teachings of Freud, among other influences, to literary works of art. In both his fiction and his poetry, Lawrence was championing a moral program which would, if put into action, cure an age of diseases almost too terrible to define.

The poem "Man's Image" is a good example of how Lawrence often uses poetry to develop a doctrine. "Bavarian Gentians," a truly fine poem, not marred by Lawrence's urge to convert his readers to his own moral system—as are many of his poems—contains much of the best he was able to achieve. Here the flowers are clearly symbolic and the speaker in the poem can easily be seen as a hero who is able to transcend the world of petty and corrupt values and merge with natural forces.

B   *Renaissance*

[*Renascence*]   We have bit no forbidden apple—
                 Eve and me—
                 Yet the splashes of day and night
                 Falling round us no longer dapple
                 The same Eden with purple and white.   5

                 This our own still valley
                 My Eden, my home
                 But the day shows it vivid with feeling
                 And the pallor of night does not tally
                 With the dark sleep that once covered the ceiling.   10

                 My little red heifer—go and look at her eyes—
                 She will calve tomorrow—

Take the lantern, and watch the Sow, for fear she grab her
    new litter
With red snarling jaws; let yourself listen to the cries   15
Of the new-born, and the unborn; and the old owl and the
    bats as they flitter
And wake to the sound of the woodpigeons, and lie and listen
Till you can borrow
A few quick beats of a woodpigeon's heart—then rise   20
See the morning sun on the shaken iris glisten
And say that this home, this valley is wider than Paradise.

I have learned it all from my Eve,
This warm dumb wisdom,
She's a finer instructor than years,
She has shown me the strands that weave
Us all one in laughter and tears.   25

I didn't learn it from her speech—
Staggering words:
I can't tell how it comes
But I think the kisses reach
Down where the live web hums.   30

A   *Renascence*

We have bit no forbidden apple,
    Eve and I,
Yet the splashes of day and night
Falling round us, no longer dapple
The same valley with purple and white.   5
This is our own still valley,
    Our Eden, our home;
But day shows it vivid with feeling,
And the pallor of night does not tally
With dark sleep that once covered the ceiling.   10

The little red heifer: tonight I looked in her eyes;
    She will calve tomorrow.
Last night, when I went with the lantern, the sow was
    grabbing her litter

With snarling red jaws; and I heard the cries
Of the new-born, and then, the old owl, then the bats that
      flitter.   15

And I woke to the sound of the wood-pigeon and lay and
      listened
  Till I could borrow
A few quick beats from a wood-pigeon's heart; and when I
      did rise
Saw where morning sun on the shaken iris glistened.
And I knew that home, this valley, was wider than Paradise.   20

I learned it all from my Eve,
  The warm, dumb wisdom;
She's a quicker instructress than years;
She has quickened my pulse to receive
Strange throbs, beyond laughter and tears.   25

So now I know the valley
  Fleshed all like me
With feelings that change and quiver
And clash, and yet seem to tally,
Like all the clash of a river   30
  Moves on to the sea.

C   *Violets for the Dead*

[*Violets*]   "Did yer notice that lass, sister, as stood away back
By a head-stone?"—
"Nay, I saw nöwt but th' coffin, an' th' yeller clay, an' 'ow
      th' black
Was blown"—

While th' parson was prayin', I watches 'er, an' she wor fair
      shaken   5
To bits"—
"I could think o' nöwt but our Ted, an' 'im taken
In his wild fits."—

"When you'd gone, I slipped back, ter see who she might be—
Poor thing"—   10
"No good, I warrant; this trouble is such as she
Helped to bring."

"You should 'a seen her slive up when we'd go
You should 'a seen her kneel an' look down.
I couldna' see her face, but her little neck shone   15
White, when the wind shifted her hair; that was soft and
          brown,

—An' 'er body fair shook again
Wi' little sobs as you scarce could hear
An' she undid 'er jacket neck, an' then
A lot o' violets fell out of er bosom on 'im down theer.   20

"They was wild ones, white and blue;—I could tell
Because they was warm, an' the wind blew
Us a little wift, an' I knew the smell
Then she rummaged her hand in 'er bosom, an' kissed the last
          little few.

"I come away, for fear she should see   25
Me watchin'. Dost think there was öwt between 'em?
Tha knows 'e'd a winsome way wi 'im, an' she
Was th' little, lovin' sort, as 'as nöwt ter screen 'em."

B   *Violets*

Sister, tha knows while we was on the planks
     Aside o' th' grave, while th' coffin wor lyin' yet
On th' yaller clay, an' th' white flowers top of it
     Tryin' to keep off'n him a bit o' th' wet,

An' parson makin' haste, an' a' the black   5
     Huddlin' close together a cause o' th' rain,
Did t' appen ter notice a bit of a lass away back
     By a head-stun, sobbin' an' sobbin' again?

—How should I be lookin' round
    An' me standin' on the plank
Beside the open ground,
    Where our Ted 'ud soon be sank? 10

Yi, an' 'im that young,
    Snapped sudden out of all
His wickedness, among 15
    Pals worse n'r ony name as you could call.

Let be that; there's some o' th' bad as we
    Like better nor all your good, an' 'e was one.
—An' cos I liked him best, yi, bett'r nor thee,
    I canna bide to think where he is gone. 20

Ah know tha liked 'im bett'r nor me. But let
    Me tell thee about this lass. When you had gone
Ah stopped behind on t' pad i' th' drippin wet
    An' watched what 'er 'ad on.

Tha should ha' seed her slive up when we'd gone, 25
    Tha should ha' seed her kneel an' look in
At th' sloppy wet grave—an' 'er little neck shone
    That white, an' 'er shook that much, I'd like to begin

Scraïghtin' my-sen as well. 'En undid her black
    Jacket at th' bosom, an' took from out of it 30
Over a double 'andful of violets, all in a pack
    Ravelled blue and white—warm, for a bit

O' th' smell come waftin' to me. 'Er put 'er face
    Right intil 'em and scraïghted out again,
Then after a bit 'er dropped 'em down that place, 35
    An' I come away, because o' the teemin' rain.

A

Violets

Sister, tha knows while we was on th' planks
        Aside o' t' grave, an' th' coffin set
On th' yaller clay, wi' th' white flowers top of it
        Waitin' ter be buried out o' th' wet?

An' t' parson makin' haste, an' a' t' black   5
        Huddlin' up i' t' rain,
Did t' 'appen ter notice a bit of a lass way back
        Hoverin', lookin' poor an' plain?

        —How should I be lookin' round!
                An' me standin' there on th' plank,   10
        An' our Ted's coffin set on th' ground,
                Waitin' to be sank!

        I'd as much as I could do, to think
                Of 'im bein' gone
        That young, an' a' the fault of drink   15
                An' carryin's on!—

Let that be; 'appen it worna th' drink, neither,
Nor th' carryin' on as killed 'im.
                        —No, 'appen not,
My sirs! But I say 'twas! For a blither
Lad never stepped, till 'e got in with your lot—   20

All right, all right, it's my fault! But let
Me tell about that lass. When you'd all gone
Ah stopped behind on t' pad, i' t' pourin' wet
An' watched what 'er 'ad on.

Tha should ha' seed 'er slive up when yer'd gone!   25
Tha should ha' seed 'er kneel an' look in
At th' sloppy grave! an' er' little neck shone
That white, an' 'er cried that much, I'd like to begin

Scraïghtin' mysen as well. 'Er undid 'er black
Jacket at th' bosom, an' took out   30

Over a double 'andful o' violets, a' in a pack
An' white an' blue in a ravel, like a clout.

An' warm, for th' smell come waftin' to me. 'Er put 'er face
Right in 'em, an' scraïghted a bit again,
Then after a bit 'er dropped 'em down that place,   35
An' I come away, acause o' th' teemin' rain.

But I thowt ter mysen, as that wor th' only bit
O' warmth as 'e got down theer; th' rest wor stone cold.
From that bit of a wench's bosom; 'e'd be glad of it,
Gladder nor of thy lilies, if tha maun be told.   40

B   *The Piano*

Somewhere beneath that piano's superb sleek black
Must hide my mother's piano, little and brown, with the back
That stood close to the wall, and the front's faded silk both torn,
And the keys with little hollows, that my mother's fingers had worn.

Softly, in the shadows, a woman is singing to me   5
Quietly, through the years I have crept back to see
A child sitting under the piano, in the boom of the shaking strings
Pressing the little poised feet of the mother who smiles as she sings.

The full throated woman has chosen a winning, living song
And surely the heart that is in me must belong   10
To the old Sunday evenings, when darkness wandered outside
And hymns gleamed on our warm lips, as we watched mother's
        fingers glide.

Or this is my sister at home in the old front room
Singing love's first surprised gladness, alone in the gloom.
She will start when she sees me, and blushing, spread out her hands 15
To cover my mouth's raillery, till I'm bound in her shame's heart-
        spun bands

A woman is singing me a wild Hungarian air
And her arms, and her bosom, and the whole of her soul is bare,
And the great black piano is clamouring as my mother's never could
        clamour

And my mother's tunes are devoured of this music's ravaging
     glamour.   20

A   *The Piano*

Softly, in the dusk, a woman is singing to me;
Taking me back down the vista of years, till I see
A child sitting under the piano, in the boom of the tingling strings
And pressing the small, poised feet of a mother who smiles as   5
     she sings.

In spite of myself, the insidious mastery of song
Betrays me back, till the heart of me weeps to belong
To the old Sunday evenings at home, with winter outside
And hymns in the cosy parlour, the tinkling piano our guide.   10

So now it is vain for the singer to burst into clamour
With the great black piano appassionato. The glamour
Of childish days is upon me, my manhood is cast
Down in the flood of remembrance, I weep like a child for the past.

C   *Morality*

[*Man's*   What a pity, when a man looks at himself in the glass
Image]   He doesn't bark at it, like a dog does,
           Or fluff up in indignant fury, like a cat!
           What a pity he takes himself seriously, and draws a moral lesson.

                           Morality

B
      Man alone is immoral
      Neither beasts nor flowers are.

      Because man, poor beast, can look at himself   5
      And know himself in the glass.

      He doesn't bark at himself, as a dog does
      When he looks at himself in the glass.
      He takes himself seriously.

It would be so much nicer if he just barked at himself
Or fluffed up rather angry, as a cat does,
Then turned away and forgot.   10

A   *Man's Image*

What a pity, when a man looks at himself in a glass
he doesn't bark at himself, like a dog does,
or fluff up in indignant fury, like a cat!

What a pity he sees himself so wonderful,
a little lower than the angels!   5
and so interesting!

D   *Glory of Darkness*

[*Bavarian   Blue and dark
Gentians*]   Oh Bavarian gentians, tall ones
                  make a dark-blue gloom
                  in the sunny room

                  They have added blueness to blueness, until   5
                  it is dark: beauty
                  blue joy of my soul
                  Bavarian gentians
                  your dark gloom is so noble!

                  How deep I have gone   10
                  dark gentians
                  since I embarked on your dark blue fringes
                  how deep, how deep, how happy!
                  What a journey for my soul
                  in the dark blue gloom   15
                  of gentians here in the sunny room!

C   *Glory of Darkness*

                               ....

                  it is dark
                  and the door is open
                  to the depths

it is so blue, it is so dark
in the dark doorway   5
and the way is open
to Hades.

Oh, I know—
Persephone has just gone back
down the thickening thickening gloom   10
of dark-blue gentians to Pluto
to her bridegroom in the dark
and all the dead
and all the dark great ones of the underworld
down there, down there   15
down the blue depths of mountain gentian flowers
cold, cold
are gathering to a wedding in the [winter] dark
down the dark blue path

What a dark-blue gloom   20
of gentians here in the sunny room!

B   *Bavarian Gentians*

Not every man has gentians in his house
In soft September, at slow, sad Michaelmas.
Bavarian gentians, tall and dark, but dark
darkening the daytime torch-like with the smoking blueness
        of Pluto's gloom,
ribbed hellish flowers erect, with their blaze of darkness
        spread blue,   5
blown flat into points, by the heavy white draught of the day.

Torch-flowers of the blue-smoking darkness, Pluto's dark-blue
        blaze
black lamps from the halls of Dis, smoking dark blue
giving off darkness, blue darkness, upon Demeter's yellow-
        pale day
whom have you come for, here in the white-cast day?   10

Reach me a gentian, give me a torch!

let me guide myself with the blue, forked torch of a flower
down the darker and darker stairs, where blue is darkened on
       blueness
down the way Persephone goes, just now, in first-frosted
       September.
to the sightless realm where darkness is married to dark   15
and Persephone herself is but a voice, as a bride,
a gloom invisible enfolded in the deeper dark
of the arms of Pluto as he ravishes her once again
and pierces her once more with his passion of the utter dark
among the splendour of black-blue torches, shedding fathom-
      less darkness on the nuptials.   20

Give me a flower on a tall stem, and three dark flames,
for I will go to the wedding, and be wedding-guest
   at the marriage of the living dark.

A   *Bavarian Gentians*

Not every man has gentians in his house
in Soft September, at slow, sad Michaelmas.

Bavarian gentians, big and dark, only dark
darkening the day-time, torch-like with the smoking blueness
       of Pluto's gloom,
ribbed and torch-like, with their blaze of darkness spread
       blue   5
down flattening into points, flattened under the sweep of
       white day
torch-flower of the blue-smoking darkness, Pluto's dark-blue
       daze,
black lamps from the halls of Dis, burning dark blue,
giving off darkness, blue darkness, as Demeter's pale lamps
       give off light,
lead me then, lead the way.   10

Reach me a gentian, give me a torch!
let me guide myself with the blue, forked torch of this flower
down the darker and darker stairs, where blue is darkened on
       blueness

even where Persephone goes, just now, from the frosted Sep-
    tember
to the sightless realm where darkness is awake upon the
    dark   15
and Persephone herself is but a voice
or a darkness invisible enfolded in the deeper dark
of the arms Plutonic, and pierced with the passion of dense
    gloom,
among the splendour of torches of darkness, shedding dark-
    ness on the lost bride and her groom.

MARIANNE MOORE

1887–1972

I N 1967, WHEN MARIANNE MOORE, THE GRANDE DAME OF
American poetry, issued a new edition of her *Complete Poems*, the
famous poem "Poetry" received a startling revision. For reasons
unknown to the reader, the poet decided to write a new poem
out of her old one. Though this final version contains the very lan-
guage of the 1921 poem, and represents its tone and point of view, a
totally new experience is received as a result her new concision—a
dramatic amputation. Here it is hardly a matter of which poem is bet-
ter or pleases most; we must accept each version as a separate expres-
sion or perception. One may question the value of the material left
out and the many reasons that may have prompted Moore to recreate
her poem. Also, we cannot rule out a "sense of play." After all, this is
at the heart of the earlier poem in the first place.

Final
version in
the   *Poetry*
Complete
Poems   I, too, dislike it: there are things that are important beyond
                 all this fiddle.
          Reading it, however, with a perfect contempt for it, one
          discovers in it after all, a place for the genuine.
                 Hands that can grasp, eyes
                    that can dilate, hair that can rise   5
                       if it must, these things are important not be-
                       cause a

          high-sounding interpretation can be put upon them but be-
          cause they are
                 useful. When they become so derivative as to become un-
                 intelligible, the same thing may be said for all of us, that
                 we
                    do not admire what   10
                    we cannot understand: the bat

holding on upside down or in quest of some-
    thing to

eat, elephants pushing, a wild horse taking a roll, a tireless
wolf under
    a tree, the immovable critic twitching his skin like a horse
    that feels a flea, the base-
    ball fan, the statistician—   15
          nor is it valid
          to discriminate against "business documents and

school-books"; all these phenomena are important. One must
make a distinction
    however: when dragged into prominence by half poets,
    the result is not poetry,
    nor till the poets among us can be   20
          "literalists of
          the imagination"—above
          insolence and triviality and can present

for inspection, "imaginary gardens with real toads in them,"
shall we have
    it. In the meantime, if you demand on the one hand,   25
    the raw material of poetry in
          all its rawness and
          that which is on the other hand
              genuine, you are interested in poetry.

Collected Poems, 1963

Final
version   *Poetry*

I, too, dislike it.
    Reading it, however, with a perfect contempt for it, one dis-
    covers in
    it, after all, a place for the genuine.

The Complete Poems of Marianne Moore, 1967

JAMES EMANUEL

1921–

J AMES EMANUEL, THE FIFTH OF SEVEN CHILDREN, GREW UP IN the small prairie town of Alliance, Nebraska, where he worked odd jobs, was a cowboy and farm hand, but also showed promise as a student. As a young man he yearned for various horizons, and lived for periods in Washington, D.C., New York, London, Warsaw, and Paris. A dedicated poet, Emanuel is still prolific as both a writer and a presenter of his work in Europe, Africa, and the Middle East. In 1996 he received the Sidney Bechet Creative Award in Paris, which recognized his innovative jazz-and-blues haiku. Yet Emanuel, despite extensive traveling, appearances in anthologies, 13 books of poetry, and a reputation throughout Europe and especially France, his adopted country, is not widely known in his homeland. His long stay abroad, plus the long tradition of racism in America, accounts for this.

In 1984 he retired as professor of literature at City College in New York, having been hired in 1957 as the English Department's first African American professor. The title of his first book of poems, *The Treehouse and Other Poems, 1968,* was suggested by Langston Hughes, whom Emanuel came to know while working on his critical biography, *Langston Hughes.*[1] The next year he co-edited, with Theodore Gross, the seminal anthology *Dark Symphony: Negro Literature in America.*[2] Although he lives in Paris, he maintains voluminous correspondence with many writers and educators in America, and continues to publish books in the U.S., primarily with the two guardians of Black literature, Lotus Press and Broadside Press. In 1991 Lotus issued *Whole Grain: Collected Poems 1958-1989.* His most recent book of poems is *Jazz from the Haiku King.*

This last book is unique, for each poem is translated into one of six languages. These poems, like the ones printed here, evolved as an experiment in form. He has commented: "My 'breakaway haiku' in *Deadly James and Other Poems* (1987) had begun my experiments with the Japanese 3-line form, adhering to its 5-7-5 syllabic pattern, but widening its sensory impact beyond the capacity of the usual single impression. My haiku added the toughness of poverty and racial injustice,

Bill Clinton ~~jazz~~ haiku

idea for
haiku
series
65 bis...
Paris
[Clinton not
wild?]

plop:
Arkansas ~~swimming~~ hole
~~feel buddy~~ ~~hot line~~ [Clinton not
jogging suit
mud flat swimmin' hole tune/tone

Bill Clinton ~~jazz mute 98~~ [Cruiser of Jazz]

65 bis
9.10.97,
9:23 p.m. –
9:56

1. ~~Sax blows~~ ~~straight up~~
"Sax   smiles, blows straight up,
like sunflower yellow topped
by rainbows   ~~BEBOPPED~~ BEBOPPED.

2. Presidential ~~note~~:
~~what won't sink~~ all floating JAZZ, baby,
~~some sinks, some float~~ JAZZ, baby,
don't need no lifeboat.

I. Sax smiles, blows ~~sinks~~ STRAIGHT UP,
~~its~~ sunflower yellow   topped
by rainbows BEBOPPED.

II. ~~Presidential note~~:
The President — note
blows SINK, blows FLOAT. JAZZ, baby,
don't need no lifeboat.

II. Sax smiles, blows STRAIGHT UP,
its sunflower yellow   bent
to point where JAZZ went.

IV. The President's sax
blows SWIM, blows FLOAT. HIS jazz
don't need no lifeboat

Hotel ~~Adou~~
Anfa,
Casablanca
11.10.97,
7:a.   7:23
au verse →
III

Cruises of   Bill Clinton
Jazz series

III. White House playground: JAZZ,
~~teeter-totter time, expert~~
~~alone on teeter-totter —~~
~~a~~ one-seat teeter-totter
JAZZ has White House fun:
his one-seat teeter-totter,
HAPPY   at both ends.

Hotel Anfa
Anfa, Casablanca,
11.10.97,
1:35–3:12 p.m.

for GUISES OF JAZZ 5 déc 98
*Thought out in bed
in morning
before rising*

Tina Turner

If she aint jazz, AINT
no jazz. Give me two of EACH
of what she has.   JA-A-AZ!

(copied for Godelieve on 1 April 2000, chez elle)

TINA TURNER DANCING

If TINA aint jazz,
AIN'T no jazz! I'll take   TWO each
of each   riff   she has.

chez Godelieve, 2 April 2000, 11H55-12H06

TINA TURNER   haiku #2
                                3.4.2000, 55 bis
                                                        [haiku #1
If her LEGS aint jazz,   If TINA   aint jazz,
SHA-A-AME   AIN'T no jazz! I'll take   TWO each
SHAME on jazz. I NEED   of each   riff   she has]
of all I can reach.   two each
all I   can   reach.   Tina Turner jazz - haiku #2
a-a-all   REACH.   3-8-2000, 14H45-15H06   + #3
7 April 2000. ca 14H30 -14H39
TINA TURNER   True, she rocked-'n'- rolled,
                                                  she rocked 'n' rolled, true.
stanza haiku # 2 or 3   But when her story's told,   JAZZ
True, she rocked 'n' rolled,   gata leg-up.   Hold!
rhythm steady, blues controlled. 3.5.2000, 22H10 - 22H20.   ②
JAZZ! Never gets old.   True, she rocked-'n'- rolled,
                                                  got a leg-up JAZZ. Fine!
#3 6.5.2000, 55 bis... Paris   Just wish it was mine.   ③
When she rocked
She gets a leg-up   4.5.2000 (composed in bed before rising)
approx.   -> Yess, she rocked 'n' rolled.
True, she rocked-'n'- rolled;   thighs pumped honey, hips shook gold
thighs like drumbeats in my head, She stayed jazz - years - old
jazzmatazz.   'nough said.   When she rocked she rolled; >10H45 changed
                                                  stays (13H05)

the declarative emphasis made possible by narrative style, and the technical challenge of rime."[3]

By 1939 James Emanuel had become "what I would always be: a person whose civil rights were inviolable." This deeply humanistic stance informs the body of his work.

While there is much tenderness, especially in his poems for and about children, there is also a checked anger, regulated by poetic form and the pleasures of language. His enterprise has been to put his life and his life's observations on record; his desire to get the record straight goes to the heart of poetic revision.

Final version

Bill Clinton*

Sex smiles, blows STRAIGHT UP,
its sunflower yellow bent
to point where JAZZ went.

The President's sax
dives, blows SWIM, blows FLOAT. HIS jazz
don't need no life boat.

JAZZ has White House fun:
his one-seat teeter-totter
HAPPY at both ends.

*Composed in Casablanca's Hotel Idou Anfa,
11 October 1997 B.M. (Before Monica)

Final version

Tina Turner

If TINA ain't jazz,
AIN'T no jazz!   I'll take   two each
of each   riff   she has.

True, she rocked-'n'-rolled,
rhythm steady, blues controlled.
She stayed   jazz-years-old.

If her LEGS ain't jazz,
SHA-A-AME on jazz. I NEED   two each
of all I can reach.

Yes, she rocked-'n'-rolled:
thighs like drumbeats in my head,
JAZZMATIZED.   'Nough said.

(Haiku set by James A. Emanuel)

Author's note: This four-haiku poem (shown here as given to my saxophonist before our presentation of 18 May 2000) will be first published in my book *The Force and the Reckoning*, due this year (2000) from Lotus Press of Detroit. Copyright James A. Emanuel.

New *Tina Turner* jazz haiku (finished 7 May 2000) to be read to end my program with Chansse Evanns on the sax at Le Merle moqueur, Paris, 18 May 2000, as our 20-minute part of the annual Festival franco-anglais de poésie.

Notes

1. James Emanuel, *Langston Hughes* (New York: Twayne 1967).
2. James Emanuel and Theodore Gross, eds., *Dark Symphony: Negro Literature in America* (New York: Free Press, 1968).
3. James Emanuel's autobiography appears in Vol. 18 of *Contemporary Authors Autobiography Series* (Detroit: Gale Research, Inc. 1994).

ALICIA OSTRIKER

1937-

THE WORK OF ALICIA OSTRIKER, ONE OF OUR MORE prominent U.S. poets, also a Professor of English Literature and Creative Writing at Rutgers University and a critic, stands well alongside that of outstanding writers such as Marilyn Hacker, Grace Schulman, Sandra Gilbert, June Jordan, and Alice Walker—creative artists who have been socially engaged as political activists, editors, literary or social critics. Ostriker is the author of eight collections of poetry; a healthy sampling is reprinted in *The Little Space: Poems Selected and New, 1968-1998.* Her opus includes *The Imaginary Lover* (1986), which received the William Carlos Williams Award of the Poetry Society of America, and *The Crack in Everything* (1996), which was a National Book Award finalist and won both the Paterson Poetry Award and the San Francisco State Poetry Center Award. In addition to poetry, she has produced critical works including *Writing Like a Woman* (1983), *Feminist Revision and the Bible* (1993), and *The Nakedness of the Fathers: Biblical Visions and Revisions* (1994). After publishing a critical book, *Vision and Verse in William Blake* (1965), she edited and annotated the Penguin edition of *The Complete Poems of William Blake* (1977). It would not be difficult to trace the interfaces between her poetry and prose; one might regard the critical work as an outgrowth of her poetic process.

While writing in free verse—her preferred approach after the early formalism of her first collection, *Songs* (1969)—she still demonstrates a formal control. The two poems printed here show her precise and unaffected voice, her lyricism, and her pictorial sense charged by subjective awareness. Her own comments on the revision process are particularly interesting and illuminating.

Final version :xtaposed th earlier variants

The Dogs at Live Oak Beach, Santa Cruz [*original title: The Dogs*]

As if there could be a world
Of absolute innocence
In which we forget ourselves
The owners throw sticks

And half-bald tennis balls
Toward the surf
And the happy dogs leap after them
As if catapulted—
Black dogs, tan dogs,
Tubes of glorious muscle—
Pursuing pleasure
More than obedience
[*First draft variant*: Like diving birds—confused only a funny]
They race, skid to a halt in the wet sand,
[*First draft variant*: Moment, before they snap and sink]
Sometimes they'll plunge straight into
The foaming breakers

Like diving birds, letting the green turbulence
[*Second and third draft variant*: The ocean's anarchy brings]
Toss them, until they snap and sink
[*Second and third draft variant*: As if they were diving birds]
[*Second and third draft variant*: Brief confusion, then they'll
        snap and sink]
Teeth into floating wood
[*Second and third draft variant*: Teeth into treasure, and bound
        back to their owners]
Then bound back to their owners
Shining wet, with passionate speed
For nothing,
For absolutely nothing but joy.

The Kiss of Judas [*final version juxtaposed with variants*]

A Among many, one panel: [One panel among many]
   Perhaps it catches the eye   [it catches the eye, but why,
   Due to its symmetry   [because of the symmetry]
   Or its subject, betrayal.   [or the subject?]

   Giotto is simple.
   What does "simple" mean?
   Soldiers, torches, a friendship, [A faith, an apple   a friendship]
   Money, a kiss.

Two profiles: one looks upward,   [The two profiles]
Lips protrude with intention,   [One slightly frowning]
Brow slightly frowns.   [lips protruding]
And one receptive, brunette,   [with intention]
                                          [and one receptive, brunette]

Eyes almost Byzantine,
Grave if not solemn,   [grave but not solemn,]
Brow smooth, neck bare   [you might say]
To show absence of fear,   [Fully present]
                                          [wholly]

Judas wears a cloak
To reveal that he's hidden.
His embrace also hides   [Giotto has painted him]
The other's body.   [And has thrown it round]
                                          [like everyone else] [The other's body]

Could Judas wish to become   [As if to protect, capture,
Joined with his Lord's body?   [or become one body.]
Giotto has painted him
Like almost everyone else

In the Scrovegni Chapel,
Slightly rounded, short,   [Softly rounded, short]
Not too far from being
A dog or a bird.

B Isn't it hard, though, to leave?
   Pope Leo liked them. We too,   [Pope Leo liked [loved] them]
   Those soft Giotto blues,   and we. We too.
   Those rose tints, those greens.   [Those rose tracts,...]
                                          [drapery] [unostentatious]
   I was never in a church   [We were][I was never in a church]

C More comforting than this one.   [more cosy than this one] [comforting]
   Imagine if women's wombs   [consoling]
   Had paintings like this one.   [Imagine if wombs]
   We would all be born
   Wise and good, then.   [Wise, then, and good, then.]

[But Jesus is taken
[There is also a crowd]
[The central drama]
[a design of staves xxx??? or torches]
[fills the upper half]

The Kiss of Judas

One panel among many
It catches the eye, always,
because of the symmetry
who or the subject?

Giotto is simple
would does "simple" mean?
A faith, an apple, a friendship
money, a kiss!

Judas wears a cloak
to reveal that he's hidden.
Giotto has painted him
like everyone else

In the Scrovegni Chapel,
slightly rounded & short
Not too far from him
A dog or a bird.

one panel among many
does it hold our eye

why does it catch

why does it catch the eye

because of the symmetry
or the subject?

The two profiles,
one slightly frowning
lips protruding
with intention

And one receptive, brunette,
grave but not solemn,
you might say
fully present.
wholly

drapery
unostentatious

Is it hard, though, to leave?
rope her like them I and us.
Those bright Giotto blues,
Those rose tints, those greens.
tracts

we too.

we were
I was never in a church
more cosy than this one.
Imagine if the wombs this one.
had paintings like

we would all be born
wise and good, then.
then,

comforting
something
well
good

Judas wears a cloak
& to reveal that he's
hidden

But Jesus is taller

There is also a crowd

A crowd of men surrounds
the central drama
a design of staffs or torches
fills the upper half

The man is short, who knows what
about displaying

But Jesus is taller

You might say
fully present
Judas wears a cloak
to reveal that he's hidden.
And has flung it round
The other's body

As if to protect, capture or hide ...
or become one body..

STAN ROGAL

1950–

STAN ROGAL, born in Vancouver and currently living in Toronto, is the former Toronto representative for the League of Canadian Poets, serving on the League's Freedom of Expression Committee. His published volumes of poetry include *Lines of Embarkation, Personations, The Imaginary Museum, Sweet Betsy From Pike,* and *Geometry of the Odd* (Wolsak and Wynn, 1999); his writing has appeared in numerous magazines, journals and anthologies in Canada, the U.S. and Europe. Rogal is also a playwright, and has had his plays performed across Canada. *Perfect Strangers,* a play adapted from a short story in his second collection, *Restless* (Insomniac Press, 1998), was premiered at the Toronto Fringe Festival in 2000. In addition to his writing endeavours, Rogal co-ordinates the Idler Pub Reading Series in Toronto, and has been co-artistic director of Bald Ego Theatre for the past ten years. Rogal's first novel, *The Long Drive Home*, was published by Insomniac press in 1999.

"Sub Rosa Transformation: 4" is from a collection of poems titled *The Sub Rosa Project*. This series began as a poem that might be used as text in the "program and show openings" of an artist friend. Very much concerned with "ideas of transformation and myth," one or two paintings and poems grew into a total of eight pictures and 30-40 poems.

Regarding his poetry, Rogal says: "My biggest challenge is to break from straight narrative without making the poems too muddled. My goal is to write something that's evocative rather than narrative. I want to allow room for my readers to interpret or to crawl into and mull around, to devise their own 'meanings' or whatever."

Sub Rosa Transformation: 4

Watch and pray that ye enter not into temptation:
the spirit indeed is willing but the flesh is weak.

— Matthew 26:41

What suggests this scape? What makes suggestive?
An outrage of petals? A whorl of fronds?
An oyster of pure, unadulterate light?   [originally placed before
line 6]
A moon that draws on blood fierce as any vampire?
A bubble of egg symbolizing procreation & cultic promiscuity?
A figure prone to excess; to access —   [earlier: "every excess"
"every access"]

venal, vernal, vernacular:
Displays:
chirrup-chirrup grind of legs
slippering *gurgle-purr* of hips
rubadub-halloo roil of breasts
racket of arms belling the ears
mouth huzza-hurrah a vaginal cleft
intoning enchantment
perhaps sudden
out-of-the-blue *yap-shriek* intercourse
of sax & violins
sacral *plash-clang* penetration of colour   [final version only]
mainly: red, white, black   [final version only]
What might be made to situate the so-called consummate
Virgin/whore rushes all feeling to extremities.
'Beauty being in the eye; ear in the heart,' *et cetera*...
Makes plain Heisenberg's uncertain principles. [final version only]
As before a mirror speculation begins & ends
with the fatal brash image
& *Shazam!* we behold what we want to behold.
["Shazam!": final version only]
Whether dazed & confused *auto-da-fé*
Romantic
Or some such other-
Wise driven Mandrake

Conjures variant
Autoerotic
Eve, on the one hand,
her teeth & lips as yet undone by the love apple.
On the other, Sara, Asmodeus a bat up her ass
Prodding thrust & shove
Death
of seven cardinal husbands.
Interpretation few dare entertain [last three lines: final version
                                        only]

Frames each digression an entrance
Long ago & far, far away.

<table>
<tr><td>A com-</td><td>What suggests this scape?</td></tr>
<tr><td>posite</td><td>What makes suggestive?</td></tr>
<tr><td>based on</td><td>An outrage of petals?</td></tr>
<tr><td>first and</td><td>A whorl of fronds?</td></tr>
<tr><td>second</td><td>A bubble of egg symbolizing</td></tr>
<tr><td>drafts</td><td>Procreation and cultic promiscuity?</td></tr>
</table>

A com-
posite
based on
first and
second
drafts

What suggests this scape?
What makes suggestive?
An outrage of petals?
A whorl of fronds?
A bubble of egg symbolizing
Procreation and cultic promiscuity?
An oyster of pure, unadulterate light?
A moon that draws on blood
Fierce as any vampire?

Note:
undecided
choices
are in
brackets

A figure prone to vernal excess:
cricket singing chirrup-chirrup
grinding legs
Slippering hips
Roiling breasts
                              [an apostrophe of arms upraised]
Curved bracket of arms around the head
                              [a racket of arms belling the ears]
      Apostrophized supplication
the mouth [wound to] huzza-hurrah a vaginal cleft
      bordering (on) [dense] otherwise
         dazed or confused enchantment? [intoning enchantment]
            Perverse?
What might situate the so-called virgin/whore
Rushes all feeling to extremities.
'Beauty being in the eye," *et cetera*...
As in a mirror
Speculation begins & end with the fatal

Image
Whether dazed & confused *auto-da-fé* Romantic
    Or some such otherwise driven
        (autoerotic) can also paint a pretty picture.
Eve, let's say, her teeth first penetrating the love apple.
Sara, let's say, Asmodeus at her back
        Prodding the deaths of seven husbands.

JILL BATTSON

1958–

JILL BATTSON was born and raised in southern England. After receiving an education in film production, she moved to Toronto, where she became active in the electronic media, film, and literary communities. In addition to having her poetry published in literary journals throughout North America and the U.K., she has had five chapbooks of poetry published, as well as a full book of poetry, *Hard Candy* (Insomniac Press), which was shortlisted for the 1998 Gerald Lampert Memorial Award. Her poetry has also been included in various anthologies, including *Playing in the Asphalt Garden, The Urban Wanderer, Invisible Accordion,* and now *Visions and Revisions.* Battson believes, though, that poetry is meant to be spoken as well as written, and to that end she has coordinated many reading series, including *The Poet's Refuge, Festival of the Spoken Word, Wordapalooza* and *Poetry Express* (at the Toronto Fringe Festival), as well as producing the *Word Up!* project, a series of poetry videos airing on MuchMusic.

Also a poetry activist, Battson tries to bring poetry to a wide variety of people, especially those whose voices are often ignored. One of her activities is to visit high school classrooms, read her poetry, and interact with the students not only about her own poetry, but about their poetry as well. She believes that young people often write, in one form or another, about the angst and confusion they experience. Because they do not see themselves represented in the poetry that is traditionally taught in school, they possibly do not consider what they write to be important. By presenting herself to these students as a contemporary poet who writes and, perhaps more importantly, speaks about relevant urban issues, Battson provides these students with a chance to experience poetry in a vibrant, meaningful way, and to recognize their own writing as part of a community, or genre, of writing.

Both of the following poems appear in *Hard Candy.* In "Parasites of Age and History," the narrator keeps pace with a series of memories or insights about her father that seemingly explain why she "never read[s] men through him." In "Desert Woman," an older woman remembers and informs, while a younger woman has not yet had the experience.

Battson's second collection of poems, *Ashes are Bone and Dust*, will be published by Insomniac Press in 2001. She currently lives in Taos, New Mexico.

Final version

Parasites of Age and History

The story of my father
is the story of the smell of wood
his hard muscle shape
what the parasites of age and history leach from you
and why I never read men through him

forgetting bends a man
ancient memories adorn his life
air temperature shapes his body

The story of my father
rendered daft by fear
his outer casing shifts and empties
manifold tales disseminated by consequence
beyond hair loss and fading sight
  to the core of how we waste our lives

The last remaining story of my father

Composite of early drafts with deletions in square brackets

[untitled]

The story of my father
is the story of the smell of wood
[in which he will never wrap his arms around me]
his hard muscle shape
[what age and history can leach from you]
the parasites of age and history
and why I never read men through him

[It is the story of how] forgetting bends a man
ancient memories adorn [one's life]
air temperature shapes the body

The story of a man rent daft by fear
[the] outer casing shifts and empties
[A] manifold deseminated by consequence

[It is the story] beyond hair loss and failing sight
to the core of how we waste our lives

This [is the] story [that] displaces others
the last remaining one.
The story of my father.

Final   *Desert Woman*   *for two voices*
version

Swooping in over another picked clean carcass
vulture glides in
opening closing claws feet around spine
     somewhere under her knee a fragment
seashell shaped fragment
holey bone pinches flesh
catwalking old life spine to skull
she bears it
ground is live
security in death
sun's energy heatwaving out of the desert
she sits
absorbing the heat of the land
shimmering over hot granite
noontime land
     bone into flesh pinching
     heat soaking into thigh bones
rocking the bird into myriad oily colours
     into ball and socket
     arcing between legs
     in a heat energy horizon
tortoiseshell quality of horn
geographic wafers of cells
obligation to evoke desire gone
splitting away from lubrication
so much heat here
feels like the inside of her
heat relaxes lungs and mind

Menopause for two voices [working title]

Swooping down over another picked clean carcass
vulture glides down
opening & closing it's claws over spine
catwalking it's way to the skull
[There is security in the ground] The ground is live
[Security in death]   There is security in death
[The sun's heat]
The sun's energy heatwaving it's way out of the sand
shimmering [over] above hot granite
rocking the vulture into a myriad of oily colours
[longhorned cow]
the [tortoise] tortoiseshell quality of horn
gently [...] in layers of cells
splitting through lack of nutrients
the bones impervious

II
Somewhere under knee a fragment
a seashell shaped fragment
of holey bone pinches flesh
but she sits there
absorbing the heat of the land
the noontime land
into her flesh into the pinching
the heat soaking up into her [the] big bones
[of her legs]
the joints
arcing between her legs
in a heat energy horizon
Somehow she feels more comfortable
in men's clothes
the baggy shirts [...] her hot [flesh] skin
the flexibility in stiff [...] legs
not obliged to look [beautiful] desirable
or even [...]
at last people (read men) take her for what she is
[a mind] an intellect
The sand of the desert

little dust fumes
spit into her cheeks
there is so much heat
it feels inside of her
relaxes lungs
relaxes mind

APPENDIX

TRANSLATIONS

This group of translations provides a further example of the way the content and the effect of poetry are determined by shifts in language. We have noted throughout how with slight shifts in words, phrasing, and rhythm, the subject or theme of a poem is altered. The vision of a poem is often changed as a result of minor changes in language. A close examination of these various translations will extend the discipline already acquired by the reader in the body of this book. There is no need here to examine the original poem; what is important is the way different poets make separate poems out of a single experience. Here the experience is actually someone else's poem. While two translations resemble the original in many aspects, each poem is to be regarded as an independent work, manifesting those very same qualities we find in original works of poetry.

THE HOLY BIBLE

Psalm 15 (1611)

Lord who shall abide in thy tabernacle? Who shall dwell in
      thy holy hill?
He that walketh uprightly, and worketh righteousness, and
      speaketh the truth in his heart.
He *that* backbiteth not with his tongue, nor doeth evil to his
      neighbor, nor taketh up a reproach against his
      neighbor.
In whose eyes a vile person is contemned; but he honoureth
      them that fear the LORD. *He that* sweareth to *his*
      own hurt, and changeth not.
He that putteth not out his money to usury, nor taketh reward
      against the innocent. He that doeth these *things*
      shall never be moved.

                     The Holy Bible, King James Version

Psalm 15: A Psalm of David (1917)

Lord, who shall sojourn in Thy tabernacle?
Who shall dwell upon Thy holy mountain?
He that walketh uprightly, and worketh righteousness,
And speaketh truth in his heart;
That hath no slander upon his tongue,   5
Nor doeth evil to his fellow,
Nor taketh up a reproach against his neighbour;
In whose eyes a vile person is despised,
But he honoureth them that fear the Lord;
He that sweareth to his own hurt,   10
And changeth not;
He that putteth not out his money on interest,
Nor taketh a bribe against the innocent.
He that doeth these things shall never be moved.

The Holy Scriptures according to the Masoretic Text

A Psalm of David: 15 (1952)

O Lord, who shall sojourn in thy tent?
Who shall dwell on thy holy hill?
He who walks blamelessly, and does what is right, and
        speaks truth from his heart;
Who does not slander with his tongue, and does no evil
        to his friend, nor takes up a reproach against his
        neighbor; in whose eyes a reprobate is despised,
but who honors those who fear the LORD; Who swears
        to his own hurt and does not change; Who does not
        put out his money at interest,
and does not take a bribe against the innocent. He who
        does these things shall never be moved.

The Holy Bible, Revised Standard Version

HOMER

Odyssey XI (1616)

Arrived now at our ship, we launched, and set
Our mast up, put forth sail, and in did get
Our late-got cattle. Up our sails, we went,
My wayward fellows mourning now th' event,
A good companion yet, a foreright wind
Circe (the excellent utterer of her mind)
Supplied our murmuring consorts with, that was
Both speed and guide to our adventurous pass.
All day our sails stood to the winds, and made
Our voyage prosperous. Sun then set, and shade
All ways obscuring, on the bounds we fell
Of deep oceanus, where people dwell
Whom a perpetual cloud obscures outright,
To whom the cheerful sun lends never light;
Nor when he mounts the star-sustaining heaven,
Nor when he stoops to earth, and sets up Even,
But night holds fix'd wings, feather'd all with banes
Above those most unblest Cimmerians.

Translated by George Chapman

The Odyssey XI (1673)

When we were come unto the sea-side, where
    Our ship lay, which we shov'd into the deep;
We rear our mast, pull up our sails, and bear
    Aboard with us one male, one female sheep.
And so for Hell we stood, with fears in mind,   5
    And tears in eye. But the fair Circe sent,
To bear us company, a good fore-wind
    That kept our sails full all the way we went.
To winds and steerage we our way commend,
    And careless sit from morning till 'twas dark;   10
Then found ourselves at th' Ocean's farthest end,
    Where up to land the wind had forc'd our bark.

Translated by Thomas Hobbes

Odyssey XI (c. 1673-1677)

First came my soldier Elpenor's spirit
    Which left the body just when we set sail,
So that we had no leisure to inter it;
    His heavy fate I did with tears bewail.
How now, quoth I, Elpenor? art thou here   5
    Already? Couldst thou me so much outstrip?
I first came forth, and left thee in the rear
    Hast thou on foot outgone my good black ship?
Then said Elpenor: Issue of Jove, divine
    Ulysses, I had come along with th' bark,   10
But the Devil and excess of wine
    Made me to fall, and break my neck i' th' dark.
I went to bed late by a ladder steep
    At top o' th' house the room was where I lay,
Wak'd at the noise of party, half asleep,   15
    Headlong I hither came, the nearest way.
        Translated by Thomas Hobbes

Odyssey XI (1897)

But the first that drew anigh me was our friend Elpenor's
    shade
For as yet he was not buried beneath the Earth wide-wayed;
We had left his body unburied, unwept, in Circe's hall,
Since other need and labour on our fellowship did fall.
So I wept when I beheld him and was sorry for his sake,   5
And I sent my voice unto him and a wingéd word I spake:
"How camest thou, Elpenor, beneath the dusk and the dark?
And swifter afoot has thou wended than I in my coal-black
    bark."
God's doom and wine unstinted on me the bane had brought
I lay in the house of Circe and waking had no thought   10
To get me back and adown by the way of the ladders tall:
But downright from the roof I tumbled, and brake my neck
    withal
From the backbone, and unto Hades and his house my soul
    must fare.
        Translated by William Morris

CATULLUS

Caeli, Lesbia nostra: Poem LVIII (1931)

Caelius, my Lesbia, that one, that only Lesbia,
Lesbia whom Catullus loved more than himself and all
       things he ever owned or treasured.
Now her body's given up in alley-ways,
on highroads to these fine Roman gentlemen,
fathered centuries ago by the noble Remus.

                      Translated by Horace Gregory

Caeli, Lesbia nostra: Poem LVIII (c. 1949)

My Lesbia, *that* Lesbia, whom alone Catullus loved
More than himself and all who are most dear to him,
Now in cross-roads and alleys trading her charms
      Fleeces the lordly descendants of Remus.

                      Translated by R.C. Trevelyan

Lesbia me dicit: Poem XCII (c. 1735)

Lesbia for ever on me rails,
To talk of me, she never fails,
Now, hang me, but for all her art
I find that I have gained her heart.
My proof is this: I plainly see   5
The case is just the same with me;
I cursed her every hour sincerely,
Yet, hang me, but I love her dearly.

                      Translated by Jonathan Swift

Lesbia me dicit: Poem XCII (1931)

Lesbia, forever spitting fire at me, is never silent. And now
if Lesbia fails to love me, I shall die. Why
do I know in truth her passion burns for me? Because I am
      like her,
because I curse her endlessly. And still, O hear me gods,
I love her.

Translated by Horace Gregory

PETRARCH

Sonetto in Vita 91 (1557)

The Long Love That in My Thought Doth Harbor

The long love that in my thought doth harbor,
And in my heart doth keep his residence,
Into my face presseth with bold pretense
And there encampeth, spreading his banner.
She that me learns to love and suffer   5
And wills that my trust and lust's negligence
Be reined by reason, shame, and reverence
With his hardiness takes displeasure.
Wherewithal unto the heart's forest he fleeth,
Leaving his enterprise with pain and cry,   10
And there him hideth, and not appeareth.
What may I do, when my master feareth,
But in the field with him to live and die?
For good is the life ending faithfully.

Translated by Sir Thomas Wyatt the Elder

Sonetto in Vita 91 (1557)

Love, That Doth Reign and Live Within My Thought

Love, that doth reign and live within my thought,
And built his seat within my captive breast,
Clad in the arms wherein with me he fought,
Oft in my face he doth his banner rest.

But she that taught me love and suffer pain,   5
My doubtful hope and eke my hot desire
With shamefast look to shadow and refrain,
Her smiling grace converteth straight to ire.
And coward Love, then, to the heart apace
Taketh his flight, where he doth lurk and plain,   10
His purpose lost, and dare not show his face.
For my lord's guilt thus faultless bide I pain,
Yet from my lord shall not my foot remove:
Sweet is the death that taketh end by love.

Translated by Henry Howard, Earl of Surrey

Sonetto in Vita 91 (1892)

Hither from her, whence Shame hath sped away,
And Good hath perished in the evil clime,
From Babel, den of dole and dam of crime,
Fleeing I come, to eke my mortal day.
Alone, as Love admonishes, I stray,   5
Culling now flower and herb, now verse and rhyme,
With meditated hope of better time
Cheering my soul, that there alone finds stay.
Fortune and multitude I nothing mind,
Or much myself, or of poor things have heed,   10
Or burn with outer or with inner heat.
Two souls alone I crave, and would indeed
For her, more gentle mood toward me inclined;
For him, his proved stability of feet.

Translated by Richard Garnett

ACKNOWLEDGMENTS

THE AUTHOR AND THE PUBLISHER HAVE MADE EVERY attempt to locate the authors of the copyrighted material or their heirs or assigns, and would be grateful for information that would allow correction of any errors or omissions in subsequent editions of the work.

Acknowledgment is gratefully made to the following authors and publishers for permission to reprint copyrighted material:

W.H. Auden, "Taller To-day," "Consider," "In Memory of W.B. Yeats," and "At the Grave of Henry James," from *W.H. Auden: Collected Poems* by W.H. Auden, copyright © 1976 by Edward Mendelson, William Meredith, and Monroe K. Spears, Executors of the Estate of W.H. Auden. Used by permission of Random House, Inc.

Jill Battson, "Parasites of Age and History" and "Desert Woman" first appeared in her collection *Hard Candy*, published by Insomniac Press, 1991. Reprinted by permission of the author and publisher.

Catullus, "Poem LVIII" and "Poem XCII" from *The Poems of Catullus*, trans. Horace Gregory (New York: Grove Press, 1956). Copyright © 1956 by Horace Gregory. Reprinted by permission of the Estate of Horace Gregory.

James Emanuel, "Bill Clinton" and "Tina Turner" from *Jazz from the Haiku King* (Detroit: Broadside Press 1999). Reprinted by permission of the author.

Robert Frost, "In White" and "Design" from *Poetry of Robert Frost: The Collected Poems, Complete and Unabridged* (New York: Holt, Rinehart and Winston, 1979). Reprinted by permission of Henry Holt and Company. From *The Poetry of Robert Frost*, edited by Edward Connery Lathem, ©1936 by Robert Frost, 1964 by Lesley Frost Ballantine, 1969 by Henry Holt and Company. Reprinted by permission of Henry Holt and Company, LLC

Room, in 2 vols (The Porcupine's Quill, 1997). Reprinted by permission of the author and the publisher.

Sylvia Plath, "Burning The Letters," "Lady Lazarus," "Medusa," "Ariel," "Words," and "Edge" from *The Collected Poems: Sylvia Plath*, ed. by Ted Hughes (New York: Harper & Row, Publishers, 1981). Copyright © 1960, 1965, 1971, 1981 by the Estate of Sylvia Plath. Editorial material © 1981 by Ted Hughes. Reprinted by permission of HarperCollins Publishers, Inc., and Faber & Faber, Inc.

Stan Rogal, "Sub Rosa Transformations: 4." Reprinted by permission of the author.

Dylan Thomas, "The Hunchback in the Park," "If I were tickled by the rub of love," "Especially when the October wind," and "The force that through the green fuse drives the flower," from *The Poems of Dylan Thomas*. Copyright © 1939 by New Directions Publishing Corp. Reprinted by permission of the publisher. Drafts of these poems are from Ralph Maud, ed., *The Notebooks of Dylan Thomas* (New York: New Directions, 1967). Reprinted by permission of Harold Ober Associates.

Stephen Watson, "Rainmaking with a Bow-string," "The Tobacco Pouch: A Song," "Sorcerers Are Like Lions," "Presentiments," "The Rain That Is Male," and "The Abandoned Old Woman" from *Return of the Moon: Versions from the /Xam*. Cape Town: The Carrefour Press, 1991; reprinted as *Song of the Broken String*, New York: Sheepmeadow Press, 1995. Reprinted with permission of Sheepmeadow Press and the author.

William Carlos Williams, "The Locust Tree in Flower" and "Young Woman at a Window" from *The Collected Poems of William Carlos Williams, 1909-1939: Volume 1*. Copyright © 1938 by New Directions Publishing Corp. Reprinted by permission of NewDirections Publishing Corp.

William Butler Yeats, "A Cradle Song," "The Sorrow of Love," "A Dream of Death," "The Hosting of the Sidhe," "The Two Trees," and "The Cap and Bells." Copyright © 1906 by The Macmillan Company, copyright renewed © 1934 by W.B. Yeats. Variants from Peter Allt and Russell K. Alspach, eds., *The Variorum Edition of the Poems of W.B. Yeats* (New York: Macmillan, 1957). Reprinted by permission of Simon & Schuster and by A.P. Watt Ltd., on behalf of Michael B. Yeats.

ABOUT THE EDITORS

Barry Wallenstein is the author of five collections of poetry; the most recent being *A Measure of Conduct* (Ridgeway Press, 1999). His poetry has appeared in over 50 journals in the U.S. and abroad, in such places as *Transatlantic Review*, *The Nation*, *Centennial Review*, and *American Poetry Review*. He teaches literature and creative writing at City College in New York and is also an editor of the journal, *American Book Review*. Currently he is the Director of City College's Poetry Outreach Center. A special interest is his involvement in the performance of jazz and poetry together. He has made four recordings of his poetry with jazz collaboration, the most recent being a CD, *Tony's Blues* (Cadence Jazz Records, 2001).

Robert Burr currently lives and works in New York City and has, over the past three years, taught freshman composition at Bronx Community College, Medgar Evers College, and The City College of New York. Mr. Burr's poetry was recently published in chapbook form under the title *Trading Bits of Dream* (Ridgeway Press, 1999); his essay, "Wallace Stevens: Gaining the Light" was also recently published in *The Wallace Stevens Journal* (Spring, 1999).